MOBILITY AND MODERNITY

MOBILITY AND MODERNITY

~

Panama in the Nineteenth-Century
Anglo-American Imagination

ROBERT D. AGUIRRE

THE OHIO STATE UNIVERSITY PRESS

COLUMBUS

Copyright © 2017 by The Ohio State University.
All rights reserved.

Library of Congress Cataloging-in-Publication Data
Names: Aguirre, Robert D., author.
Title: Mobility and modernity : Panama in the nineteenth-century Anglo-American
    imagination / Robert D. Aguirre.
Description: Columbus : The Ohio State University Press, [2017] | Includes bibliographical
    references and index.
Identifiers: LCCN 2017016259 | ISBN 9780814213445 (cloth ; alk. paper) | ISBN 0814213448
    (cloth ; alk. paper)
Subjects: LCSH: Panama Canal (Panama)—History—19th century. | Panama—History.
    | Panama Railroad Co.—History. | Travelers' writings, British. | Travelers' writings,
    American. | Panama Canal (Panama)—Description and travel. | Panama Canal
    (Panama)—In literature. | Panama Canal (Panama)—Pictorial works.
Classification: LCC F1569.C2 A38 2017 | DDC 972.87—dc23
LC record available at https://lccn.loc.gov/2017016259

Cover design by Andrew Brozyna
Text design by Juliet Williams
Type set in Adobe Minion Pro

♾ The paper used in this publication meets the minimum requirements of the American
National Standard for Information Sciences—Permanence of Paper for Printed Library
Materials. ANSI Z39.48–1992.

9   8   7   6   5   4   3   2   1

CONTENTS

ILLUSTRATIONS

ACKNOWLEDGMENTS

~

I AM GRATEFUL to the faculty, staff, and students of Wayne State University, where this project took shape and was completed. It is a privilege to work at a university that prizes humanities research and perceives it as fundamental to its core mission and values.

Wayne M. Raskind, dean of the College of Liberal Arts and Sciences, has been an unfailing champion and a model of intellectual curiosity in his own discipline. My fellow colleagues in Old Main—Donald Haase, Christy Chow, Peter Hoffmann, Heather Dillaway, Ratna Naik, Joseph Kieleszewski, Caroline Brzuchowski, Jessica Archer, Elizabeth Stone-Hall, and Kim Mason—have assisted me in ways large and small. I owe special thanks to Paul Clemens for intellectual camaraderie and an unyielding passion for the written word.

My colleague Professor Ellen Barton gave needed encouragement at early and late stages of this project; I will be forever thankful for her instruction in the fine arts of the "research hour." Professors John Reed and Michael Scrivener trained their intelligent eye on early drafts, while Arthur Marotti helped refine a grant proposal at a critical stage. I benefited more informally from the innumerable hallway chats and coffee breaks with colleagues that make life in a large, intellectually vibrant department so rewarding. I thank particularly my former students, Shashi Thandra and Justin Prystash, whose own intellectual commitment has been an inspiration. Many colleagues farther afield have lent their ears, eyes, and opinions. I mention, in particular, Helena Michie, Ross Forman, Karen Racine, Jennifer Hayward, and Jessie Reeder. Parts of this project were presented to helpful audiences at the North American Victorian Studies Association, the Dickens Project in Santa Cruz, the Trollope bicentenary in Leuven, the Rice University Humanities Seminars, and the University of Guelph, Ontario. Lindsay Martin at the Ohio State University Press believed in this project from the start; her expertise with external readers has been particularly helpful. Their comments prompted me to think in productive new ways about my hypotheses and methods.

A yearlong fellowship at the University of Michigan, Ann Arbor, generously funded by the Public Goods Council and the Andrew E. Mellon Foundation, gave me the chance to spend an enriching year in the well-stocked archives of the Clements Library of Americana. At a later stage, a fellowship from the Huntington Library in San Marino gave me time both to write intensively and to deepen my knowledge of California letters while reading in its extraordinary collections. Conversations with library fellows and staff were invaluable; Anne Blecksmith pointed me toward other collections in the local area and suggested research strategies for my work on James Stanley Gilbert. Staff at the Getty Research Institute and the Getty Museum, both in Los Angeles, generously shared their time and expertise. The days I spent among the Muybridge collections at the Getty convinced me I needed to write about his photographic work. I was also fortunate to gain access to the Muybridge collections at the Bancroft Library at Berkeley, where conversations with James Eason shaped my research. I also owe thanks to the staff of the following archives and libraries for their professionalism and service: the British Library; the Library of Congress; the Harvard University Libraries; the Kingston Museum in Kingston Upon Thames; the British Postal Archive in London; the New York Public Library; the California State Library in Sacramento; the UCLA Special Collections; the University of Michigan Libraries; the Detroit Public Library; the Library of Congress; and the Wayne State University Libraries, especially the inter-library loan office, which made many distant sources available for me in Detroit. I received valuable research and editing expertise from Claire Daniels and Ruth Boeder. It is a privilege to thank them here. I also thank the editors of *Victorian Literature and Culture* for permission to reprint an earlier version of chapter 2.

My greatest debts are to the friends and family members who have sustained me over the years I've worked on this project. Raphael Gunner, John Friedman, Alice Kimm, and Carol Ann Johnston, each in their own ways, have left their stamp on this work and its author. My siblings Hedy, Paul, Erika, Eva, Eleanor, Susan, Frank, and Constance have been there at key moments, as have my late mother and father, whose own journeys of immigration and mobility continue to amaze me after all these years. I am blessed to share a home and a life with Danielle E. Price, a writer and scholar whose devotion to her craft continues to be an inspiration. This book is dedicated to her and our sons, Mateo and Stefan, for all the light they bring.

Mobility and Modernity

Without steam, there is not a sufficient base of operations. With it, New Panama may as much outshine Old Panama, as the sun is more brilliant than the dimmest star of the heavens.

—*PANAMA STAR*, AUGUST 4, 1849

Invitations are out for the most sublime and magnificent nuptials ever celebrated upon our planet—the wedding of the rough Atlantic, to the fair Pacific Ocean. An iron necklace has been thrown across the Isthmus. . . . Across the bosom of the Isthmus, the golden products of our Pacific borders and the incalculable treasures of the distant Orient are destined to flow in unremitting streams.

—*THE CALIFORNIA FARMER AND JOURNAL OF USEFUL SCIENCES*,
MARCH 29, 1855

Iron and steam, twin giants . . . have put a girdle over rocks and rivers, so that travellers can glide as smoothly, if not as inexpensively, over the once terrible Isthmus of Darien, as they can from London to Brighton.

—MARY SEACOLE, *WONDERFUL ADVENTURES*, 1857

TODAY'S MELTING polar ice cap has not only sparked fears of rising oceans and swamped coastlines. It has also revealed a forgotten seaway, the Northwest Passage, the legendary arctic route whose frozen expanses bedeviled maritime explorers from John Cabot to John Franklin. The thaw has predictably spurred a scramble for influence, as trading nations seek to claim this new global shortcut. The Chinese have declared that "there will be ships with Chinese flags sailing through this route in the future."[1] Denmark, not usually given to warlike stands, has jostled to control tiny Hans Island, a desolate, ice-encrusted rock off the Greenland coast whose possession might legitimate claims of arctic sovereignty.[2] Even at the risk of ignoring the Inuit, who have lived in the arctic for millennia, Canadian politicians from across the spectrum have recently sought to rename the route the "Canadian Northwest

Passage."³ Beneath the posturing lies a strategic concern: command over sea lanes that would draw Europe, North America, and Asia into closer commercial proximity by cutting the London to Tokyo passage from 15,000 to 8,500 nautical miles. While diplomats scramble to halt global warming (the Paris Climate Agreement was reached in 2015), global capital mobilizes to profit from its unexpected effects. And because the widened ocean path is not simply an economic channel but a strategic one, military power ensures it is properly securitized.

In 1848, at the critical, coal-dominated moment of the Anthropocene called the Industrial Revolution, the discovery of gold in California set off a similar rush, focused less on commercial shipping and more on passenger mobility, desires for increased global interconnection, and emerging patterns of white settlement. Seeking an alternative to the treacherous route around South America, thousands of fortune seekers from the United States and Europe crossed over forty-nine miles of Panamanian jungle to reach the Pacific, there to board ships for San Francisco and the gold-rich foothills beyond.⁴ Bayard Taylor, an early traveler, called the overland journey by mule and canoe "novel, grotesque, and adventurous," and Ulysses S. Grant recounted losing one-third of his regiment to a cholera outbreak.⁵ By 1849, New York entrepreneurs had appealed to Congress for aid to build a railroad across the Panama isthmus. Completed in 1855, the iron necklace cut a four- to eight-month oceanic journey of 13,600 miles around Cape Horn to a 5,000-mile one that could be accomplished in less than a month: twelve days by steamer from New York to Chagres, on the Atlantic side of the Isthmus; four hours by rail overland to Panama; and twelve days by steamer from Panama to San Francisco. Period maps of the crossing (fig. I.1) depict a frictionless conduit connecting disparate parts of the globe. In these maps, vast distances collapse into the direct, uncomplicated lines of a mobility system. Distance is conquered; nature tamed. The ocean expanses, uncrossed by any border, appear empty and unclaimed, as if global movement were a simple matter of connecting dots. The essential question here is not only one of distance (how many nautical miles from Europe to California or Japan?) or even of time (how long will it take?), but also of the social relations that shape the understanding and experience of both measures. For as we will see, the railroad's effects were also social and political. By exchanging a system of pedestrian mobility for a mechanized and self-contained one, the new crossing shaved precious days off the isthmian journey and enabled foreign travelers to circumvent the locals, on whom trans-isthmian passage formerly depended. The new isthmian passage was political.

Although the canal overshadows it in the popular and scholarly imagination, the railroad's significance is difficult to overestimate—both as a trans-

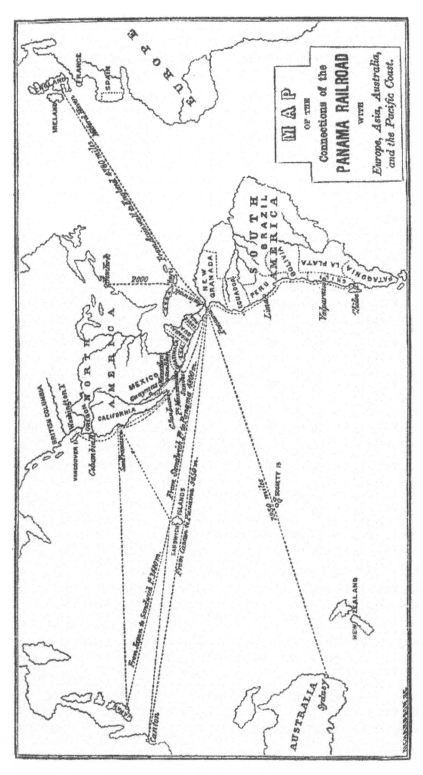

FIGURE I.1. Panama as Global Center. F. N. Otis, *Illustrated History of the Panama Railroad* (1861).

formative reality in its own time and a harbinger of the canal, now a crucial geopolitical link.[6] The development of rapid isthmian transit in the 1850s fueled the aptly named gold *rush* and hastened the westward expansion of the United States during the era of Manifest Destiny. By supporting emergent patterns of white settlement along the Pacific Coast and spreading U.S. culture southward, it served the nation's larger imperial ambitions and territorial designs. For unlike distant Cape Horn, Central America was geographically proximate to the United States and comfortably situated within imaginative and military reach of a nation whose armies had already marched on Mexico City. Not least, the coming of the railroad changed Panama forever. It presaged not only the canal and all that came in its wake but also more recent episodes in the history of globalization. Indeed, it is striking that in the present moment—a moment wedded to the digital as the evolutionary and seemingly inevitable replacement for a vanishing industrial economy of iron and steam—large-scale global shortcuts have returned with a vengeance. In 2016, as melting ice opens shipping lanes across the Northwest Passage, Panama has completed its decade-long, $5 billion project to widen the canal and double its capacity. Meanwhile, despite warnings of ecological disaster from notable figures such as the poet Ernesto Cardenal, Nicaragua is forging ahead in its partnership with the Chinese billionaire Wang Jing to construct its own rival passageway.[7] The world's attention on massive transport infrastructure has never been greater.

During the nineteenth century, writers from across the United States, Britain, and Europe hailed the development of an isthmian connection as a sign of a new age, casting it in explicitly political terms. Charles Dickens employed the language of collapsed frontiers to suggest the advent of a golden era of international cooperation in which "every short cut across the globe" would bring forth "concord, prosperity, and peace."[8] The Frenchman Félix Belly, an early supporter of a water route between the oceans, declared grandly that the project to pierce the isthmus belonged to a generation sworn to pulling down barriers and suppressing distances ("d'abaisser les barrières et de supprimer les distances").[9] Additionally, the naturalist Berthold Seemann connected the scheme to innovations in transport and communications that promised to overcome the problem of planetary scale, a conceptual breakthrough necessary for any understanding of globalization. In his vision, steamers would "ascend the mighty rivers, railroads break in upon the stillness of the virgin forests, and silent telegraphs flash along intelligence, telling of the great deeds of mankind."[10] The prospect of a Panamanian shortcut engendered a new politics of mobility and a new utopian vocabulary in which to express it—both of which are very much alive today.

Focusing on nineteenth-century U.S. and British travel writing, photography, and lyric poetry, and with attention to Panamanian responses, this book engages two broad questions: how did British and U.S. cultural and political figures make sense of this newly important place, and what implications did such representations have for British and U.S. political interests in the period before Panama separated from Colombia and the United States began construction of the canal? I argue that by defining pre-canal Panama as a site of traversal, a location between, these representations laid the discursive ground for its incorporation into a world transport system whose centers of command lay elsewhere. As Panama became defined in this period as a global, industrialized throughway, the needs of distant travelers and commercial enterprises predominated above all else. These "geopolitical exigencies," according to the Panamanian historian Alfredo Castillero Calvo, resulted in the isthmus entering the "imperialist orbit" of an emboldened and increasingly "hegemonic" United States.[11] Although the United States sent warships several times to Panama to safeguard its interests and the railroad employed vigilantes to patrol the isthmus, power was also wielded by controlling "representational machines"—canals, bridges, railways, highway systems, side-wheel steamers, telegraph stations—that projected U.S. power through the mastery of technology.[12] These devices reshaped the hemisphere and defined modernity as a function of technological prowess. My argument is that U.S. and British literary and pictorial representations, by forging new vocabularies and ideological frames, splintered traditional notions of place. Employing powerful aesthetic techniques, they spatially redefined pre-canal Panama as a site between, a disjointed locale serving a technologically driven modernity geared to global movement and speed. Texts and images reframed Panama as a zone through which the foreigner could speed as quickly as possible on the way to somewhere else, clearing the imaginative ground for undermining local culture and asserting foreign control. Here, routes took precedence over roots.[13] By characterizing Panama's residents as primitive and resistant to modernity, the discourse privileged foreigners' unfettered movement as the highest good, even if that meant delegitimizing and dominating the labor, culture, and personhood of local inhabitants. The discursive construction of Panama as an in-between zone, the geographical servant of other masters, was constitutive of a bold new order in which the capital needs and settlement patterns of distant powers could redefine, almost overnight, a sovereign territory as a link of empire.

In this period, a vast body of U.S. and British representations constructed the isthmus as a place between: lodged between the Atlantic and Pacific, North and South America, primitivism and modernity. For foreigners neither a destination per se nor a site of formal colonization, it was consistently described as a connection to other places, a temporary way station. An article in Dickens's popular magazine, *All the Year Round,* put it this way: "Panama is, to the world in general, only part of the road leading to better, more genial places."[14] This ubiquitous formulation located Panama at the juncture of a larger network, a term defined as far back as Dr. Johnson's *Dictionary* (1755) as "any thing reticulated or decussated . . . with interstices between the intersections."[15] Less than a century after Johnson's tortuous definition, the term would name not only Britain's web of interlinked railroad lines and stations but also a vastly larger transportation network whose ships, ports, coaling stations, and mail depots spanned the empire, including such critical junctions as Panama. Today, of course, the word has assumed new meanings that derive from other encompassing systems: computing, information technology, communication, and media.[16] As the Panama Papers scandal of 2016 shows, the word *network* also describes the shadowy world of off-shore banking and capital sequestration, where Panama continues to play a role that dates to the establishment of tax havens in the post-canal period.

After 1840, demands from afar dictated the region's emergence as a crucial network node. Distant events, such as the sight of glittering metal in a California stream, an administrative decision in London to reconceive the routes of the Royal Mail Steam Packet, and the incorporation of the Panama Railroad Company in New York, even more than local needs and rights, fashioned Panama as a link in a world travel system. The gold rush; U.S. Manifest Destiny; evolving patterns of migration and settlement; changing flows of itinerant labor; the rapid development of new forms of industrial technology such as steamships, locomotives, trestle bridges, telegraphs, and steam printing presses—these remote occurrences profoundly shaped the modernization of the isthmus. Anticipating the current meaning of networks, the isthmus also became a place where postal and telegraphic messages, the information packets of their day, were routed to faraway places: Lima, San Francisco, Vancouver, and Hong Kong. The rapid movement of these messages shaped the economic, military, and political fate of distant nations and the affective bonds that connected far-flung individuals to each other and the state.[17]

Scholars of hemispheric American studies have moved productively "beyond the national frame to consider regions, areas, and diasporan affiliations that exist apart from or in conflicted relationships to the nation."[18] Panama's fashioning as an in-between place, a site of transit and mobility serving travelers bound for California, is certainly an important moment in this expanding frame. The prospect of shortening the distance between New York and San Francisco sparked the imagination of U.S. politicians and writers, who sought to extend their nation's reach not only westward toward

the Pacific but also southward into Central America, part of a larger project of hemispherical dominance that would reach its apogee in the Spanish-
American War. Yet to view nineteenth-century Panama merely in terms of
a hegemonic United States is both to simplify a complex story that involved
multiple actors and risk reinscribing imperial assumptions about U.S. dominance within the scholarly field that addresses it.[19] Great Britain, which had
vast overseas interests across the Pacific, took a keen interest in the idea of
a communication between the two great oceans. In the Atlantic context, the
isthmus's proximity to Jamaica, the traditional seat of British power in the
Caribbean, and to British Honduras and the Mosquito Coast, Britain's strategic footholds in Central America, meant that Panamanian matters loomed
large in the agendas of the Foreign and Colonial Offices. These interests, in
turn, brought Britain into conflict and cooperation with its upstart rival across
the Atlantic, also expanding its influence. As well, Panamanians across social
classes were not the passive recipients of shaping external forces, but exerted
themselves in manifold ways to forge their own destinies in a rapidly modernizing world, in which a happy geographical location between the seas could
become both an asset and a liability. To capture these multiple crossings of
imperial power, and how they shaped Panama at a crucial moment in its own
history, this study proposes a multinodal approach in which the perspectives
of hemispheric critique, which illuminate north-south political formations,
join with Atlantic models to open east-west vectors.[20]

I also turn away from celebratory accounts of the canal as a technological and engineering marvel, a wonder of the world, toward a more contested
history understood through the theoretical paradigm of "mobilities." This
work arises from social science research on aspects of urbanization such as
traffic, the automobile, crowds, airports, mass transit, and networked communication. It explores a variety of speculative questions occasioned more
generally by movement and flow, particularly though not exclusively those
instigated by human agency.[21] And it studies the "various complex systems,
assemblages, regimes and practices" of the mobile and immobile. Yet crucially for my purposes here, mobilities research examines not only motion,
but also the forces that resist, retard, or inhibit it in a dynamic set of interactions among differential energies, not a simple binary between motion and
stasis.[22] The historian Tim Creswell usefully calls this dynamic the "politics of
obduracy."[23] Such resistant forces are Janus-like: for the hurried and harried,
they may appear as irritants or obstacles to overcome; for those who do the
resisting—in this case many Panamanians themselves—a stubborn obduracy,
or even a hesitation about embracing new modes of movement, such as the
locomotive, may assume the form of a political act or even a bloody rebellion.

At its best, mobilities research thinks through this politics of friction to correct accounts of a networked world that overemphasize connectivity and flow to the detriment of understanding global inequities and the unevenness of the capitalist mode. Hence, I examine mobility here not as an absolute good, but a force that conflicts with other forces that have their own rationales and legitimacy, an imperative that jostles uncomfortably with other imperatives in the isthmian space. Finally, in the larger hemispheric and global contexts that concern me here, work on mobilities prods questions about national frames and the exceptionalist narratives they have frequently produced. Any study that deals with how transnational formations (oceans, sea lanes, transit, global communication) clash with more traditionally defined national concerns, such as sovereignty and rights, must probe the tension between that which is nation-bound and that which crosses borders.

CULTURE ON THE MOVE

It is impossible to understand nineteenth-century Panama apart from the changes in transit and transport that altered its landscape and culture, as well as the places to which it connected—changes that in their scale and speed remain shocking to this day. In 1848, before news of California's gold had traveled far, just 335 foreign travelers made their way across the isthmus. By 1852, that number had spiked nearly a hundredfold, to 31,826, and by 1865 the railroad had carried more than 400,000 people across.[24] In 1848, California's population stood at 20,000. One year later it had risen to 100,000, and by 1852 had reached 225,000.[25] Noel Maurer and Carlos Yu calculate that during the 1850s travel across Panama "contributed no less than twenty one percent" of California's total population growth.[26] The isthmus became a massive throughway for wealth; from 1855 to 1867, the railroad conveyed 750 million dollars of specie (money in coin), mostly from California.[27] The communications of two empires—Great Britain and the United States—surged through as well. The *California*, the first Pacific Mail steamship to serve the Panama to San Francisco route, carried 6,000 letters in its hold on its maiden voyage in 1848–49. Within months the number had risen to 36,000.[28] In the space of twelve years, 300,000 bags of mail were conveyed across the isthmus.[29] Writing in 1869, Berthold Seemann, the naturalist who collaborated with the British naval officer Bedford Pim on several Central American projects, commented on the isthmus's centrality to communication, describing it as the central spot for "obtaining information and news, and carrying on trade with the East and the West, the North and the South."[30] Persons, currency, state communications, and letters—all these, as well as private and commercial freight, ideas, texts, and images, moved from one ocean to another in a seemingly endless stream, first by mule and canoe, then later by rail. The isthmus quickly became a quintessential contact zone, a place where various peoples intermingled and sometimes clashed. The sizeable number of U.S. citizens that crossed through, unusual throughout all Latin America, brought with it extra tensions, as the military and economic backing of a large and powerful nation gave an extra charge to interactions between these highly mobile foreigners and the locals.

Through, across, over, by way of, and between—the language and ideology of isthmian transit (in Spanish, "transitismo") became dominated by the prepositional phrase, a constant reminder in everyday language of the region's discursively in-between status and of relational space itself. "The first parcel [was] brought across the isthmus . . . 23 days from the Pacific," proclaimed the *Panama Star & Herald* in 1857. "The whole expense of delivering it in New York, taking it from ship's tackles on the Bay of Panama, is only nine cents per gallon."[31] Shipping maps and elaborate timetables of arrival and departure coordinated the mobiles—the things and people that moved relentlessly across—locating them ever more precisely in space and time. The latter half of Otis's best-selling handbook, *The History of the Panama Railroad . . . Together with a Traveller's Guide and Business Man's Hand-Book* (1861), is filled with page upon page of railway and steamship schedules. These tables implicitly acknowledge that place has yielded before a new, reigning order: temporality. The tables slice time into segments meaningful to the foreign traveler, the human agent of mobility Panama came to serve, and capitalism, the system that transformed the isthmus into what Otis calls the "natural culminating point for the great commercial travel of the globe."[32] Otis's tabular representation of connections through Panama anticipates the insights of railway historians, that the chaos of multiple regimes of temporality that prevailed before the advent of standardization would finally bend to the needs of modern travelers, who demanded to know, to the minute, where they stood in time, even at the cost of submitting to what Hobsbawm calls the "gigantic . . . complex and interlocking routine symbolized by the railway table."[33] In Otis's scheme, we see how Panama became enmeshed in, and subject to, modernity's insatiable demands for speed, mobility, integration, and global connectivity, forces that pose the greatest threats to "sedentarist" accounts of location-bound meaning.[34]

To the extent that Anglo-American travelers identified Panama, variously, as a way station, a hub, a thoroughfare between more important points, a site of transit and exchange, and sometimes a bottleneck where movement slowed or ground to a halt, their representations fractured the meaning of place itself—a recurrent theme in mobilities research and a pressing concern throughout the discourses I examine here.[35] As nineteenth-century Panama reveals, the trammeling forces of rootlessness, travel, environmental degradation, and global commerce undermined the traditional understanding of place as a locus of significance for its inhabitants, a coherent center of meaning shaped by culture and language, or the site where people make their lives. The geographer David Harvey, writing in another context, describes what happens when the conflict between "place-bound fixity" and the "spatial mobility of capital" erupts: "The geographical configuration of places must then be reshaped around new transport and communications systems and physical infrastructures, new centers and styles of production and consumption, new agglomerations of labor power, and modified social infrastructures."[36]

In mid-nineteenth-century Panama, a swiftly globalizing world hastened the land's radical transformation. The pickaxes that swung in the California foothills echoed in faraway Colón and Cruces, thousands of miles away. The demand for more rapid communication to and from California—of bodies, things, and capital—drove the leveling of mountains, the filling of gorges, the laying of railroad ties, the establishment of foreign businesses, and the texture of interactions between travelers and Panamanians. The land's visual scarring highlighted the altered fabric of social relations between foreigners and the permanent residents of the isthmus, for whom Panama was not an intersection or throughway but a home. For Panamanians, the economic benefits of these sweeping changes remained elusive. Describing the followers of Mammon ("capitalistas extranjeros") who swept down upon the isthmus, Castillero Calvo points out that they reshaped the local economy by immediately investing in and controlling the assets of the region's most lucrative businesses: mule trains, horse stables, banks, gambling and entertainment, newspapers, hotels, and restaurants. He notes that the benefits of this commerce on the local economy, and particularly on Panama's commercial elite, have never been ascertained.[37]

TEMPORALITIES

If hurried and impatient Anglo-American travelers—steamship and railway schedules in hand—defined Panama as a spatial and temporal shortcut, they also shaped the world's perception of it in other crucial ways. By far the most important was their insistence on seeing the isthmus through a deeply pernicious anthropological lens, itself conjoined to ideas about time. Described by Johannes Fabian as the "denial of coevalness" and Anne McClintock as the creation of "anachronistic space," this cognitive structure positions Western observers and their native subjects in *allochronic* temporalities, one specified as modern and technologically advanced, the other as primitive, backward, and progress-less.[38] As McClintock puts it, the colonized in this framework "exist in a permanently anterior time within the geographic space of the modern empire as anachronistic humans, atavistic, irrational, bereft of human agency."[39] Government officials, military officers, geographers, and anthropologists routinely drew on the trope to justify colonial policy as well as schemes of economic development, and it became a staple of both nineteenth-century fictional and nonfictional writing about the tropics.[40] In 1851, at the inception of the Panama Railroad, an article in *Household Words* depicts a journey into the Central American jungle as a frightening scene of submission to primordial nature: "We are enclosed on all sides by a forest wall. The course of the broad stream is hidden by its windings; trees, piled upon trees environ us."[41] By century's end, the metaphor would organize the colonial ideologies of modernism. Conrad's *Heart of Darkness*, the locus classicus of jungle penetration, figures the journey across the Belgian Congo as a regression in time; the farther Marlow, the novella's narrator, travels along the Congo, the further back in human history he goes. Aboard his trusty steamboat, an emblem of mechanized modernity, Marlow describes the journey upriver as "traveling back to the earliest beginnings of the world, when vegetation rioted on the earth and the big trees were kings." "We were wanderers on a prehistoric earth," he says, "travelling in the night of the first ages," hearing the splashes of what seems an "ichthyosaurus" bathing in the river.[42] Such metaphors are far more than decorative touches in an armature of natural description; primordial nature here stands as a thinly disguised metonym for primitive culture. Tropes of allochronic temporality, as Fabian writes, constitute "ideologically construed instruments of power," tools in the larger domination of one part of humankind by another that achieve their discursive force by immobilizing colonial subjects in a time anterior to the forward-moving temporality of anthropologists, travelers, and readers.[43] As we shall see, to the extent that Panamanian space was rendered prehistoric and outside a progressive logic, it could be wrested away in the service of cultural enlightenment and economic development.

Yet if the specification of allochronic temporalities—one forward moving, progressive, and modern; the other primitive and underdeveloped—was a key component of the Anglo-American discourse of Panama, it was also complicated by Panama's own differential regimes of time. As throughout Latin America, Panamanian history was comprised of indigenous, colonial, and modern temporalities. Indigenous peoples such as the Kuna (discussed in chapter 4) clung ferociously to their traditional ways of life on the isthmus, even as modern machines transformed the terminal cities. The colonial remnants of Old Spain—forts and battlements, roads and bridges, decaying churches—were ubiquitous and stood alongside the signs of a modernity that had accelerated rapidly with the coming of the railway but was in clear development before, evidenced by a lively newspaper and periodical culture, local and national institutions, and a transport system that was efficient in its own way. Panama was clearly a place with a history and a future. Neither its three-hundred-year-old colonial culture nor its modern-day people could be easily dismissed by reference to a simple binary between civilization and barbarism. To accomplish this ideological move, it was necessary both to reconceptualize Panama as a place between—evacuating its local culture by constructing it as a non-place—and to privilege rapid mobility as the sine qua non of modernity itself.[44] This discursive remapping was accompanied by the reshaping of the land, first to accommodate the railroad and accompanying Yankee Strip and later the canal.

Speed was central to this new world order, both as a metonymic shorthand for modernity and a physical reality with manifold affective consequences. In a recent study of this phenomenon, Enda Duffy argues that speed is "the only new pleasure invented by modernity." Updating Stephen Kern's *Culture of Time and Space: 1880–1918*, Duffy locates this new pleasure in the automobile age, which offered for the first time "the promise, through technology, of an experience lived at a new level of intensity . . . hurtling through space at speed." Delivering "a new pleasure to the masses," the automobile stood against "the excruciating slowness of inefficient transport" such as steamships and railways, which could only deliver a "passive experience" of velocity.[45] Like a speed-crazed driver himself, Duffy takes the reader on a whirlwind ride through modernism's romance with the car, but in doing so succumbs to technology's own progressive narrative, which is that newer is always better (or more "modern"). He thus minimizes, predictably so, the psychosocial effects of earlier transport revolutions that scholars of nineteenth-century culture, since at least Wolfgang Schivelbusch's *Railway Journey* (1977), have identified as equally important in the intensification of a desire for speed. The exhilarating sensation of speed Duffy associates with the experience of commanding an automobile was in fact one of the first effects noticed by early railway passengers. As Schivelbusch notes, a whole medical literature arose to analyze the strain, disorientation, delirium, fatigue, and even nausea produced by traveling at what Jonathan Grossman more recently describes as the "almost unthinkable velocity of movement" introduced by railway travel to a generation raised on the horse-drawn carriage.[46] Consider Laurence Oliphant's account of riding the Panama Railroad, published in 1860:

To one only accustomed to see[ing] a thickly populated and highly cultivated country traversed by railways, and familiar with tropical jungles only
when they are penetrated by the devious little paths of the woodcutter or
the hunter, this dash through the virgin forest at the tail of a locomotive is
very imposing, and presents, with unusual force to the mind, the important
change which steam is destined to effect on the face of nature.[47]

Or, rather, on the face of culture, and indeed politics. For here Duffy is correct
in arguing that speed, properly considered, "should be thought of as political."[48] That valence is particularly acute in the literature and photographic
images examined throughout this book, where we encounter a form of coloniality built on the opposition between capitalism's speed compulsion—signaled
by railway and steamship, above all—and the slower rhythms of local culture
it constructs as its antagonist. In this world, modernity's addiction to speed is
part of the larger ensemble of colonialism's practices.

U.S. and British writers represented the Panama Railroad and the larger
network of mobilities they encountered as proffering wholly new experiences
of time. Their accounts stress the exhilaration of crossing forbidding geographies with unprecedented speed and implicitly a new world order that would
be wedded, via the iron bands of capital, to the pursuit of ever-swifter movement and interconnection of persons, things, and information. The history of
capitalism, as David Harvey puts it in his discussion of "time-space compres-
sion," is characterized by the "speed-up in the pace of life, while so overcoming spatial barriers that the world seems to collapse inwards upon us."[49] What
Marx described in the *Grundrisse* (1857–58) as the "annihilation" of space and
time quickly became associated in the writers examined here with the project
of a communication across Panama, which in turn was part of the larger tra-
jectory of globalization: the establishment of global shipping; railway expansion; the telegraph system; and spatial and temporal "shortcuts" such as Suez
and Panama. The Anglo-American champions of a rapid capitalist tempo
delighted in setting their desire for speed against forces—human and nonhu-
man—that appeared to oppose it. In the 1850s, a series of articles in Dickens's
Household Words both argued vehemently for new, faster global pathways and
decried the failure of earlier British capitalists to realize them.[50] "Short Cuts
Across the Globe" (1850) states that "till the discovery of the new Gold country
how contentedly they dawdled round Cape Horn; creeping down one coast
and up another; but now such delay is not to be thought of."[51] The U.S. writer
Joseph Fabens, who described his own crossing in the early 1850s, captures
the sense of haste that prevailed at the Atlantic port of Chagres: "Over and
above everything else one great feeling predominates in the minds of men at

Chagres, an impatience to be away."[52] And in *The Gate of the Pacific* (1863), Bedford Pim reminds us that "a few years ago, loss of time was not considered of any moment," whereas now a passenger would feel "deeply aggrieved if the train arrives a few minutes late."[53] Panama's emergence around 1848 as an indispensable shortcut between the Atlantic and Pacific—a project to collapse space—became explicitly joined in the Anglo-American mind to a new sense of hurry driven by the desire to speed up and monetize time itself.

Geography posed one obstacle to the speed of travel and thus the mobility of travelers and capital. The beleaguered California-bound traveler confronted either the "provoking peculiarity" of going "thousands of miles out of his way," via Cape Horn, or the "virgin swamp, covered with a dense growth of the tortuous, water-loving mangrove, and interlaced with huge vines and thorny shrubs," via Panama.[54] Some travelers simply gave up. An 1851 article in *Chambers's Edinburgh Journal* described the conditions in Chagres as so unpleasant that one traveler, having sold everything to settle in California, abandoned his journey, declaring that "nothing on earth would induce him to cross the Isthmus."[55] When they did persist, Anglo-American travelers represented the prerailroad crossing as a chaotic scramble through confusing terrain. In his 1855 travel account, Francis Marryat, son of the adventure writer Captain Marryat, put it this way:

> With our mules in a string we plunged at once into a narrow rocky path in the forest, where palm trees and creepers shut the light out overhead—splashing through gurgling muddy streams, that concealed loose and treacherous stones—stumbling over fallen trees that lay across our road—burying ourselves to the mules' girths in filthy swamps, where on either side dead and putrid mules were lying—amidst lightning, thunder, and incessant rain, we went at a foot-pace on the road to Panama.[56]

In an accompanying image (fig. I.2), travelers, mules, and horses pull in all directions. Marryat's image also depicts precarious local labor positioned at the cusp of rapid modernization; *silleteros* carry some travelers on their backs, and guides tend the horses and mules of others. According to Mary Seacole, the mixed-race Jamaican woman who ran a hotel at Cruces, these interactions were shot through with racialized conflict invisible in Marryat's image: "Terribly bullied by the Americans were the boatmen and muleteers, who were reviled, shot, and stabbed." Her account makes clear that this rough treatment was conditioned by racial attitudes travelers carried with them from the North: "They would fain whop all creation abroad as they do their slaves at home."[57]

FIGURE I.2. Pedestrian Mobility. Frank Marryat, *Mountains and Molehills* (1855).

Nineteenth-century U.S. and British narratives sweep aside these conflicts to describe the coming of the railroad in mythic terms, invariably presenting the new technology as a magic, almost salvific force, a machine power that subdues the resistant natural and cultural order. The widely quoted *History of the Panama Railroad* (1861) typifies the pattern:

> Two American citizens, leaping, axe in hand, from a native canoe upon a wild and desolate island, their retinue consisting of half a dozen Indians, who clear the path with rude knives, strike their glittering axes into the nearest tree; the rapid blows reverberate from shore to shore, and the stately cocoa crashes upon the beach. Thus unostentatiously was announced the commencement of a railway, which, from the interests and difficulties involved, might well be looked upon as one of the grandest and boldest enterprises ever attempted.[58]

Symbolizing the larger project of the civilizing mission, whereby the United States brings the benefits of industrial technology to the underdeveloped parts of the hemisphere, the energetic foreigners clear the forbidding jungle with their glittering axes, accomplishing in a few swift strokes what had only recently been described as impossible. The swift submission of the "stately cocoa," a common image of tropical fecundity, illustrates the magic power of Anglo-Saxon energy to remake the resisting wilderness.

Yet Otis's picture of the natives feebly hacking away with their "rude knives" reveals that Anglo-American writers located obduracy not only in a resistant geography but also in the human inhabitants that populated it. Indeed, images of native futility and foot-dragging are a stock feature of this discourse and combine in the Panamanian context with representations of allochronic time to further justify Anglo-American hegemony. When Fabens asks the native boatmen who guide him up the Chagres how much farther to the village of Gatun, they reply, "Poco tiempo"—here meant to indicate an infinitely elastic period somewhere between minutes and days.[59] At Chagres in 1849, Bayard Taylor describes California-bound travelers running "up and down the beach shouting, gesticulating, and getting feverishly impatient at the deliberate habits of the natives."[60] Similarly, the British telegraph engineer Lionel Gisborne, who surveyed the isthmus in 1852, complains that long delays compounded the "difficulty of exploring a country covered with dense forest," to the point that he begins to agree with a U.S. engineer who tells him, "Everything here is Mañana."[61] Even Mary Seacole proclaims that "Central Americans should adopt the hammock as their national badge; but for sheer necessity they would never leave it."[62] Yet beyond the familiar stereotype of the languid Latin American lies a more troubling set of views about the ability of local Panamanian people to embrace progress at all. As often, these ideologies found a focal point in the question of transport. Guided by deep-rooted cultural attitudes about the inability of black and mixed-race laborers to participate in Panama's transformation, Anglo-American travelers failed to recognize what the Panamanian boatmen had in fact achieved—a "resource-fulness," as Marixa Lasso puts it, that adapted to a changing technological world and efficiently conveyed thousands across the isthmus.[63] Viewed from the perspective of U.S. and British travelers, the transport revolution was not simply about replacing canoes with steam locomotives but also stamping an image of modernity on Panama that erased the local people themselves, who were perceived as obstacles to the capitalist dream of a frictionless flow of goods and people across the globe.

Such views found sanction not only in the writings of travelers but also in the budding discipline of anthropology, whose rise as a codified area of study coincided with the period treated here. In learned societies on both sides of the Atlantic, prophets of vanishing races took special aim at racial mixing, such as was common throughout the Americas. As George Stocking and Patrick Brantlinger have shown, racial theories of human extinction were closely connected to the larger project of Anglo-American imperialism, and they had a particularly sharp edge vis-à-vis the mixed race inhabitants of Spanish America.[64] In 1863, the anthropologist and South American specialist William Bollaert argued in a substantial demographic study of New World races that the "morally and physically" detrimental habit of mixing races would cause the Spanish American population to decline.[65] Seemann described the native race as "an amalgamation, as it is, between white, Indian, and negro" and argued that "a day must come when the greater part of Spanish America will be cleared of its present occupants."[66] As we will see, the champions of isthmian transport read the coming of the railway as a decisive technological break that would hasten the large-scale demographic changes predicted by Victorian anthropology. They saw the steam locomotive not simply as a new machine, but as the emblem and embodiment of a broader historical and cultural shift that would complete the triumph of the Anglo-Saxon races.

Among the most influential boosters of a mechanized system of isthmian transport was the English-language *Panama Star,* which began publication in February 1849. Its immediate readership was the community of gold rushers and the businessmen who sprung up to serve them on their way to California, and yet its reach extended far and wide, as its columns about life in Panama were widely reprinted in newspapers across the United States and cited in Britain. In a lead column entitled the "Iron Horse," published in August 1849, the *Star* cheered the railway's advent in racialized terms that went well beyond the paeans to technological speed and efficiency we have examined previously. The column begins by describing the coming technology as a swift and powerful emblem of the Anglo-American hegemony that would collapse distance and conquer geography: "What a revolution that iron horse has made in the world, and what an upturning he will make here, leveling mountains, and setting at defiance the obstacles which now perplex the weary Californian."[67] Initially, those obstacles are geographical, which the *Star* hopes the railroad will overcome by crossing the isthmus in rapid time. It soon becomes clear, however, that the *Star* locates obduracy not so much in nature as in the human inhabitants of the isthmus: "What will the swarthy natives of this peaceful Isthmus say, when they see him coming—puffing, steaming, whizzing, and with lightning speed lifting his burthen at Lemon Bay and laying it down at Panama in two or three short hours?" The *Star* represents the railroad not as a benign instrument of increased human communication, but as a terrifyingly personified brute with a maw that "cannot be fixed" and an "appetite which cannot be satiated." The railroad "snorts—he puffs—he blows his shrill trumpet and moves off majestically on his Pacific-bound course." In this harrowing account, the machine in the garden has come horribly alive as a merciless destroyer.

What did the smoke-belching monster come to ravage? The answer lies in the picture of the "bewildered negroes of Chagres stupefied with amazement," leading lives a "century behind the spirit of the age," wedded to "paddles, oars, and mules," a classic formulation of allochronic time that locates Panamanians outside modernity's perceived blessings. The *Star*, itself a shrill trumpet, prophesies that the railroad will swiftly spell the end of the preindustrial, local economy in which black and mixed-race people guided white travelers—all too slowly for the *Star*—over footpaths and along rivers. For just as the column's celebration of the annihilation of space ("levelling mountains") is a familiar component, as we have seen, of the techno-enthusiastic rhetoric of railway promotion, so is its location of obduracy and frustration in a racialized account of the local people: "What else could be expected of you, when you have never seen a steam engine?" Clearly the "upturning" the *Star* has in mind is social as well as technological, one that would leave the "bewildered" local people with no language to understand the change and no recourse but to try their hands "at something new." For the *Star*, the railroad was a disruptive technology whose purpose was to harden the distinction between forward-moving, modern Anglo-Americans and the colonial other they displaced. In this new age, according to the *Star*, "you must become tinctured with iron, or perish under it."

PANAMANIAN VOICES

Of course Panamanians had their own ideas about the isthmian transformation. Like the Anglo-American representations with which they stand in tension, these voices reflect a complex and heterogeneous culture, fraught with its own inconsistencies, exclusions, and inequities. Moreover, the archive that preserves them is, like all archives, necessarily selective, an artifact of power relations rather than a transparent container of information; its contents and organization reflect the dominant social structures of the culture that assembled and preserved it. Describing the archival turn that has redefined repositories as objects of study in themselves, Ann L. Stoler writes that such changes signal "a new grappling with the production of history, what accounts get authorized, what procedures were required, and what about the past it is possible to know."[68] One might add to this list the problem of the conditions and limits on speech itself, a preoccupation of postcolonial theory at least since the 1980s.[69] This problem matters especially much in an archive that privileges elite perspectives, where the infrequently heard voice of the subaltern, whether Chinese, black, or indigenous, is usually mediated through other forms (the newspaper, the government document, the statesman's treatise, or the traveler's account), and not given under the privileged sign of authorship. This context assumes further urgency in nineteenth-century Panamanian culture, which was riven by internal conflicts between a large black population, which comprised sixty-three percent of the country in the late eighteenth century, and the creole elites, who worried about becoming "another Haiti," a revolutionary state that would wreck their dream of a trade-based Hanseatic republic and a Panamanian identity, or *Latinidad*, based on the denial and repression of blackness.[70]

These tensions erupt in the writings of Justo Arosemena (1817–96), the most well known and prolific of mid-century Panamanian writers. A towering figure in politics and letters, the statesman and orator advocated Panama's increased participation in global trade, even suggesting the creation of a commerce-based state that, as Peter Szok has pointed out, would be protected for a decade by the United States, Great Britain, Sardinia, and France, a position that flirts dangerously with the acceptance of annexation.[71] In a brief 1842 essay, "Estado económico del Istmo," he expressed his wish for an easy communication ("fácil comunicación") across the isthmus that would permit Panama to benefit from its fortunate geographical position between the seas.[72] He elaborated this view at much greater length in his 1846 treatise, *Exámen sobre la franca comunicación entre los dos Océanos por el Istmo* (1846), which evaluates the interests of the great economic powers of the day (England, France,

and the United States) in building such a route. Recognizing that cries for
faster transit were revolutionizing communication and travel, he noted that
Britain had already sent steam packets to the isthmus's Atlantic coast and was
seeking to expand its Pacific trade, and that France was steadfastly pursuing
scientific exploration in the region.[73] Arosemena argued that the United States
stood most to benefit from any crossing. To allay concerns about its increased
influence, he observed that it had "not formed a single colony" and was occupied with peopling its own vast terrain.[74] In his early writings, Arosemena
revealed himself a shrewd and informed supporter of the Hanseatic ideal that
would position the isthmus at the center of international trade. He thus exemplified a larger pattern in which Latin American elites, as Bradford Burns puts
it, became "increasingly convinced that Europe and the United States offered
solutions to the problems they perceived in their societies."[75]

By the 1850s, however, in the aftermath of the gold rush, the U.S. invasion of Mexico, and growing U.S. designs on Cuba, Arosemena's views had
noticeably darkened. In an 1850 article in *El Panameño* entitled "¡¡¡Alerta Istmeños!!!, To Be or Not To Be," Arosemena summoned the Prince of Denmark's famous soliloquy to draw attention to increasing threats to Panama's
sovereignty. Writing just as construction on the railroad had begun and a year
after the establishment of the *Panama Star,* he identified the foreign press as
a special threat to Panamanian interests. He pointed to the "alarming" tone
of the commercially aligned *Star,* which had challenged Panamanian attempts
to regulate the growing number of steamers that carried gold seekers to and
from California. The paper's increasingly bellicose and hostile positions, as
evidenced by articles such as the "Iron Horse," suggested a new front in the
battle for Panamanian self-determination. For Arosemena, the central question, as always, was national sovereignty, the ability to make one's own laws for
the interest of Panamanians, not foreign travelers or commercial enterprises
such as steamship and railway companies. However, he couched this concern
in a larger argument about U.S. imperialism itself, and the power of print culture to advance it: "Lo que vemos en todas estas publicaciones es la convicción
de que el Istmo es una tierra de conquista" (What we see in these newspapers
is the conviction that Panama is a land of conquest). Against a warlike foe
like the United States, which he likens to a hungry wolf, Panamanians must
decide "to be or not to be: to be an independent people, with their own laws
and customs; to be the owners of their own lands which they inherited from
their forefathers; or to be the humble servants of other proud races, that never
will grant them the name of 'civilized peoples.'"[76]

By 1855, Arosemena had taken an even more pessimistic view. By then the
establishment of the Yankee Strip and the arrival of adventurers in Central

America such as William Walker crystallized the threat of U.S. economic hegemony and imperial expansion. In his most famous work, *Estado Federal*, published in 1855 just as the railroad was being completed, Arosemena surveyed
his people's economic and political fortunes. He concedes that prior to 1849
the economy had been in a woeful state ("lamentable estado de postración"),
a condition he illustrates by citing the famous saying of Rufino Cuervo, the
Colombian statesman, to the effect that "whoever wants to see Panama should
hurry because it would soon be finished." For despite the injection of massive
U.S. capital, local industry had decayed, as many of the products that Panama
formerly had produced were soon imported from afar.[77] A year later, in his
"Contra la expansión colonialista de Estados Unidos," his arguments assume
a harder political edge as he takes special aim at the concept of Manifest Destiny, linking it strongly to the excessive ambition ("desmedida ambición") of
the United States. He criticizes as well, however, the "prodigal" concessions
that were given to the railroad company and the generosity extended to what
he calls the "implacable speculators." But rather than speak of these matters in
purely economic terms, he puts the problem in the stark political language of
self-determination and autonomy. Arosemena summons a sharp, nationalist
rhetoric to lay down a fundamental principle: to give land is to forfeit sovereignty ("señorío"), and to relinquish it for permanent and expensive infrastructure, such as the railroad, is just the same as giving up territory.[78] He
concludes by calling on his countrymen to fulfill the destiny afforded by a
happy geographical location between the seas ("la opulenta Península, ceñida
por dos océanos") by standing up to what he calls the "enemy race" of the
Anglo-Saxons.[79] In a subsequent essay, he would again employ this overt language of distinct races to contrast the peaceful and religious "raza latina" with
the warlike expansionists of the North, who would cry from their New England redoubts, "I need another world; this is mine; and I will conquer you
entirely."[80] Their mission, he writes, is to subdue, and in a compelling burst of
anti-imperial rhetoric, he assembles evidence of a larger hemispheric imperialism emanating from the United States. He describes the expansion across
the "deserts" of the West and the annihilation ("aniquilando") of the indigenous races that lived there.[81] Not content with Mexico's submission, the Anglo-
Saxons, he argues, had used diplomatic means to steal California, and now
they were intent on spreading their "corruption" throughout the hemisphere.
They were ultimately a distinct race: materialist, thieving, a grave threat to
Latin America and the future of universal commerce itself.[82]

Yet along with Arosemena's anti-imperialism, one must also confront the
statesmen's racism that was its unfortunate counterpart. For the "American
question" that Arosemena describes was not confined solely to two races: the

Anglo-Saxon and the Latin. Panama's black majority presented a quandary not only for U.S. travelers unaccustomed to evidence of black political empowerment but also for the creole population of maritime-commercial elites who were engaged in a process of cultural and national self-fashioning predicated on the suppression of this demographic reality.[83] Arosemena's "American question" was written in the immediate aftermath of the so-called "Watermelon Riot," or as it is known in Panama, "El incidente de la tajada de sandía" (the incident of the watermelon slice), one of the most extensively documented events in nineteenth-century Panamanian history.[84] On April 15, 1856, in Panama (City), Jack Oliver, a drunken U.S. traveler, approached a black fruit seller, José Manuel Luna, asking for a slice of watermelon. It seems likely that Luna, identified elsewhere as a silversmith, was one of those economically harmed by the Yankee irruption on the isthmus. He was associated with the *arrabal*, a poor neighborhood that formed the center of black life in the city. When Oliver, after taking a bite, threw the melon on the ground, issued a vulgar insult, and refused to pay, Luna said to him *in English*, "Careful, we are not in the United States here." This utterance, which comes to us, like so many subaltern voices, through newspaper accounts and official reports, has been correctly interpreted as a reminder of the limits of U.S. hegemony. It is also a strong declaration of New Granadian sovereignty, which included the abolition of slavery, the establishment of universal manhood suffrage, and access for blacks to the mayoralties of various towns throughout the republic. It is clearly a sign that Panama's black residents would not treat white travelers with the deference they were accustomed to at home. After this exchange a riot ensued, with loss of life on both sides, official inquiries, and eventually the arrival of the U.S. Navy in a show of force, the first of many military interventions in the long, troubled relationship between the nations.[85]

All this is quite well known. Arosemena's interpretation of the incident reveals an additional layer of complexity, the existence of a significant rupture in the very idea of "Latinidad."[86] For after recounting the surrounding events, Arosemena performs a delicate excision, absolving the people ("pueblo") of Panama from any blame and laying it instead on the shoulders of "negros advenedizos." Arosemena's adjective "advenedizo" most simply means upstart, but may also connote an outsider, a foreigner, a person without employment or office, or even someone who comes into a fortune and begins to put on airs. In the context of anxieties about assertive black empowerment in Panama, the word may have also suggested an unseemly grasping for political influence among those perceived as undeserving. Indeed, as Verena Martinez-Alier documents, mid-nineteenth-century Cuban officials used similar language to register their fears of the "ambitious pretensions" of free blacks in the realms of economic and professional achievement. White Cubans implored the government to prevent any "slackening of the links of obedience and respect which the colored race should entertain for the white."[87] As for Arosemena, he crucially defines these ambitious upstarts as foreigners who had arrived from several countries, but particularly from the Antilles, and shows his disdain by referring to them as "escoria corrompida," corrupt riffraff or "scum" that congregate in the world's terminal cities and commercial highways. White Panamanians, he insists, had not engaged directly in the conflict but merely witnessed it.[88] As Arosemena's comments reveal, the riot hardened the division not only between Panama and the U.S., but also between white and black Panamanians themselves, as the former seized the occasion to delimit the very definition of a Latin American.[89]

We can see further evidence of this emerging racial division and internal coloniality in elite Panamanian literary culture of the time. Among the era's most important poets was Tómas Martín Feuillet (1832–62), described by Rodrigo Miró as a prototypical romantic and vital participant in the flowering of Panamanian literary culture.[90] Author of the famous poem celebrating Panama's national flower, "La flor del Espíritu Santo," and the acerbic lyric on his society's cash-nexus, "¿Cuánto tiene?," where everything has a price, Feuillet was also acutely conscious of growing U.S. power in the region. Like Arosemena, the Chilean poet Francisco Bilbao (1823–65), and the Colombian lyricists Rafael Pombo (1833–1912) and José María Torres Caicedo (1830–89), Feuillet captured the deleterious effects of the new Yankee domination. Although Kirsten Silva Gruesz suggests that two of Pombo's unpublished poems from 1856 constitute the "first directly anti-imperialist verse about the United States," an examination of Feuillet's corpus suggests a simultaneous political awakening in Panama, perhaps, as Miró hypothesizes, the result of the civil disturbances of April 1856.[91] Certainly, Feuillet's "Al ciudadano gobernador D. Bartolome Calvo," published in October 1856 during a period of rising anti-Yankee sentiment in the Panamanian press, gives a ringing defense of Panamanian sovereignty against northern aggression and expansionist tyranny.[92] In these powerful verses, he asserts that the "sons of the noisy Niagara" will no more plant their "starry flag" in Panama ("¡más no los hijos del ruidoso Niágara, / su estrellado perdón aquí alzarán!").[93] The extraordinary metonym, associating the North Americans with the "noisy Niagara," brilliantly locates the expansionist character of the United States in a traditional symbol of its landscape and national identity—a waterfall on a border attached to a major canal. Implicitly drawing the connection, Feuillet interprets the falls as more terrible than beautiful, capturing their ferocious power and connecting them to the larger hemispheric aggression that was threatening Latin America.

The anti-imperialism announced in Feuillet's poem—that the brash Yankees will sweep down on the region in an unstoppable flood—assumes an even
richer form in his 572-line patriotic masterpiece, "A un amigo." Employing the
language of landscape description and nostalgia to register the speaker's pride
in his homeland, Feuillet's poem expresses its nationalism by condemning the
increasing foreign presence in Panama. In a familiar logic, the poem bolsters
Panamanian nationalism by representing instances of the Anglo-American
threat. It laments that the land has rotted since so many foreigners came from
the United States and Great Britain. Everyone on the isthmus is American
now, and all of them want to speak English. It would be better if the earth
would simply swallow up the "gringo" intruders.[94] Yet in this poem, Feuillet,
like Arosemena, performs a characteristic double move, defining Panamanian
"Latinidad" both against the aggressive Northern expansionists and the internal threat of a black underclass. For the speaker he chooses to deliver these
condemnations is not someone from his own, elite social stratum but a "zamba
rancia" (a rank woman of black/indigenous mixture), born in the poor *arrabal* neighborhood of "Rajaleña," a person he describes as a true representation of the Panamanian lower class ("pueblo bajo"). As Walter Mignolo points
out, the operative racial hierarchy in Spanish America from the seventeenth
century onward located Spanish creoles at the top; mestizos/as and mulattos/
as "in the next social group down"; and zambos, blacks, and the indigenous
"at the bottom of the pyramid."[95] Feuillet captures this status by marking her
birthplace in the *arrabal,* her race as a "zamba," and, most importantly, her
speech in a dialect that grates against his lyric's own polished and urbane
surfaces. When she complains about the many "gringos," she notes they come
from "Engalaterra" [*sic*], and when she identifies the North Americans, she
calls them "yankeeks" [*sic*]. "Toitos quieren hablá inglé" (They all want to
speak English), she says, again in dialect. At once the voice of anti-imperialism and an object of the poet's satire, a knowing political commentator and
a representative of the illiterate black underclass, she occupies an ambivalent
position. Although the collision of European and indigenous languages in the
Americas would later produce the affirmative tradition of *poesía negra,* as in
the work of Cuban poet Nicolás Guillén, Feuillet's use of dialect serves a different, stigmatizing purpose. The poet provides a rare subaltern voice, a striking linguistic instance of Panama's cultural heterogeneity, but couches it in his
own verse. This enfolding both contains subaltern expression and sets it apart
as a stereotypical sign of otherness and cultural immobility.[96] Although this
voice from below registers Panamanian resistance to U.S. domination, it also
vividly embodies the black underclass threat against which Panamanian elites
sought to define their own identities as Latin Americans.

CHAPTER OUTLINES

A profoundly in-between character, Feuillet's "zamba" is one of many characters from the margin examined in the chapters to follow. Although my archive
is primarily the Anglo-American representations that were published in the
English-speaking world, the presence of these marginalized figures is everywhere just beneath the surface, and sometimes front and center. In the chapters that follow, I explore the tensions alluded to in Fueillet's "A un amigo,"
examining a range of literary, governmental, and photographic archives that
demonstrate the discursive remapping of Panama as a place between, especially in the critical period from the gold rush to 1903. In chapter 1, I analyze the Central American transport career of John Lloyd Stephens and his
role in bringing massive technological infrastructure to the isthmus in the
form of the Panama Railroad. Most celebrated today for his best-selling literary accounts of Maya cities in Honduras, Guatemala, and Mexico, Stephens
worked throughout the 1840s to leverage his expertise on the ground and his
relationships with government officials in Washington and Central America to
realize the dream of a swift isthmian passage. Completed in 1855, the Panama
Railroad represented an important extension of U.S. hegemony in the Americas, establishing an informal zone of influence and laying the groundwork
for the eventual digging of the canal, which followed its path across Panama.
It conveyed thousands of passengers to and from the Pacific, as well as gold,
mail, and commercial goods. Established and policed by U.S. citizens (though
built with foreign labor), it formed the spine of the so-called "Yankee Strip,"
a zone of U.S. control in the otherwise sovereign territory of Nueva Granada
(now Panama). At the time the largest U.S. capital outlay in Central and South
America, the railroad reshaped the land and, just as importantly, social relations between U.S. citizens and the local people of Panama.

The question of an isthmian passage was of concern not only to Americans but also to the governments of France (later associated with De Lesseps's
failed canal project) and Great Britain. In chapter 2, I read the British novelist
Anthony Trollope's *The West Indies and the Spanish Main* (1859) in the context of British concerns about communication through Panama to its colonial
holdings in the Pacific, and tensions between the United States and Great
Britain over expanding U.S. influence in the region. Trollope went to the West
Indies and the isthmus on an official mission from the British Post Office to
streamline mail service, and in the course of this work, conducted a detailed
survey of communication routes through and across Central America. The
few critics who have examined this work focus exclusively on Trollope's attitudes toward race in the West Indies. My analysis considers these comments

but within a larger context afforded by his extensive journeys through Central America. As a well-placed government official gifted with a keen novelist's eye, Trollope was in a unique position to assess competing transit plans, Central America's possibilities as a nexus for global transit, and shifting geopolitical dynamics as a result of growing U.S. power in the region.

After the boom times of the 1850s and 1860s, the fortunes of transit companies serving the isthmus suffered a notable decline in the 1870s. Both the Pacific Mail Steamship Company and the Panama Railroad Company, the largest concerns, were damaged by the completion of the transcontinental railroad across the United States in 1869, which made the isthmian route less attractive to westbound travelers. In chapter 3, I consider this period through a close examination of an important, though heretofore neglected, body of visual images, the stereographs and large-plate photographs of the British photographer Eadweard Muybridge. In 1875, the steamship company sent Muybridge to Central America to promote U.S. tourism and trade, particularly the nascent Guatemalan coffee industry, whose shipments it conveyed. The steamship company was a key force in Panama's emergence into trans-Pacific modernity, controlling passage from the isthmus to San Francisco and other ports in the United States and Asia. By the time of his Central American journey, Muybridge was already celebrated as a landscape photographer and a pioneer in the modernization of his medium. His work for Leland Stanford laid the groundwork for the development of cinema. As regards his Panamanian journey, the company hoped that the powerful new medium of photography would stimulate foreign investment by representing the beautiful landscapes of Central America and a docile and contented native work force, safe from revolutionary undercurrents. Muybridge's images, however, tell a different story, exploring tensions among labor, indigeneity, and sexuality in ways that question U.S. control of the isthmus.

In chapter 4, I recover the once popular but now forgotten work of James Stanley Gilbert, a U.S. poet who resided in Panama in the decades before the canal was begun and produced what his *New York Times* obituary called a document of isthmian life. The expatriate community's unofficial bard, Gilbert was associated with the poet Tracy Robinson and other resident U.S. authors. Through a close reading of his oeuvre (two volumes of poems, photographs, and many prose sketches), I argue that his reputation as an unabashed supporter of imperialism—the "Kipling of the isthmus"—ignores his profound unease about the Americanization and transformation of Panama. While some poems celebrate that process, others paint a darker picture, focusing on debilitating tropical diseases and uneasy relations with the locals, which present a moral challenge to the colonizer. Like Muybridge before him, Gilbert emerges as an ambivalent commentator, both indulging in the conventional tropes of the tropical idyll and showing their limitations.

In a brief epilogue, I consider Panama's transformation into a pleasurable spot on newly invented leisure maps. As the mighty locks opened for the first time, and the Canal Zone filled with U.S. citizens, writers produced a flurry of texts to guide the new class of urbane subjects who descended on the isthmus. These works offered information about practical matters such as the post, the telegraph, currency, and schedules for ocean transport to faraway places. They also recommended suitable tropical attire and the best shops for jewelry and oriental rugs, Japanese silks, and the ubiquitous Panama hat—all metonyms for the canal's function in global trade, which, in a fulfillment of its first champions, brought the products of distant markets near. Several of these works romanticize the era of the Panama Railroad, seeing it as the beginning of a long process of economic development that transformed the region from an insalubrious swamp to the epitome of modern, Jazz-age prosperity. The development of a touristic discourse suggests at least one prominent direction for the rhetorics of travel, transport, modernity, and development examined in this book.

The chapters that follow thus present a cultural history of a certain place and time, one that, as a result of geographical accident, of isthmian thinness, became defined as a way station, a passageway, or in the old-fashioned phrase of the nineteenth century, a "communication." Through, over, and across this narrow neck or strip of land, culture moved, technology developed, people and things traveled, and political forces were unleashed. As a site of mobility that paradoxically engendered varieties of immobility, a place of flow that met with fixity and resistance, the isthmus produced representations that are here brought together for the first time. There remains much more to do, of course, as the archive of literature, pictorial images, and government documents has yet to be plumbed, even in the current golden age of information. By writing this book, this communication, I hope to point the way toward further study in this area.

CHAPTER 1

~

Short Cuts

The Panama Railroad and the Making of the Yankee Strip

Where is it written in the book of fate that the American republic shall
not stretch her limits from the capes of the Chesapeake to Nootka Sound,
from the isthmus of Panama to Hudson Bay?

— *DEMOCRATIC CLARION AND TENNESSEE GAZETTE*, APRIL 28,
1812

It seems to me that if the world had to choose its capital, the Isthmus of
Panama would be ideal for this august purpose, situated as it is in the
center of the globe, looking toward Asia on one side and toward Africa
and Europe on the other.

— SIMÓN BOLÍVAR, "LETTER TO GENERAL FRANCISCO DE PAULA
SANTANDER," MAY 30, 1825

Cut through this Isthmus, 'Uncle Sam' will then turn the corner, and
England will be distanced. Instead, then, of meeting us in India, China,
and even on our own Pacific coast with the advantage of some ten days'
sail, or more, the scales will be turned, and we shall have the advantage.

— M. F. MAURY, "MAURY'S ESTIMATE ... OF THE IMPORTANCE OF
INTEROCEANIC COMMUNICATION," JULY 2, 1849

BEFORE THE Panama Canal, there was a railroad. Upon completion in 1855,
it reduced the New York–San Francisco ocean route from 13,600 to 5,000
miles, and from four months to one. The hemisphere's first transcontinental
line, stretching forty-nine miles from Colón on the Atlantic to Panama on the
Pacific, it constituted in its day the largest outlay of U.S. capital in both Central
and South America. As an investment, it became one of the most profitable

offerings on the New York stock exchange, realizing an average annual return
as high as forty-eight per cent. Relative to the U.S. economy of its time, the
$8 million investment in 1858 would equal $28.5 billion dollars in 2009, or
roughly three times the relative scale of the Golden Gate Bridge.[1] But there
was more to the railroad than investment capital. It demonstrated the power
of industrial technology to reorder time and space: reshaping hemispheric
and global politics, modernizing California and Panama, and altering Central
American trade and commerce.[2] Laborers arrived from Ireland, the United
States, China, South America, the West Indies, and Africa to work on its construction.[3] They were the first to move, arriving long before any passengers
would enjoy the train as a vehicle for their own mobility. Other displacements
followed. The isthmian population boomed, tripling in the city of Panama
alone between 1840 and 1860.[4] The railroad prodded the making of a mobile
world of migration, dislocation, and diasporic wandering. And along with the
war against Mexico, efforts to annex Cuba, U.S. incursions in Central America, and the appropriation of pre-Columbian artifacts by travelers and antiquarian researchers, the railroad signaled a new, more aggressive era of U.S.
imperial ambition. Its sheer mechanical reality—the steam locomotives, ties
and rails, switches, trestle bridges, stations, and telegraph wires—suggested
the tentacular power of U.S. technology to expand southward and integrate
Central America within its dominion.

The land on which the line was built lay formally within the sovereign territory of Nueva Granada, formed along with Ecuador and Venezuela after the
breakup of Gran Colombia in 1831. Yet the overland railway path and its associated infrastructure became widely known as the "Yankee Strip," a zone of
commerce and culture designed to provide the goods, services, and comforts
demanded by Anglo-American travelers. This represented a linguistic concession to a new, albeit contested, reality, in which throngs of foreign travelers
crossed the isthmus but primarily enriched the expatriate community, not the
locals. California gold, according to the Panamanian historian Alfredo Castillero Calvo, did as little for the local economy in the 1850s as silver in an earlier
era from the mines of Potosí; the Panama Railroad and "los capitalistas neoy-
orquinos" absorbed all the transit and almost all the resulting economic benefits.[5] Indeed, "Isthmian sacrifices," as Alex Pérez-Venero puts it, were primarily
for the "benefit of two foreign nations—Colombia and the United States."[6]
Even the British naval officer Bedford Pim, not known for sympathizing with
Panamanians, noted in 1863 that since the railway bypassed the city of Panama
"all merchandise therefore passes through the country without in any way
affecting the prosperity of the city."[7] What's more, many of the foreigners were
rough and ill-mannered, a motley and frequently unsavory band compris-

ing, according to one Panamanian observer in 1857, all manner of travelers, businessmen, two-bit speculators, profiteers, gamblers, keepers of gambling houses, shoplifters, thieves, and assassins ("pasajeros, comerciantes, especuladores de menor cuantía, logreros, jugadores, gariteros, rateros, ladrones, asesinos"). Flouting the rule of law, they settled disputes with "la pistola, el rifle, el puñal [dagger], y el machete."[8] Contemporary observers, such as the Jamaican creole Mary Seacole, noted the specifically racial quality of these interactions, which appear to have been shaped by the perception that laws and customs on the strip were somehow in suspension, and that travelers in this in-between zone were under no obligation to conform to reasonable standards of conduct. Seacole's *Wonderful Adventures* (1857) vividly recounts the tensions that welled up on the isthmus as "the extreme class of [U.S.] citizens" encountered a society where blacks, who were in the majority, were not only free, but held important positions in public life. Seacole's transnational experience of travel had taught her that "Americans (even from the Northern States) are always uncomfortable in the company of coloured people, and very often show this feeling in stronger ways than by sour looks and rude words."[9] As she subsequently put it, the "New Granadan's experiences of American manners have not been favourable."[10]

The sudden inundation was particularly hard on Panama's working classes, the majority of whom were "gente de color," defined by Aims McGuinness as "all people who were perceived to descend at least partially from Africans."[11] The newcomers not only undermined the local economy but also encroached on working-class neighborhoods such as La Ciénaga, just outside the city of Panama, as well as other towns along the railway route. When Pim described the depressed economy of Gatún, which lay on the Chagres River near the Atlantic terminus, he noted that it "used formerly to be a stopping-place for the bongos, or native boats, and certainly throve in those days, but the rapidity of the locomotive has taken away the native breath, and the glories of Gatun may be reckoned of the past."[12] To enforce order and protect its capital investment, the railroad maintained a vigilante police force that used whippings, shootings, and the noose to frighten the locals.[13] In a period of rapid U.S. expansion, the railroad constituted nothing less than a prosthetic extension of U.S. power and culture overseas.[14]

A "representational machine" of informal empire *par excellence,*[15] the railroad was itself the subject of numerous Anglo-American representations—in legislation, journalism, travel narratives, guidebooks, and pictorial images. These representations yielded a contradictory picture. In a time of unprecedented demand for transoceanic mobility, which placed a premium on speed, the railway served as the primary conduit for moving people, commodities, and information from one ocean to another. As a new link in the global transportation system, it became associated with the advancement of industrialized modernity and capitalism itself. It thus occupied a paradoxical position. Was it a gift to humankind, a utopian instrument of increased "intercourse" and "communication"? Or was it a nationalist vehicle for U.S. control over the isthmus, the extension of *Yanquismo* southward in a larger design for hemispheric dominance?

To address these questions, this chapter examines the founding documents of what would eventually become the Panama Railroad, focusing in particular on the U.S. travel writer John Lloyd Stephens (1805–52), the project's architect and prime mover, and on links between the ideological foundations of his archaeological and transportation writing. In the late 1830s, he scoured the Central American backwoods searching for the lost cities of the Maya, publishing his findings as *Incidents of Travel in Central America, Chiapas, and Yucatan* (1841) and *Incidents of Travel in Yucatan* (1843). The former was among the century's most popular works of travel, going through twelve editions in its first three months in print.[16] Graced by the exquisite drawings of his coauthor, the Englishman Frederick Catherwood, Stephens's works were the first to publicize Maya culture to a broad audience. He did not discover the ruins, which were already known among Central Americans, but he brought them alive by enfolding them within a vivid tale of desire and national ambition, employing the same imperial logics that drove his work on the transisthmian passageway and relying on a model of colonial temporality derived from his antiquarian researches among the Maya.[17]

Popularly understood as a work about the ancient past, *Incidents of Travel in Central America, Chiapas, and Yucatan* is also a compelling brief on prospects for a newly modernized and unified America, with a "communication" between the Atlantic and the Pacific as its technological emblem and masterwork. Explorers and engineers had sought such an interoceanic shortcut across the Central American isthmus since the days of Columbus. The idea, as one writer from the 1840s put it, occupied "Monarchs on their thrones—Navigators on the ocean—Merchants at their desks—Men of science in their closets."[18] Columbus, Cortes, Humboldt: these and many more had put their minds and energies to the realization of this great project.[19] It featured centrally in Simón Bolívar's dream of a grand political confederation, which, as he makes clear in *Carta de Jamaica* (1815), centered on the isthmus' commercially strategic location:

> The states of the Isthmus of Panama as far north as Guatemala will perhaps
> form a confederation. Its magnificent strategic position between two great

oceans may in time result in a universal emporium, its canals shortening the distances between worlds and reinforcing commercial ties between Europe, America, and Asia, bringing tribute to this happy region from the four quarters of the globe. Here alone, perhaps, it will be possible to establish a world capital, as Constantinople aspired for Byzantium to become for the ancient world.[20]

By the mid-nineteenth century, Anglo-American writers came to view a trans-isthmian "communication" as vital to the realization of a globalized modernity. Stephens was well suited to bring the project to completion, and fortunate to pursue it at an auspicious moment in hemispheric affairs, when the U.S. government sought to extend its influence into Central America.[21] Inclining at first toward a water route across Lake Nicaragua, he settled on a railroad across the Panama isthmus, which was laid on a path that would eventually become the canal route. His work not only maps a geographical terrain but also the dominant discursive frameworks that would structure Anglo-American thinking about the isthmus for decades to come.

MODERNITY AMONG THE RUINS

How did Stephens succeed where others failed, and how did his experience as a traveler shape the way his contemporaries saw the region? Born into prosperous circumstances, he graduated from Columbia College at age seventeen and then pursued a law degree at Lichfield, Connecticut. Like many privileged young men, he set out on the grand tour, journeying through Italy, Greece, Poland, Russia, Turkey, Egypt, and the Levant. Adopting Arab dress to visit the hidden city of Petra, in what is now Jordan, he became only the second U.S. citizen to lay eyes on it. His prose accounts of these journeys, emblematic of European romanticism, captivated writers such as Edgar Allan Poe and Herman Melville, among many others. In 1836, while attending Robert Burford's "Panorama of Jerusalem," a large, circular painting of the Holy Land that was exhibiting in London, Stephens met Catherwood, an expert draughtsman who had also traveled extensively in Egypt and the Levant. Like Stephens, Catherwood had learned how to profit from his travels, drawing panoramas during the period of their greatest popularity. His skill in drawing meshed well with Stephens's talent in writing, and the two joined forces in seeking the ruined cities that were rumored to rest undisturbed in the Central American backwoods.[22] Equipped with a diplomatic passport from the United States, Stephens sailed with Catherwood in the fall of 1839 for Belize and then trekked overland to the suspected location of the ruins in northern Honduras.[23]

In committing his journeys to paper, Stephens turns to the durable mode of quest narrative to cast himself as a heroic explorer overcoming obstacles in pursuit of truth—a rhetoric of cognitive imperialism and masculine ideology that characterizes his larger isthmian project. So totalizing is his fantasy of solitary struggle that Catherwood, his faithful companion, frequently disappears from the narrative, as if Stephens alone were the master of all he surveys, a narrative position described by Mary Louise Pratt as a "moving eye on which the sights/sites register."[24] The landscape having been emptied of fellow travelers and local people alike, stripped of all markers of habitation or ownership, it awaits only the arrival of the imperial eye to take possession. The emplotment of the journey to the ruins becomes isomorphic with a solitary and sexualized conquest; the same, luxuriant vegetative growth that obstructs the mountain trail conceals the ruins and the secrets they contain. As he pursues nature to her hiding places, clearing the matted bush becomes both a preliminary step to beholding the ruins' unadorned beauty and a metaphor for the discovery of something valuable but hidden, the consummative awareness of a vast, cultural truth.

Stephens underscores the point by couching his realization in the emotionally charged language of the European sublime, seasoned with an exceptionalist celebration of New World antiquity as *more sublime* than any seen in Europe and the Levant:

> The beauty of the sculpture, the solemn stillness of the woods, disturbed only by the scrambling of monkeys and the chattering of parrots, the desolation of the city, and the mystery that hung over it, all created an interest higher, if possible, than I had ever felt among the ruins of the Old World. (1:119–20)[25]

As in Wordsworth's "Nutting" (1799) and other works in the Romantic tradition, nature stands as virginal and unspoiled. "The ground," Stephens writes, "was entirely new; there were no guide-books or guides; the whole was virgin soil" (1:119). In a riveting parable of unfolding consciousness, light gradually dawns on the obscure stones, revealing their history and significance. The reader bears witness to the founding of a discipline rooted in ancient time, as well as a national discourse, explicitly registered in terms of rivalry with Great Britain. This latter theme would echo throughout the discourses I examine here.[26] Stephens imagines a distinctly New World corpus of antiquity that will surpass the great British collections and vault the United States to a high place among the civilized nations. "The casts of the Parthenon," he writes, are regarded as "precious memorials in the British Museum, and casts of Copan would be the same in New-York" (1:115).

Yet this seemingly cosmopolitan desire to share the hidden treasures of Central America with the world at large soon conflicts with an equally strong desire to monetize them. Stephens's mind, tempted by commercial gain, moves quickly to the problem of how to leverage the traveler's hard-won knowledge into profit. Presaging tensions we will subsequently see in his canal and railroad work, Stephens's archaeological writing seems never to stray very far from what Carlyle called the "cash nexus," the desire, latent in almost every chapter, to view Central America as a grand investment opportunity. For example, on surveying the volcano at Mosaya, in present-day Nicaragua, he first praises the "power of the great Architect" to spread such wonders across the globe, but he quickly changes registers from the sublime to his more natural mode, the commercial, suggesting that "at home this volcano would be worth a fortune." In prose ripe for parody, he imagines something like a family-oriented theme park: "a good hotel on top, a railing round to keep the children from falling in, a zigzag staircase down the sides, and a glass of lemonade at the bottom." He notes—helpfully for any future investors—that "Cataracts are good property with people who know how to turn them to account" (2:13). Gazing on the exquisite Maya site of Copan, he sees a real estate scheme: "Hide your heads, ye speculators in up-town lots!" (1:115). Audaciously, he bargains with an unwitting landowner at Copan, one of the greatest of Maya cities, to purchase the site for fifty dollars. He justifies his ploy by a straightforward capitalist logic: "The reader is perhaps curious to know how old cities sell in Central America. Like other articles of trade, they are regulated by the quantity in market, and the demand" (1:128). In short order, he determines that the ruins "belonged of right to us," and that "ours they should be" (1:115–16). He interprets the entangled masses of trees and vines as signs of neglect that, despite the ruins' location within a sovereign nation and his own belated status on the scene, justify his acquisitive claim.[27]

Perhaps inspired by the London public's fervent enthusiasm for antiquities, Stephens pivots to the task of monetizing the ancient sculptures that lay before him. He forms a plan to "remove the monuments of a by-gone people from the desolate region in which they were buried, [and] set them up in the 'great commercial emporium'!" (1:115). The only impediment appears to be logistical: "Could the idols be removed?" (1:115). Since rapids in a nearby river were impassable, Stephens decides to chop the ruined city into portable mobiles, the better to "remove it in pieces" and "exhibit by sample" (1:115). Through it all, he gives little thought to competing claims, either by the people living nearby (who he repeatedly disparages) or the sovereign state in which the structures were located. He dismisses such claims by noting the ignorance of the locals on the one hand and the remoteness of the central government on the other. As I demonstrate below, Stephens also views the entire region through a well-defined anthropological lens, which legitimates his appropriative claims by associating the local people with the antiquities and thereby defining them as hostile to, and out of step with, a modernity predicated on speed and mobility. With little fanfare, he assumes the role of "proprietor" of the place (1:129), and within months presents himself in print as the discoverer of the ruins themselves. This imperial proprietorship, here focused on an ancient ruin, would subsequently organize a much larger project of U.S. domination. Just as Stephens had "rescued" the ruins from the jungle wastes and cultural neglect of their Central American keepers, he would later salvage failed interoceanic schemes by building his own hard won path of commerce and empire. Both projects relied on the fundamental assumption that Central Americans were ill adapted to the modernity occupied by Stephens and his U.S. countrymen.

Indeed, by arguing that the Copan sculptures should form the centerpiece of a "great *national* museum of *American* antiquities," Stephens collapses the broad, hemispheric meaning of "American" to its narrower, national sense of pertaining to the United States and incorporates Maya antiquity within it. He argues, in effect, that although the sculptures originated in Central America, they can only realize their potential greatness by becoming detached from their local habitation and absorbed into the great commercial emporium of New York and the larger narrative of capitalist modernity it represents. Thus, when he declares that the ruins "belonged of right *to us*," he does not mean merely himself and Catherwood, but a larger hegemony symbolized by a great national museum located somewhere in New York, the throbbing heart of U.S. commerce. Moreover, by including the reader in its address, the plural pronoun fashions an imperial subject, a collaborative partner in scenes of desire and appropriation. Such sentiments were common throughout the 1840s and 1850s, the decades of the Mexican War, U.S. designs on Cuba, and incursions into Central America, as traveler/antiquarians and canal promoters such as Stephens and the more bellicose Ephraim George Squier assumed unprecedented importance in the projection of U.S. power into the hemisphere.[28] Cleverly using diplomatic appointments to gain privileged access to the Central American interior, Stephens and Squier portray the ruins as the rightful property of enlightened U.S. residents, enfolding them into a new world order headed by the United States and its institutions. During a period of emboldened U.S. power and military expansionism, these writers use travel and exploration as soft forms of power to extend U.S. influence into the far reaches of the hemisphere.

TRANSPORT VISIONS

U.S. antiquarian research incorporated the "lost" Maya monuments into a narrative of advancing Western modernity, carefully detaching contemporary Maya and Creole elites from any stake in their own past. It enlisted the ruins in a story of ascendant U.S. greatness. On the one hand, the United States would embody its greatness by "discovering" sublime artifacts and displaying them in grand museums, temples of culture that themselves served as signs of cultural preeminence. On the other, it would pursue rapid, technological modernization and the consolidation of a continental empire that reached westward and southward across the continent. The "communication" across Central America that Stephens and others pursued was similarly perceived as crucial to Manifest Destiny. It promised to unite the nation by strengthening affective ties among a geographically dispersed populace bereft of modern transport and communication systems, knitting them together by means of new technologies of mobility. With Stephens's extensive experience on the ground as well as his ability to articulate bold national ideals, he was well placed to drive this project forward.[29]

After 396 pages of describing his travels to and researches at the ruins, and his (failed) search for a Central American government, Stephens takes his reader to the shores of the Pacific Ocean, at San Juan del Sur, Nicaragua. His letters to Secretary of State John Forsyth, who had authorized his diplomatic mission, make clear that he had always intended to scout for a canal route after concluding his official duties.[30] Since previous travelers had already essayed a route across Lake Nicaragua, it seems likely that Stephens had fixed this spot as a destination on his journey. He carefully narrates the scene of his arrival. Once again, as in his earlier apprehension of the lost ruins, dense undergrowth obstructs the view: "At every two or three paces I became entangled and held fast. . . . The woods were thicker than before, and the path entirely undistinguishable" (1:397). Again, he imagines himself as the explorer of virgin territory: "Since Mr. Bailey left not a person had visited it" (2:400). He and his local guide ascend a high promontory. In this liminal space, bounded on one side by the roaring ocean and on the other by the rising terrain behind, Stephens proleptically imagines the shape of a future canal. Everything points to a moment of the Humboldtian sublime: the strenuous journey; the dark passage of ignorance followed by the mountain ascent; the view from on high. But here what results, at least initially, is failure and disappointment:

> I had read and examined all that had been published on this subject in England or this country; had conferred with individuals; and I had been san-

guine, almost enthusiastic, in regard to this gigantic enterprise; but on the
spot the scales fell from my eyes. The harbour was perfectly desolate; for
years not a vessel had entered it; primeval trees grew around it; . . . it seemed
preposterous to consider it the focus of a great commercial enterprise; to
imagine that a city was to rise up out of the forest, the desolate harbour to be
filled with ships, and become a great portal for the thoroughfare of nations.
But the scene was magnificent. The sun was setting, and the high western
headland threw a deep shade over the water. It was perhaps the last time in
my life that I should see the Pacific. (2:400–401).

The hoped-for realization crumbles amidst the ocular proof of backwardness and desolation. What Stephens sees before him is the very antithesis of
modernity and development. If the magnificence of verbal description suggests the familiar rhetoric of the sublime, it is a sublime emptied of the energy
necessary to move from visionary exuberance to built reality.

The keyword in this passage is "primeval," a clue to the differential logics
of time and colonial encounter that, as discussed above, sustain the project of
modernity. In Stephens's narrative, the politics of this "schizogenic" division
of time are particularly acute. For having plunged his reader deep into the
region's pre-European past, he now describes *present-day* Central America as
similarly primitive—its people confined in darkness, the land undeveloped,
and nature itself primordial. This move lays the ideological ground for the
diminution of local sovereignty and the advance of U.S. interests, as Stephens
uses the discourse of backwardness throughout *Incidents of Travel in Central
America, Chiapas, and Yucatan* to mark the gulf between the mobile, mechanized modernity he occupies and the immobile, primitive culture he describes
as its antithesis, both when seeking the ruins and scouting a route for a canal.
Desiring information about the ruins of Copán, he asks the native people
who live nearby "who made them, and their dull reply was 'Quien sabe?' 'who
knows?'" (1:105). He dismisses the creole landowners, who insist on being
paid in cash for their land, as "barbarians" (1:111). Most tellingly, he argues
that "Indians, as in the days when the Spaniards discovered them, applied
to work without ardour, carried it on with little activity, and like children,
were easily diverted from it" (1:118). The infantilization of the colonial subject,
though deplorable, is familiar enough in the long history of European contact
with the torrid zones. More troubling is the refusal to acknowledge that the
indigenous inhabit history at all, a position that denies their three hundred
years of survival under an often-brutal colonialism. Though they inhabit the
same moment of time as Stephens, their engagement with it is delegitimized.
Describing the road approaching the port of San Juan del Sur, Stephens evokes

his Middle Eastern travels to push historical reference even further back: "The desert of Arabia is not more desolate, and the track of the Children of Israel to the Red Sea a turnpike compared with it" (2:398). All the while, he makes his reader conscious of the other who stands beside him—the "dark skin of my guide glistened with perspiration" (2:403)—a vivid anticipation of the subaltern labor that would eventually build Stephens's railroad. The employment of such figures not only locates native people outside the moving, progressively ordered time Stephens and his readers occupy but also outside Central America's history itself. In Stephens's work, the indigenous exist as anachronistic subjects, remnants of a bygone epoch not much different than the dead stones he comes to discover. The effect is of total erasure.

Again, the locals appear to disregard a site with clear monetary value for the foreign traveler: "More is known of [the proposed canal] in the United States than at Nicaragua" (2:405). By a logic related to the denial of historical experience, Stephens clears the way for his own "commercial enterprise," a transoceanic canal that would employ spectacular machines to bring economic development and modernity to what he portrays as a forgotten backwater. In breathless, rapid-fire prose, Stephens rushes within a single phrase from descriptions of primeval forests to visions of a fully developed transport infrastructure. He allows himself "to imagine that a city was to rise up out of the forest, the desolate harbour to be filled with ships, and become a great portal for the thoroughfare of nations" (2:400). Stephens's prose dissolves starkly different orders of time in a fantasy of instantaneous development. A few pages later, he repeats the fantasy in language worthy of magical realism: "What a magnificent spectacle it would be to see a ship, with all its spars and rigging, cross the plain, pass through the great door, and move on to the Pacific" (2:403).

The hallucinatory quality of these visions, while making for vivid writing, elides the violence, labor, and scarring of the landscape such a transformation would necessarily entail. As the later history of the Panama Railroad and Panama Canal makes plain, there was no easy route from uncleared forests to a highway of nations. The workers who built the railroad—from the West Indies, China, Ireland, and beyond—were part of a massive dislocation of labor, much of it indentured and exploitative, from one part of the world to the other; untold numbers died from sickness and tropical disease. The railroad became a grave, spawning a legend, since disputed, that one worker perished for each of the thousands of railroad ties that stretched across the isthmus. The case of the several hundred Chinese who were lured to the isthmus in 1854, however, is very well documented, the deplorable conditions they endured and their tragic deaths a grim reminder of the railroad's human toll.[31]

Yet Stephens's easy elision of individual laboring bodies is consistent with the imperialist imaginary, which achieves its power in part by repressing evidence of historical trauma in order to represent modernization as smooth, untroubled, and naturalized. In haste to remake the world, the imperial traveler's gaze not only levels obstacles and collapses time but overlooks the toiling bodies and colonial violence that were necessary to achieve these ends.

Moreover, like the ruins, which "belonged by right" to Stephens and his countrymen, any future passage through Central America appears to belong by right to the United States. The same desire to monetize ruins repeats itself here, and the same adjective is used to name it: "commercial." Stephens's travelogue, replete with a detailed prospectus for a canal through Nicaragua, implies that it was not only the unclaimed ruins that threw possession into doubt but also the apparently underdeveloped land near San Juan del Sur and across Central America more generally.[32] As Amy S. Greenberg has shown, U.S. expansionists during this period justified sweeping redefinitions of sovereignty and legal possession by reference to the enlightenment principle of "best use," a legal theory with which Stephens, the Lichfield-trained lawyer, would surely have been familiar. Employed by Jefferson to argue that "Indian land rights could be extinguished by virtue of failing to bring arable lands into cultivation," the doctrine was also subsequently cited by Stephens's contemporaries Sam Houston and Thomas Hart Benton to justify territorial aggression during the Mexican War.[33] At a historical moment when U.S. expansionists used signs of apparent neglect as evidence of *terra nullius*—land belonging to no one—Stephens's narration depicts the surrounding land as ripe for the taking.

Stephens's lengthy report, which concludes volume one of *Incidents of Travel in Central America, Chiapas, and Yucatan,* was made possible by the work of Lt. John Baily of the Royal Navy, a British half-pay officer residing in Central America. Baily vigorously supported various canal projects and shared his plans and elevations with Stephens. He later authored a volume urging British subjects to emigrate to Central America.[34] Although Britain and the United States frequently clashed over Central American affairs, transport was considered, at least initially, as a mutually beneficial good, as evidenced by the Clayton-Bulwer Treaty of 1850, which bound the United States and Great Britain not to seek or enforce exclusive control over any future Nicaraguan canal.[35] Indeed, Stephens closes his discussion of the proposed but ultimately unrealized canal by predicting the imminent arrival of a new, beneficent world order in which goods and people would flow effortlessly from one part of the globe to another. In rhetoric that anticipates the dense interconnectedness associated with globalization, Stephens imagines the canal as a crucial link in a modern transport system:

In less than a year, English mailboats will be steaming to Cuba, Jamaica, and the principal ports of Spanish America, touching once a month at San Juan and Panama. To men of leisure and fortune, jaded with rambling over the ruins of the Old World, a new country will be opened. After a journey on the Nile, a day in Petra, and a bath in the Euphrates, English and American travelers will be bitten by moschetoes [sic] on the Lake of Nicaragua, and drink Champagne and Burton ale on the desolate shores of San Juan on the Pacific. The random remarks of the traveller for amusement, and the observations of careful and scientific men, will be brought together, a mass of knowledge will be accumulated and made public, and in my opinion the two oceans will be united. (1:417–18)

The waterway that grounds this utopian vision of unfettered travel is here revealed to be far more than a commercial thoroughfare. Binding together the new world order, it is presented as a great unifying symbol, facilitating communication, knowledge, transport, and leisure. Although it took weeks to cross the Atlantic in 1839, Stephens imagines a world in which a traveler could enjoy his morning bath in the Euphrates and his afternoon tea on the Pacific. It is a fantastical vision of radically collapsed time and space, but one repeatedly encountered in the isthmian literature it exemplifies, and one that, in other forms, characterizes many current understandings of a networked and globalized world.

Stephens's proleptic vision of a new isthmian passageway also exemplifies the larger project of exporting U.S. development to Central America. Presented as a pure vehicle for advancing "the peaceful intercourse of nations"— an intimacy without rivalry or strife—the Nicaraguan canal is also articulated as a U.S. remedy for what ails Central America more generally. As such, it embodies the civilizing mission of empire, in which advanced nations assume responsibility for disseminating knowledge, truth, and peace to their colonial inferiors. In Stephens's view, a ship canal across Nicaragua would

> compose the distracted country of Central America; turn the sword, which is now drenching it with blood, into a pruning hook; remove the prejudices of the inhabitants by bringing them into close connexion with people of every nation; furnish them with a motive and reward for industry, and inspire them with a taste for making money, which . . . does more to civilize and keep the world at peace than any other influence whatever. (1:419; emphasis mine)

By ushering Central America into capitalist modernity, the canal project will solve the problem of shizogenic time explored previously. Central America's political dysfunction, which Stephens discusses at length in *Incidents of Travel in Central America, Chiapas, and Yucatan,* will be composed, its swords beaten into ploughshares, its local forms of labor industrialized and modernized. By instilling a love for "making money," the canal will usher in the blessings of civilization and prosperity. Even nature itself will be rejuvenated. Using an elaborate personification that evokes the doctrine of best use, Stephens imagines that Nicaragua's "magnificent mountains, and valleys now weeping in desolation and waste, will smile and be glad" (1:419). The keyword here is waste, an abuse of the land's inherent economic potential that both justified U.S. territorial claims and served as a foil for the elaborate picture of development and industry Stephens goes on to describe.

The language of "waste" and "barren[ness]" also suggests the civilizing project of cultural and spiritual renewal, as Protestant values and Anglo-Saxon energy supplant the Catholic legacy of old Spain, associated with underdevelopment and cultural stagnation. In the *Hand of God in History* (1847), the U.S. evangelical Morris Read identified the crossing as one of the providential "facilities" that would serve the "speedy and universal spread of the Gospel" and argued that its completion would "bring the moral and political *wastes* of Central America into the pale of civilization and a pure Christianity" (emphasis mine). Interweaving nationalist arguments for Manifest Destiny with evangelical ones for increased missionary effort, Read insisted that the "spread of truth" was inextricably bound with "improvements in modes of conveyance."[36] Later, when construction of the railroad began, Protestant missionaries identified the town of Aspinwall (later Colón) as a fruitful ground for spreading the gospel, arguing that "before long the influence of the Protestant commercial enterprise of the Anglo-Saxon race will, under Divine Guidance and blessing, open stand-points for the faith in the darkest places of the South American continent; portions of the great field which have been left by true Christianity for ages as entirely impracticable."[37]

Stephens's prospectus for a Nicaraguan passage attempts but ultimately fails to balance two competing agendas: advancing the canal as a global good, a manifestation of utopian ideals versus advancing it as an expression of a narrowly pursued national agenda, the project and projection of U.S. imperialism. The two stand in delicate tension throughout the work and the larger discourse it embodies. On the former, Stephens quotes a widely cited article in the *Edinburgh Review,* which described the idea as "the mightiest event in favour of the peaceful intercourse of nations which the physical circumstances of the globe present to the enterprise of man" (1:419). He summons the testimony of U.S. Senator Henry Clay, who in an 1825 letter to the Central American minister, Antonio José Cañaz, characterized a previous attempt as "highly calculated to diffuse an extensive influence on the affairs of mankind" (1:415).[38] The idea of a "communication" or channel that would usher in a new, more enlightened period in human history resonated around the Atlantic. Stephens himself descants long and lovingly on the promise of "new markets," "intercourse and communion," and the prospect of "improv[ing] the character of nations" (1:420). Additionally, in a sign of the discourse's ubiquity, Harriet Martineau could use its excesses as fodder for rich parody, mocking the poetic delirium of contemporary canal boosters:

> When the professional man perilled his savings to cut through the Isthmus
> of Panama he gloried in helping on a mighty work; and described, like a
> poet, the pouring of the one vast ocean into the other, and the procession of
> the merchant-ships of the world riding through on the new-made current.[39]

Whether the point was praise or ridicule, the association of transisthmian communication with a dawning epoch of global cooperation drove the communication's political appeal, serving to mask its economic and political motives with utopian visions of smoothly flowing information and goods. Indeed, the economic logic of laissez-faire capitalism meshed neatly with heightened interest in steam navigation to propel arguments for the canal as a solution to the long oceanic networks that inhibited trade. Canal proponents viewed the passage as a vehicle for increased human interaction and a prod to shrink the world through communication and transport.

Such utopian ideals, however, jostled uneasily with narrower political agendas arising from heightened nationalism elsewhere, particularly in the United States, where political leaders viewed the crossing as vital to the national interest. Although Stephens expresses his reluctance to speak of the project "with sectional or even national feeling," he is forced to admit that if "Europe is indifferent," it would fall to the United States to make this "greatest enterprise ever attempted by human force *entirely our own work*" (1:420; emphasis mine). He sanctions this position by referring to a long history of earlier U.S.-sponsored attempts, such as the formation of the Central American and United States Atlantic and Pacific Canal Company, which was established by New York financiers in 1826.[40] Connecting the history of Northern industrialization and canal building in the United States to Central America, he wonders whether it is too much to ask that

> in honour of services poorly paid but never to be forgotten, a steamboat,
> bearing the glorious name of Fulton, may start from the spot where he made

his first experiment, and open the great "highway of nations" to the Pacific Ocean? (ibid.)

These formulations metaphorically incorporate Central America into the historical arc of the U.S. machine age. The triumph of steam in colonial America becomes an analogue for transport thousands of miles away; Fulton conquers Panama as easily as the Hudson. Like the canals they refer to, these comparisons have the effect of collapsing geography and cultural difference, naturalizing the Central American landscape as simply a component of a larger, hemispheric entity that was centered in the U.S. industrial heartland but stretched southward to the isthmus.

FROM WORLD CHANNEL TO NATIONAL RAILROAD

If in 1840 Stephens remained ambivalent about the canal's ultimate purpose—whether it was a selfless gesture of humanitarian concern or a tool of U.S. imperial expansion—the events of 1846–48 seem to have banished all doubt. For in the immediate aftermath of the Mexican War, when the United States aggressively enlarged its territory westward and southward amidst John O'Sullivan's 1845 cry of Manifest Destiny to "overspread the continent" with our "yearly multiplying millions," Stephens twice came before the U.S. Congress to pitch a bold new plan for a railroad across a narrow strip of land in Nueva Granada, in what is now Panama.[41] Having abandoned the idea of a Nicaraguan canal as impracticable, he proposed an overland rail line that would similarly conquer geography by "connecting the waters of the Atlantic and Pacific oceans."[42] Like the planned route across Lake Nicaragua, the path across Panama had been surveyed many times before, both by U.S. and British citizens. Stephens appealed to Congress both to renew the case for the Panama route and to seek an exclusive contract for conveying military supplies and mail across the isthmus. In the process, he redefined Panama itself, transforming it from a distant, foreign place into a critical component of a newly emboldened and expansionist United States. "Viewed in its future commercial and political aspect," he argued, "this point is exceeded by none on the *American continent* in value or importance" (3; emphasis mine).

On December 11, 1848, Stephens presented the first of what would be his two memorials—formal, written petitions to Congress appealing for exclusive contracts on the proposed railroad.[43] It was an auspiciously timed appearance, occurring on the cusp of gold rush mania, amidst patriotic fervor for Manifest Destiny, and at the crux of events that radically altered the nation's geographic borders and political ideology. Two years earlier, the United States had gained a strong foothold on the Pacific by settling the Oregon Boundary question with Great Britain, which established the northern border with what is now Canada.[44] In 1846, the Mallarino-Bidlack Treaty, negotiated with Nueva Granada, gave the United States significant transit rights through the territory and, by including the isthmus in its larger hemispheric orbit, offset long-established British sway on Nicaragua's Atlantic coast and in the Caribbean more generally.[45] Ratified during the Polk administration in 1848, at the end of the Mexican War, the treaty included the obligation, as Stephens phrased it, "to protect it with their army and navy" (23), a clause that was subsequently used to exercise military control over Nueva Granada when U.S. troops were sent to the isthmus in 1856 to quell the Watermelon Riot.[46] The United States would eventually use the treaty to justify military intervention in Panama some fifty-seven times over the next several decades.[47] The Royal Mail Steam Packet, which began mail service to the West Indies in 1842, extended the post to and across the isthmus in 1846.[48] In 1847, economic depression swept through the region, causing Panamanians to search for outside investors to complete an interoceanic communication, and in the same year the U.S. Congress authorized the Navy to enter into contracts for conveying mail by steamship from New York and New Orleans to Chagres (on the Atlantic) and from Panama (on the Pacific) to Oregon.[49] William H. Aspinwall, one of Stephens's partners, would obtain the contract for Pacific service in April 1848.[50] In February 1848, the United States and Mexico signed the Treaty of Guadalupe Hidalgo, ending the Mexican War and ceding California to the United States, along with a large area comprising present-day Nevada, Arizona, New Mexico, Utah, and portions of Wyoming and Colorado. Moreover, on January 24, 1848, James Wilson Marshall discovered gold in the foothills of the Sierra Nevada—the overlap between acquisition and discovery, according to one recent historian, standing as perhaps "the single greatest piece of luck in American history."[51] Almost immediately, reports of riches beyond measure began to appear in newspapers, first in California and then farther afield.[52] By midsummer, word had reached Hawaii, Oregon, Salt Lake, and Mexico. After the *New York Herald* and the New Orleans *Daily Picayune* published the findings in August and September, the news, as we now say, went viral.[53] In this context, Stephens downplayed the rhetoric of global responsibility he had enunciated seven years earlier in *Incidents of Travel* in favor of economic, military, political, and above all affective arguments that cast the railroad through Nueva Granada as vital to the national interest and its building as a "great *American* work" (23; emphasis mine).

Employing every tool in his rhetorical arsenal, Stephens petitioned Congress to expand its notions of the national interest to include events in a faraway, little known place. Despite the spread of gold rush news, California was as yet little known, a recently acquired slice of Northern Mexico that few in New York or Washington understood in any but the scantiest terms. As Richard T. Stillson points out in his masterly analysis of gold rush information cultures, credible news from the West was nearly impossible to come by, since there was "almost no communications infrastructure" in California at this time. Rumor was rampant.[54] Panama was even more geographically and culturally remote, a lightly filled-in spot on a map that was largely terra incognita. Writing in 1849–50, George W. Hughes, of the U.S. Topographical Engineers, noted that there was "little exact and reliable information" since "few scientific observers have traversed the American Isthmus."[55] Stephens's rhetorical task, then, was to make the marginal central, the unfamiliar knowable, and the foreign unavoidably and compellingly a domestic concern.

Stephens frames his appeal by invoking the "new era" of U.S. history forged by "the acquisition of California, and the settlement of our boundary line in Oregon" (21)—events that "have fixed the period and the hands" that would finally accomplish an isthmian crossing (23). Arguing in vivid biblical tones that the "appointed time has now arrived," he summons the doctrine of Manifest Destiny to convince his readers that the United States is ordained to build it. "It has become the *destiny* of this country," he states, to "achieve an enterprise" that had been long contemplated but not realized by "the great powers of Europe" (23; emphasis mine). When Theodore Roosevelt came to build his canal, he used strikingly similar language, declaring that "if ever a Government could be said to have received a mandate from civilization to effect an object the accomplishment of which was demanded in the interest of mankind, the United States holds that position."[56] Stephens reminds his readers that no canal had been built in the three hundred years since European contact with the Americas and lays blame on the "peculiarities of Spanish dominion" (3). In the mid-nineteenth century, such a phrase was shorthand among U.S. writers for the popular belief that Spanish American apathy toward industrial development had squandered the hemisphere's economic potential. Related to the so-called "Black Legend," which condemned the brutality of the Spanish conquest and inquisition, this critique dovetails with the doctrine of "best use" summarized above. Indeed, in language that recalls his characterization of the land surrounding the ruins as desolate, Stephens complains that the isthmus has remained in "nearly the unimproved condition in which it was found by its early discoverers," and notes that on the

Pacific coast the region is "all but uninhabited" (4). The rhetoric of dereliction was central to arguments for U.S. action.

Although gold rush news had already reached the East Coast in December 1848, when Stephens addressed Congress, its future importance to the railroad's bottom line was as yet unclear. The first memorial thus makes only passing reference to the discovery, extolling the "mildness of the climate, the richness of the soil, the great promise of mineral wealth" (21). The following year the second memorial would more assertively point to "the large and brilliant discoveries of metallic riches in California," but the emphasis nevertheless remains on the railroad's capacity to promote national consolidation, commercial advantage, and military power.[57] Stephens praises the future railroad's capacity to increase "trade and intercourse" between the "widely separated portions of our common country" (3), and foresees a not-too-distant day when, through control of the isthmus, the United States will exercise "commanding authority of the trade and navigation" to Asia (17). The Georgia Congressman T. Butler King, who supported Stephens and Aspinwall from his seat on the House Committee for Naval Affairs and was a strong advocate of railway expansion, concurred: "The construction of this railroad will throw into our warehouses and shipping the entire commerce of the Pacific Ocean."[58] Stephens also stresses the railroad's importance to military logistics. With the Mexican War still resonating in U.S. ears, he focuses on the sometimes pressing occasions for the

> transportation of men, munitions of war, and naval stores for our military and naval stations on the Pacific; all of which, however great the emergency, and at whatever sacrifice of time and money, must go by the long and hazardous voyage around Cape Horn, or by the wild paths across the Rocky Mountains, for the half the year covered with snows, and entirely impracticable. (21)

According to his calculations in 1848, the railroad would permit the sending of "reinforcements" to California or Oregon in thirty days, rather than six months, via either the overland route or the passage around Cape Horn. He refers to these territories as the "newly acquired portion of our *empire*" (9; emphasis mine)—a clear indication of the military and political value he attached to this overseas arm of the nation's transportation infrastructure. Indeed, the Navy later required that the mail steamers authorized in 1847 be convertible, if occasion demanded, into warships, and inspected the first such ships of the Pacific Mail Steamship Company, launched in 1848, to ensure they were properly outfitted. British observers, predictably, lamented this expansion of isthmian power. The naval officer Bedford Pim, who urged his country's leaders to adopt a hawkish and muscular Central American policy, worried that they had instead yielded Pacific commerce and communication to their "rivals," who had the power, "in the event of war, to inflict disaster upon our squadron, menace our possessions, cut up our trade, or destroy our cruisers in detail, before we could even inform our countrymen that hostilities had broken out."[59]

Yet Stephens would ultimately argue that the railroad's economic and military value paled before its symbolic value as an expression of national unity and its ability, through technology and geographic advantage, to annihilate the distance between far-flung individuals. "An empire," Thomas Richards has written, "is partly a fiction. No nation can close its hand around the world; the reach of any nation's empire always exceeds its final grasp."[60] In the United States, the bonds of nationhood were threatened by rapid geographical expansion, which stretched the idea of union to its conceptual limits. In his memorial, Stephens employs a series of vividly told tales to dramatize the danger of a nation divided by its own expanse:

> *At this moment* hundreds of young men, full of enterprise, from our Eastern States, are buffeting the storms of Cape Horn, while in the coming spring the hardy pioneers of the West will be moving by thousands over the desolate prairies, or climbing the rugged steeps of the Rocky Mountains, to build for us new States on the Pacific. (21; emphasis mine)

He defines the nation not as a cartographical or political abstraction, but as a set of narratives in which disparate individuals are bound together by the collective struggle and suffering of travel itself.[61] His image, which would be endlessly repeated in the Panama literature, sets these hardy pioneers against a forbidding geography—storm-tossed seas, desolate prairies, and rugged mountains—and lays the rhetorical ground for the technoimperial solution offered by a short railway through Panama.

For if a forbidding geography imposed hardships on travel, it also strained the fabric of social intercourse on which national coherence depended. Stephens argues that in the absence of frequent communication, there are "no means of returning, or of personal intercourse with friends at home, except by the stormiest passage ever known at sea, or the most toilsome journey ever made by land" (21). He calls this condition the threat of being "virtually expatriated," a phrase that captures the anxiety of a still-forming nation whose strong bonds might be revealed as wispy threads. He worries that what Benedict Anderson calls the "imagined community" of nationhood will fray without more frequent interaction across its vast expanse.[62] For although the monthly steamship lines from New York to Chagres and from Panama to the West Coast had "facilitate[d] correspondence" to California and Oregon, they could not answer "the immediate and pressing want of a thoroughfare for travel" (21).

The railroad was both a technology of mobility and a conveyor of mobiles. It moved people and their communications (letters, government documents, military commands) rapidly across great distances, possessing a power that was frequently described as magical. This movement of bodies and information was vital to the project, as Stephens describes it, of "strengthening the bonds of national union" (13). In the late 1840s, as we have seen, the union's increased territorial reach had thrown into relief the problem of affectively connecting populations on the Atlantic and Pacific Coasts that had newly defined the nation's borders. Both the problem and its solution went by the same name: "communication." This mid-nineteenth-century keyword had two related but distinct definitions: the familiar meaning of transmitting information through symbols; and a more specialized sense, as the *OED* indicates, of a "connecting channel, line, passage, or opening; a route, channel, etc., by means of which transportation or travel . . . may be effected."[63] In its capacity as symbol (of modernity, progress, speed), as well in its capacity as conveyor (of messages and people), the railroad embodied these meanings. Stephens's description of the tortured progress of mail across the isthmus captures this double valence:

> It is through [the Isthmus] . . . a hitherto lifeless and forbidding region, obstructed by dense and tangled masses of tropical vegetation, that the whole public and private correspondence of the Union, between its Atlantic and Pacific portions, recently sprung up, as if by magic, and already numbering from twenty to thirty thousand letters in a single steamer, is now transported. (4)

The magic resides in the sudden eruption of a "public and private correspondence" numbering in the thousands for each steamer, which was transported by canoe and mule through the jungle's tangled mass, a tropicalized image of natural obduracy that runs through Stephens's search for the Maya ruins and his first exploration of the Nicaraguan canal route in 1840.[64] Stephens's information bottleneck arises from an all too familiar problem in modern communication: too many messages and too little capacity to convey them. By cutting a clear path through the jungle's riotous vegetation, the railroad promised to convey these messages rapidly from coast to coast, and thus strengthen the "Union," perhaps the most powerful trope of U.S. nationalism.

In 1861, F. N. Otis published a *History of the Panama Railroad and of the Pacific Mail Steamship Company History of the Panama Railroad; Together with a Traveller's Guide and Business Man's Hand-Book for the Panama Railroad.* As the subtitle suggests, Otis's book served as general guidebook to the isthmus, orienting the business traveler to the new modernity represented by the geographical shortcut between the oceans. Replete with schedules and timetables for travel, and nicely illustrated with engravings, it went through several editions in the succeeding years. Two such engravings exemplify the changes wrought by the coming of the railroad. In "Running the Lines," a fecund Panamanian jungle envelops the surveyor and his native assistant, who are mapping the railroad's path through the tangled vegetation (fig. 1.1). Drawing on common visual tropes, the image suggests the ever-present threat of dense overgrowth—an image of obduracy we have traced back to Stephens's initial contact with Central American nature in his search for ruins. But the image also maps social relations. The surveyor's tripod and transit level—instruments of the trade—occupy the center of the image, while the native subject who assists him is placed marginally. A monkey swings from the treetops as another reminder of the primitive surround. As opposed to the ocular and cognitive power that resides in the act of surveying, the half-dressed native subject has been reduced to the measuring rod he holds, charting not only a distance between points on a map but also the gulf between a new modernity, governed by the machine, and his own culture, which is depicted as passing away.

The widely reproduced frontispiece to Otis's work (fig. 1.2) carries this logic to its natural conclusion. Here, the locomotive dominates, charging out of the massed vegetation directly at the viewer, displaying the machine's power to conquer nature. The railroad now complete, the fire-breathing engine emerges from a space and time anterior to modernity, represented by the primordial jungle, and surges forth into the future, toward the viewer. As opposed to other sites of colonial possession, such as Bombay's Victoria Terminus Train Station, what we see here is not a rooted structure, a built and immovable sign of national identity, a place where one might, as Ian Baucom puts it, "come home to Ruskin's England."[65] What the image foregrounds, rather, is the transformative and destructive power of that which moves, cuts, and displaces. The iron machine, spewing black smoke, marks a fundamental transition— from fixity to motion, from colonization to traversal, and from a world of foot-bound travel to one of networked transport. There is no grand terminus here, no heirloom architecture, only an iron road, the sign of Panama's radical between-ness; and pushed to the image's side, almost out of the picture entirely, stands a further reminder of these transformations—a black worker,

RUNNING THE LINES.

FIGURE 1.1. Running the Lines. F. N. Otis, *History of the Panama Railroad* (1861).

FIGURE 1.2. Conquering the Jungle. F. N. Otis, *History of the Panama Railroad* (1861).

invisible except for his arm and bare feet, a reminder that the railroad's significance as a vehicle of global mobility rested on the displacement of the workers who came to build it. Just as his arm is a synecdoche for labor, so is his blackness a visual clue to the black labor that built the railroad. Like so many representations of colonial and racial alterity in the Anglo-American corpus, the black worker occupies a marginal position, pushed literally to the edge of the image and symbolically to the side of the story it tells. Dominated by the train, its white masters, and by extension its foreign stockholders, he stands as an image of the repressed colonial unconscious, a disconcerting reminder that the railroad's disruptive technology aimed not only to level the high mountains but also the lifeways that Nueva Granadians held dear.

CHAPTER 2

∽

Panama as St. Martin's-le-Grand

Communication and Mobility in Trollope's
The West Indies and the Spanish Main

Panamá is indeed in this particular the great centre of South American civilization—a very St. Martin's-le-Grand. All the correspondence for the whole coast of South America is distributed and despatched [*sic*] by Her Majesty's Consul at Panamá, who, with a large staff of clerks passes many a hot night in sorting and stamping letters.

—CHARLES TOLL BIDWELL, *THE ISTHMUS OF PANAMÁ* (1865)

Central America is no longer what it was & is daily becoming the most important spot of earth in yᵉ whole world: to us especially with Australia [and] New Zealand in our hands & the Chinese empire falling to pieces. We cannot, we must not see it American, I mean belonging to the U.S.

—BULWER TO CLARENDON, MARCH 1854

LATE IN 1858, the British novelist Anthony Trollope boarded the *Atrato*, owned and operated by the Royal Mail Steam Packet Company, and took passage to the West Indies and the Spanish Main. Over the next several months, he traveled by every conceivable modality: steamer, small boat, train, horseback, mule, and foot. His path took him through Britain's Caribbean colonies, the Spanish colony of Cuba, and the independent Central American republics. It was a toilsome, arduous and, if Trollope is to be believed, frequently impossible journey. Travel never felt more like travail. Trollope kept detailed notes and returned to London with a finished manuscript, as he rarely let good material go to waste. The fruit of his labors, *The West Indies and the Spanish Main* (1859), is not only a classic of Trollopian style, with all the irony and layered meaning his readers have come to expect. It is also, I will argue here, a seminal text in the British discourse of nineteenth-century Panama. For in contrast to Frances Trollope (his mother), Charles Dickens, Harriet Martineau, Matthew Arnold, and countless other Victorians who authored trans-Atlantic travel narratives, Trollope downplays the usual focus of such narratives—the special relationship between the United States and Britain—to highlight a larger set of geopolitical issues that arose from his itinerary in the global South: the Americas' complex racial landscapes; advancing U.S. territorial ambition in the hemisphere; and above all the increasing importance of Panama to interoceanic mobility in a rapidly globalizing world.[1] Few Victorian writers were as equipped to handle these difficult subjects as Trollope, and fewer still to crystallize British attitudes toward modernity and communication at this critical juncture in Atlantic history.

As he admits, however, Trollope undertook this journey not to write a travel narrative but, as he opaquely claimed, to complete "certain affairs of State"—affairs that he implies but never narrates as such.[2] Elliptically, he represents his itinerary as incidental, when in fact it sprung from an official postal mission whose motives and means were overtly imperial. By imperial, I refer not to the blunt exercise of military power, or even techniques of embargo or blockade, which the British frequently employed in South America. I mean rather a softer form of influence organized around the conveyance of paper letters, a matter that, according to an 1860 parliamentary committee on steam packets, involved "our political relations, our colonial empire, the efficiency of our army and navy, and the spread of our commerce."[3] The high importance the British government attached to such communications is reflected in the lengthy letter of instruction composed by Frederic Hill, assistant secretary in charge of the mail packets. This seven-page, twenty-seven-point memorandum directed Trollope's every move, stipulating who he was to see, what he was permitted to say (and not to say) in meetings, and the arrangements he was to make on behalf of the British government.[4] Acting on these orders and conveyed on the *Atrato*, Trollope ventured across the Atlantic to increase the speed and lower the cost of overseas mail in this crucial theater of British influence, work he later called, in his posthumous autobiography, "cleans[ing] the Augean stables of our Post Office."[5]

Like Stephens before him, Trollope undertook a journey that was as much administrative as literary. Traveling five years after the completion of the Panama Railroad, and with the isthmus as a key area of focus, he charted a path that paralleled the postal routes connecting individuals and communities across a vast imperial field. Lending credence to the assertion that "much of the historical geography of empire is the history of ship-borne communication," his journey coordinated a principal technology of mobility (the steam packet) with the principal communicative mobile it conveyed (the letter).[6] Trollope, in other words, went to the Americas to do his day job as a highly trained government servant. His narrative, though meeting travel literature's generic expectations, mirrors this official purpose by analyzing the imperial uses of mobility in a dawning era of global information. An expression of its author's own mobility as a traveling subject—an obsessive subject in Trollope's oeuvre—*West Indies and the Spanish Main* also examines how travel and mobility were reshaping Central America and more particularly Panama in the decade after the railroad's completion.[7]

Recent postcolonial criticism, seeing Trollope's text as an anticipation of the Morant Bay rebellion of 1865, has advanced a significantly different account of this enterprise, suggesting that he sailed to the West Indies, disembarked, spent most of his time commenting on the racial situation in Jamaica, and returned. Although Trollope devotes only one third of his book to the West Indies, Simon Gikandi describes Trollope's focus as "the West Indian space," "the West Indies," "the islands," and the "Caribbean landscape."[8] This partitioning drives Gikandi's influential thesis, which has guided criticism for several years: the work's "dialectical irony" both "questions and affirms Englishness" by specifying the West Indies as an anachronistic, atavistic space. Similarly, Catherine Hall's focus on formal colonial rule leads her to ignore the text's sustained attention to Spanish America, where Anglo-Saxons were few and the geopolitical issues far different than in the British colonies.[9] In his *Intellectual History of the Caribbean*, Silvio Torres-Saillant argues that attempts to understand the work in terms other than race risk complicity with the text's own deeply prejudicial logics. He accuses the Caribbean writer Fred D'Aguiar, who wrote an introduction for a paperback reprint of *West Indies and the Spanish Main*, of accepting "Trollope's ideological aggression against his [D'Aguiar's] people while celebrating the text's stylistic virtues."[10] Yet however much postcolonial criticism has taught us about Trollope's activities in Jamaica, it has remained incurious about the wider contexts of his mission, specifically the way in which Central America was becoming a global transit zone and a funnel for diasporic movement on a grand scale. This material, properly understood, can help reframe the Jamaican chapters within a broader understanding of British imperial objectives in the region, which included but was not limited to the question of abolition.

Sharing Deborah Morse's impatience with characterizations of Trollope as an "unconflicted imperialist," this chapter attempts to move beyond this critical impasse by examining a larger story of mobilities and immobilities unfolding across the "and" of Trollope's title—the Spanish Main that critics of this work, postcolonial and not, have ignored.[11] As we have seen, this region was undergoing unprecedented change. New pathways of interoceanic transit had thrust it to the center of worldwide attention in the 1850s, when throngs of U.S. citizens traversed Panama on the way to the California gold fields, and the United States sought to connect the disparate parts of its transcontinental expanse. Across the Atlantic, British officials also fretted about the isthmus. While grudgingly accepting U.S. control of the railroad as well as the Yankee Strip, British officials struggled to exert influence in the region even as their sway diminished. They were particularly concerned to ensure the smooth passage of mail to their outlying territories and sought to exploit the isthmus and its already built railroad as a shortcut to distant parts of their empire. Trollope's remit, which dealt with establishing new mail routes in the Caribbean basin and across the isthmus to the Pacific, put him in a privileged position to comment on and indeed shape these changes. Like Stephens before him, he combined official and unofficial roles, and in the process left an important literary commentary on British attitudes toward the isthmus in the wake of the U.S. railroad. Not an architect of large-scale infrastructure himself, he specialized in the analysis and improvement of already existing systems, a skill he learned well as a servant in H.M.'s government.

COMMUNICATION, TRANSIT, AND EMPIRE

In nineteenth-century Britain, the creation of long communication networks played a crucial role in the project of imperial expansion. Such networks drew together subjects across a vast global field and countered suspicions of the utter fictiveness of empire itself, a thing no one could grasp except through representations. If, as Edward Said writes, "the enterprise of empire depends upon the *idea of empire*," communication with far-flung correspondents gave this fiction a local habitation and a name.[12] For the Victorian world, the "information packet" that performed this crucial office was the letter, the antecedent of digital communication systems and a crucial marker in the story of mobilities and communication that Trollope's narrative describes.[13] For it was in this period, as Patrick Joyce brilliantly shows in *The State of Freedom*, "that there developed a remarkable extension of [the state's] communicative powers and an equally remarkable deepening of human and non-human connectedness."[14] In Britain, the mobile at the center of this broadening system, the letter, was delivered through a complex web of locally walked routes and large-scale transit infrastructure, from coaches to railways. This national system was in turn connected to a global network of ships, ports, coaling stations, and railways, facilitated by arrangements and treaties with other nations.[15] Hoping to draw

near the disparate parts of a global empire, postal officials harnessed efficiencies from evolving industrial technologies and exploited geographical short
cuts to effect dramatic increases in delivery speed. In an 1851 post office report
on steam communication with India, Robert Lowe captured the importance
of mail to colonial coherence in the terms we have been considering here:
time, space, and intimacy across great distance. He argued that "if you mean
to maintain those colonies, you must either absolutely abandon to them the
whole of the government, or else you must shorten the distance; people cannot
wait; the larger the communities become, the more impossible it is to wait."[16]
A few decades later another British official, J. Henniker Heaton, pleaded for
lower cost overseas mail by asserting that it would foster patriotism, "cement
the social and political bonds of the empire," and provide a "formidable blow
to the foreign competition with which we are threatened in colonial markets."[17]
As with the United States and its expanding geographical terrain, a growing
overseas empire demanded operations conceived at a large scale. The sheer
pace of technological change in the global communication system was breath-
taking. Until the 1830s, a letter posted from London to India would be sent
on one ship around the Horn of Africa and arrive five to eight months later,
providing monsoons did not delay it further.[18] By the 1850s, the journey had
been segmented, rerouted, and distributed across various modes of transport,
with a consequent decrease in time. Letters traveled first by rail across France,
then steamer to Alexandria, camel to Suez, and steamer again to Calcutta or
Bombay, all in thirty to forty-five days. Later, the advent of transoceanic cables
cut these times to mere hours, and by the 1920s, telegraph messages circled the
globe in eighty seconds. Small wonder, then, as Daniel Headrick puts it, that
many Britons "thought the world empire they had acquired was a not unrea-
sonable reward for the amazing ingenuity of their industry."[19]

Trollope joined the Post Office as a clerk in 1834, witnessing both a period
of unprecedented reform and an enormous increase in postal volume, as
chargeable letters rose from 75.9 million in 1839 to 410.8 million in 1853.[20]
After several agonizing years of lackluster performance as a lowly clerk, he
took a position as a postal surveyor in the west of Ireland, where his ability to
grasp the complexities of the delivery system made him a valued employee.
The same passion for efficiency and the mastery of time that would later drive
his legendary writing habits—arising at 5:30 a.m. to write by the clock—also
motivated his work as a postal surveyor, in which he analyzed multiple steps
in a vast, interlinked network of delivery that was increasingly driven by the
need for speed. Rowland Hill, his superior at the Post Office, described the
work as the application of analytical rigor to personal movement: "The surveyor determines the length of a walk a letter carrier might reasonably make

in a day, arranges the walk to include as many villages and hamlets as he can, determines whether the weekly volume of letters for those places be sufficient to pay the expense . . . [and] establishes the route."[21] According to his biographers, Trollope walked his routes religiously: "It was," he said, "the ambition of my life to cover the country with rural letter carriers."[22] After his stint in Ireland, he assumed responsibility for reviewing mail service in several English counties (Gloucestershire, Herefordshire, Monmouthshire, Oxfordshire, Wiltshire, Worcestershire), the six southern Welsh counties, and the Channel Islands, where he recommended the experiment of roadside letter collection (fig. 2.1).

Susan Zieger has recently framed the Post Office's growing power to coordinate information as a "foundational example of logistics," arguing that it discovered in Trollope someone particularly skilled at this quintessentially modern form of management.[23] Indeed, Trollope's work in this period demonstrates his sophisticated understanding of the post *as a system*, first locally and then abroad. In 1858, he was sent to Suez—then just in the beginning stages of canal construction—to forge an agreement for mail delivery to colonial possessions in India and Australia. With characteristic acumen, he assessed each strand in the complex multinodal web, going so far as to calculate, timepiece in hand, "the normal speed of a camel" across the desert sands.[24] The next year, having won his superiors' confidence (he was praised by name in the Post Office annual report of 1859), he sailed to the Americas to carry out a similar analytical project. Like the work at Suez, another in-between place, a zone of contact and conflict, his task in Central America entailed the harnessing of his own mobility to the study of a vast structure of other mobilities. Only by bringing his logistical talents to bear, as he did in Ireland and Suez, could he rationalize and reconfigure the delivery system. The letters of instruction he carried with him reinforced this requirement. He was informed that on "visiting Colon and Panama the experience derived from your recent mission to Egypt will aid you in examining thoroughly the arrangements connected with the transit of mails across the Isthmus."[25] He was directed to reconceive individual segments in view of the large, multipoint network that led across the Atlantic to the Caribbean, over the isthmus, and finally to cities and towns throughout the Pacific: Victoria (British Columbia), Sydney, and Canton (fig. 2.2). He reports in *The West Indies and the Spanish Main* that he deemed the Panama route superior to a competing route across Honduras on the basis of efficiency. For he had measured the speed of the prevailing trade winds and calculated that a steamer from Belize to Jamaica "is timed only at four miles an hour," while one from to Honduras "is timed at eight miles an hour" (322), a piece of data collection lifted directly from his official reports to

FIGURE 2.1. "I tarnt reach.—Christmas Eve." Postcard, 1860. © Royal
Mail Group Ltd. Courtesy of The Postal Museum.

the Post Office.[26] Convinced of Panama's importance to the imperial project of
communication—it was one of the "high-roads to Australia" (242)—Trollope
threw his efforts behind making isthmian mail swifter and cheaper.

Part of that project entailed the adroit use of economic might to drive
advantageous bargains with local officials who were in a position of economic
dependency—a key component of Britain's informal imperialism in the Americas.[27] Yet his behavior in this regard also illustrates key differences between
British and U.S. dealings on the isthmus. The Post Office wanted efficiencies
and lower costs, and thus his instructions included forging new, more favor-
able economic agreements with the government of Nueva Granada and the
Panama Railroad Company, both of which levied tariffs on transisthmian
mail. Trollope was particularly concerned about the practice of taxing *individual* letters, which he felt would discourage personal communication by post.
As explained in a substantial letter to his superior, Rowland Hill, he raised the
matter with the U.S. engineer George Totten of the Panama Railway Company,

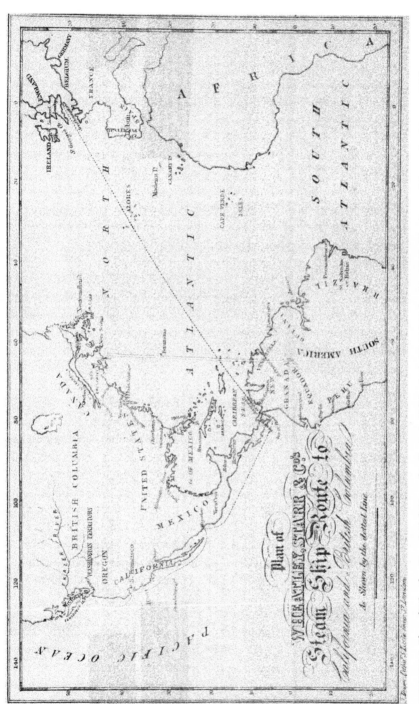

FIGURE 2.2. Plan of Wheatley, Starr & Co.'s Steamship Route to California and British Columbia (1861). Huntington Library, San Marino, California.

who advised him that the United States simply ignored the Nueva Granadian levy.[28] Such disregard of local sovereignty, of course, typifies the larger
and more aggressive U.S. domination in the 1850s that Panamanian officials
such as Justo Arosemena bitterly decried. In "La cuestión Americana" of 1856,
Arosemena described the nonpayment of taxes as an insult to national sovereignty and a sign of disrespect to Nueva Granada's laws and moral traditions.
In light of the concession across the isthmus that enabled the railroad, the
refusal to pay fees and tariffs was particularly galling to Panamanian officials.[29]
Great Britain was in no position to act similarly, but it is striking that rather
than refuse to pay, as Totten had recommended, Trollope chose another path,
negotiating the tax downward. His solution produced the required result—
lowering the cost—but avoided the tensions created by a heavier-handed U.S.
approach. This was not, then, simply a matter of logistical thinking, but a
demonstration of the power of soft influence and the deft negotiation of different sovereignties.

As I have noted, the prospect of a shortcut to the Pacific, whether by paved
road, railway, or canal, drew increasing attention in the years preceding Trollope's journey and was perceived on both sides of the Atlantic as critical to
nation building and global empire. In the same year Stephens and Catherwood were preparing to explore the Central American backwoods, the noted
Scottish geographer James MacQueen authored *A General Plan for a Mail
Communication by Steam, between Great Britain and the Eastern and Western
Parts of the World* (1838), which proposed the development of steam packets
to the West Indies, the carriage of mail across the isthmus, and further service
to Canton and Sydney. Identifying the analogic relationship between local and
global technologies of communication, MacQueen defined steam packets as
"the mail-coaches of the ocean" and described their function in carrying communication as central to the informal armature of British imperialism:

> The rapidity and regularity with which such communications can be made,
> gives to every nation an influence, a command, and advantages such as scarcely
> anything else can give, and frequently extends even beyond the sphere of that
> influence and that command which the direct application of mere physical
> power can obtain.[30]

In 1842, one year after Trollope began his work as a surveyor in Ireland, the
Post Office introduced adhesive postage stamps, began biweekly steam packets
to the West Indies, and landed its first steamer at the isthmus.[31] Three years
later, Captain W. B. Liot scouted the mail route across the isthmus, which was
duly established in 1846, soon connecting established Atlantic routes with new

ones branching into the Pacific.[32] By 1852, the Royal Mail had established a line from Savannah to Chagres and would soon begin mail service through the isthmus to Australia.

Victorian writers understood the project to cross the isthmus not only as an end in itself but as part of a larger ensemble of practices and technologies that closed distances and united far-flung individuals. Dickens's *Household Words* framed the connection this way:

> Now that we can shake hands with Brother Jonathan in twelve days by means of weekly steamers; travel from one end of Great Britain to another, or from the Hudson to the Ohio, as fast as the wind, and make our words dance to distant friends upon the magic tight wire a great deal faster . . . it seems extraordinary that the simple expedient of opening a twenty eight mile passage [*sic*] between the Pacific and Atlantic Oceans . . . has not been already achieved.[33]

Steamship, iron horse, and telegraph: the passage endows these instruments of human and informational mobility with magical power, as words dance and travelers hurtle across space. We see the enthusiasm that greets every new technology and the feelings of freedom prompted by the promise of an unfettered, frictionless flow of persons, things, and information. Minimizing the political and engineering challenges involved in such a project—and reducing a forty-nine-mile distance to twenty-eight—the writer is dumbfounded that it "has not already been achieved." The techno-enthusiastic language also expresses the genuine hunger for intimacy, the prospect of being in closer and more frequent touch not only with kindred cousins (Brother Jonathan) but also far-flung members of the imagined community of empire. Indeed, the English Vice Consul Bidwell, writing in 1865, captured the emotions produced by the imminent arrival of letters: "One of the most refreshing sights to a European stationed at Panamá is, I think, the sight of the long row of mule-carts bearing towards the English consulate their goodly loads of British mail-bags."[34]

Colonial officials strongly supported such short cuts. Just as U.S. writers on the isthmian crossing stressed the railroad's importance in connecting their nascent transcontinental empire, British writers were similarly interested in joining remote parts of the empire, as evidenced in my epigraph from Bidwell, who likens Panama's mail processing to St. Martin's-le-Grand, the famous General Post Office in London. Bidwell was writing in 1865, but in the early 1850s, a letter from London to Victoria, British Columbia, took on average three months to arrive, with assistance from Hudson Bay ships and Native American canoes. When gold fever struck the Fraser Valley in 1858,

James Douglas, British Columbia's colonial governor, pleaded with the Colonial Office for a direct steamer line from Panama to Vancouver Island, which he represented as "advantageous to British interests in this part of the world."[35] MacQueen claimed that by cutting through the isthmus "the valuable, but almost unknown, British territory on the west coast of North America, would be brought near, and cleared, and cultivated," and that more generally, the opening of such a passage would benefit the cultural mission of British imperialism.[36] It would do more, he wrote, "to people, to cultivate, and civilize the world, than any other effort—than all other efforts made by the world at large, when combined and brought together." No nation, he argued, was better suited to realize this great dream than Great Britain itself.[37]

RACE AND SLAVERY

Achieving these efficiencies, however, was not just a matter of drawing new lines on a map. British and U.S. travelers consistently characterized local populations as the principal threat to schemes of greater mobility. They defined their own sense of modernity as a function of speed and haste, and interpreted any alternative human tempo as a sign of incurable backwardness and barbarity. The discourse of tropical obduracy relied on a largely anecdotal though widely accepted body of racial thought influenced by the abiding issue of West Indian slavery. It is in this context that Trollope's notorious writing about racial tension in postemancipation Jamaica must be considered. Like many British travelers bound for the Americas, he viewed the region through the prism of the Caribbean, where the steam packets initially landed when bringing the Atlantic mail. Not coincidentally, then, his opening three chapters deal explicitly with Jamaica, the largest and richest Caribbean colony. Each is influenced by the writings of Thomas Carlyle, especially the reactionary Carlyle of the notorious "Negro Question" essay of 1849, which shaped British thought about the West Indies in the years leading up to the Morant Bay rebellion of 1865.[38]

Carlyle's thinking informs Trollope's disdain for the philanthropic perspective of "Exeter Hall" abolitionism (61) and his picture of the emancipated slave "now eating his yam without work" (65). It shapes his crude comparison between the robust "Saxon energies fresh from Europe"(47) and black "squatting" (62), and the distorted logic that would trace the woes of the planter class not to the end of a reviled system of human trafficking but to Jamaica's tropical fecundity, which provided "too many good things in Jamaica for the number who have to enjoy them" (65), a luxuriance that Trollope found inimical to habits of industrious labor. As a fervent adherent to the gospel of work,

which he credited for his own success, Trollope followed his mentor in dis-
missing the prospect of a life free from its dictates. As he put it, "Man's energy
is brought to its highest point by the presence of obstacles to be overcome, by
the existence of difficulties which are all but insuperable" (263). Trollope turns
Carlyle's infamous portrait of "Quashee," the idle ex-slave, to caricature in an
invented dialogue of the freed slave's response to a call for work: "No massa;
no starve now; God send plenty yam" (64). James A. Froude would later give
the subject an odious theological gloss by claiming that "these poor children
of darkness have escaped the consequences of the Fall" by living "surrounded
by most of the fruits of Adam's paradise," where "yams and cassava flow without effort."[39] Bedford Pim, writing just after the Morant Bay Rebellion and
during his affiliation with the racist Anthropological Society of London, was
even more caustic: "Your body corporate is rotten to the core, whilst your
thews and sinews, the negroes, are worse than useless: the men ignorant, bru-
tal, and slothful; the women degraded." Pim did not wish for slavery's return,
but like many conservatives of his age, thought Jamaica would decline further unless the "stalwart, well-fed turbulent negro population do their duty
in that state of life in which it has pleased Almighty God to place them."[40]
These writers were blinded, of course, to the reality that in postemancipation
Jamaica, where economic opportunities for former slaves were scant, pious
invocations to the muse of work were absurd. Trollope himself gives the fate
of free black slaves second billing to how white planters would fare in a world
without compulsory labor and the protections afforded by high sugar tariffs
on slave holding territories such as Cuba and Brazil. Although, like Pim, he
considers slavery morally "repugnant" (90) and accepts the abolitionist credo
that the Negro was both a "man and a brother" (94), he leaves no doubt about
Britain's future dominance. Jamaica would continue to "be governed by us
English" (99).

Abhorrent as these sentiments are, Trollope elsewhere moves beyond
rigid antinomies to a wider, regional view informed by his own experience
of mobility and his analysis of changing labor patterns in the Caribbean. This
is a more interesting and expansive Trollope, though still not without problems. He explores, even if he does not fully develop, a "Jamaica theory of
races" (196) that seeks to account for how migration, particularly from east
to west, was changing the island's familiar dynamics. Driven by a perspective
that extends beyond the Caribbean, this argumentative thread begins with a
discussion of the varied lineages and roving nature of the British people themselves: "No Englishman, no Anglo-Saxon, could be what he now is but for
that portion of wild and savage energy which has come to him from his Van-
dal forefathers" (63). Moving to the West Indian context, he valorizes "mix-

ture" (73) and "amalgamation" (75), especially between people of West African stock and immigrants from India and China that arrived in the West Indies as indentured servants after emancipation.[41] Many of these immigrants came to work on the Panama Railroad, and many thousands more would eventually labor on the canal. Lauren Goodlad is certainly right in arguing that "in climates deemed hospitable to Anglo-Saxon settlement, Trollope envisions no role for racial intermixture," but there is no doubting his praise for Jamaica's mixed-race population: "They practise as statesmen, as lawyers, and as doctors in the colony" (80).[42] Trollope goes so far as to speculate that the colony's future prosperity lay with further mixing and immigration, even though its price would certainly be diminished British power. These seemingly progressive stands, of course, must be weighed against his blunt assessment of Jamaica's economic decline ("The palmy days of that island are over" [99]), which Trollope believes resulted from the necessity of competing against the slave-holding sugar economies of Cuba, Brazil, Puerto Rico, and the southern United States (107). Foreshadowing how globalization devalues work by pitting one group of laborers against another, Trollope argues that greater productivity can be squeezed from emancipated black slaves by placing "the Coolie or Chinaman alongside" (214), populations whose arrival in the region were remapping racial lines and the politics of labor, as we have seen in the context of the Panama railroad.[43] Trollope's Caribbean, like his Panama, is a world being radically transformed by patterns of global mobility—of goods, information, and people.

If Trollope's succeeding chapters demonstrate his interest in examining race and imperialism beyond the confines of British colonial relations, and in considering the threats posed by expanding U.S. influence, his visit to the Spanish colony of Cuba reveals a subtle understanding of the geopolitical forces at work in the broader Caribbean basin. This context frames his consideration of the island's troubled relationship to the United States and particularly questions of annexation and national sovereignty, which had broad implications for U.S. policy in Central America, and particularly Panama. Insofar as the question of Cuba's status involved a dispute between the United States and Spain, the matter fell formally outside British concern. Yet as Trollope understood, the United States' various attempts to annex Cuba inevitably involved larger issues of sovereignty and imperialism at issue throughout the Americas.[44] John Quincy Adams famously put the case for absorbing Cuba in terms of natural affinities:

> If an apple, severed by a tempest from its native tree, cannot choose but fall
> to the ground, Cuba, forcibly disjoined from its own unnatural connection

with Spain, and incapable of self-support, can gravitate only towards North American Union, which, by the same law of nature, cannot cast her off from its bosom.[45]

Four years before Trollope's arrival, James Buchanan, U.S. Minister to the Court of St. James, used similar arguments in the Ostend Manifesto to declare that the U.S. government ought to purchase Cuba from Spain. It "must be clear to every reflecting mind," he wrote, that Cuba's proximity made it "as necessary to the North American republic as any of its present members, and that it belongs *naturally* to that great family of states of which the Union is the providential nursery" (emphasis mine). If Spain refused to sell, Buchanan claimed, the United States had every right to "wrest" it by force, on the same principle that "would justify an individual in tearing down the burning house of his neighbor if there were no other means of preventing the flames from destroying his own home."[46] For Buchanan and his followers, Cuba held out the tempting prospect of extending Manifest Destiny across the seas.

In the mid-nineteenth century, the term filibuster was used to describe the much-despised practice whereby rogue U.S. militia forces invaded foreign territories with the intent of fomenting discontent and revolution. British officials and Latin American leaders alike railed against filibusters such as William Walker, who sought to overthrow Nicaragua in 1855, seeing them as little more than "piratical marauders."[47] When in 1856 Walker set himself up as a dictator in Nicaragua and seized the British-controlled settlement of Greytown along the Mosquito Coast, Britain responded with a threat of naval blockade, which nearly sparked a war with the U.S.[48] Panamanian officials worried that the isthmus would be overrun. Yet beyond Walker, the outrages perpetrated by filibusters stoked deeper fears of U.S. territorial ambitions, already aggravated by the Mexican War and the acquisition of Texas and California. Bidwell, the British Vice Consul, fretted openly that the U.S. might "*annex* Panamá" and take full control over the commercial railroad across it.[49] U.S. actors in Central America were equally suspicious. When Ephraim George Squier was appointed to a diplomatic post in Nicaragua, Charles Eliot Norton asked him whether he would be safe "there in that nation made up of Chatfields and Palmerstons or worse men than they,—all anxious and eager to plunge their daggers in the hearts of every American?"[50] Competitive tensions were fueled by the discovery of gold in California and the sudden demand for transit across the isthmus, putting Central America "at the center of world attention."[51] Despite the Clayton-Bulwer Treaty of 1850, which prohibited Britain and the U.S. from acquiring further territory in Central America, tensions ran high. The pronounced and frequently reiterated anti-imperialist concerns of Panamanians, who had the most to lose by annexation, seem to have been disregarded, and never enter into Trollope's account.

Throughout *West Indies and the Spanish Main* Trollope turns to the issue of future, or proleptic, U.S. expansion, imagining a monstrously enlarged U.S. extending its imperial footprint to the Caribbean:

> I saw the other day a map, "The United States as they now are, and in prospective;" and it included all these places—Mexico, Central America, Cuba, St. Domingo, and even poor Jamaica. It may be that the man who made the map understood the destiny of his country; at any rate he understood the tastes of his countrymen. (225)

In this image, a prospective United States engulfs not only Mexico and Central America but also, more worrisomely for Trollope, Britain's Caribbean colonies. Indeed, Trollope wonders whether in the future "the whole district" (i.e., Central America) would one day be nothing more than an "outlying territory belonging to the United States" (238). This anxiety resonated not only with Britons fearful of diminished regional influence but also with Panamanians such as Arosemena, who opens his important 1856 essay, "Contra la expansión colonialista de Estados Unidos," with a dark warning about the aggressive habits of the eagle of the north ("águila del norte"). This rapacious force, Arosemena writes, has already directed its acquisitive eyes on Nicaragua and Cuba, and threatens to realize in the not too distant future even greater plans for regional domination ("consumar sus vastos planes de conquista un día no muy remoto").[52] As far as British officialdom was concerned, a specific threat was intelligence security, the opening of confidential dispatches and government letters. In his argument for steam packet service to the West Indies, MacQueen noted that it was "quite notorious, that from almost every quarter of the western world the earliest intelligence is almost uniformly received through the United States," and fretted that official British dispatches to foreign states were "sent through the United States, because they go earlier to their place of destination."[53] Writing in 1863, Bedford Pim employed stark, geopolitical terms to argue that "the time has arrived when the eyes of the public ought to be opened to the true aspect of affairs in Central America. Sooner or later, nothing but disaster will be the result of tamely submitting to this close monopoly of the transit." Noting that the British minister had been unable to communicate with the colonial governor in British Columbia for six weeks, owing to the fear of dispatches falling into hostile hands in Panama, Pim urged his government to take a much more aggressive stand. Pim believed that the United States, "by monopoly of the Panama Railway transit, virtually *holds the key* of the Gate of the Pacific."[54] Such sentiments were widespread.[55]

Written in the context of these transatlantic tensions, Trollope's discussion of Cuban annexation articulates a remarkable stance of critical self-reflection on the course of empire, one that has significant implications for his views of Panama and expanding U.S. power:

> It may be fair for us to consider whether we have not in our younger days done as much in this line as have the Americans—whether Clive, for instance, was not a filibuster—or Warren Hastings. Have we not annexed, and maintained, and encroached; protected, and assumed, and taken possession in the East—doing it all of course for the good of humanity? (132)

Trollope's equation of British colonial rule in India with U.S. filibustering challenges two central rationales for British imperialism: its difference from other imperialisms and the use of moral grounds to justify territorial aggression. First, if one cannot distinguish between kinds of imperialism, on what grounds can it be upheld? What distinguishes the colonial enterprise in India from William Walker's incursions into Central America? Do these differences matter? Trollope's extraordinary question leads him from moral superiority to realpolitik: "Let them fulfil their destiny in the West, while we do so in the East" (137). Drawing on the familial trope that structured the discursive relationship between Britain and the U.S., he claims that "the world is wide enough for us and for our offspring" (137), even if at times "the weaning of the baby will always be in some respects painful to the mother" (138). Cuban annexation, for Trollope, appears as a local irritant in a broader geopolitical reality wherein culturally allied empires assume their place in the global order. Filibustering, "called by that or some other name, is the destiny of a great portion of that race to which we Englishmen and Americans belong" (132). Again, however, in assenting to an expanded U.S. role, Trollope leaves little room for Spanish-American self-determination.

The text goes further still by questioning the opposition between colonizer and colonized and the moral logic that would reject annexation under any circumstances. Trollope notes significant differences among Cubans themselves, asserting that some "would be glad enough to see the transfer effected" (133)—a view upheld by recent scholarship in the field. Hugh Thomas, for example, has shown that Cuban plantation owners worried that "abolitionism might capture the minds of the Spanish officials"; Louis A. Pérez, similarly, demonstrates that creole elites saw annexation as an end to the "onerous system of Spanish taxation on foreign imports" as well as "North American tariffs on Cuban products."⁵⁶ Along with this emphasis on elite opinion, Trollope highlights the oppressive colonial conditions under which Cubans suffered: subservience to a distant power; a military and bureaucracy staffed by Spaniards; and a total lack of political representation. Since "no Cuban has any voice in his own country," what "love can he have for Spain?" (133). Setting aside Trollope's blindness to similar conditions in British colonies, and his faulty conflation of elite with working-class opinion, these anticolonial claims are worth examining for another reason: his belief that annexation was the surest way to end the slave trade, which he loathed.

Trollope's argument for justifying U.S. territorial ambition finally hinges on the abolitionist rhetoric of sympathy for the enslaved—the legally immobile— distinguished here from their free, mobile black brethren in post-emancipation Jamaica. This use of abolitionism runs against his earlier formulations. In the Jamaica chapters, he had critiqued the application of abolitionist language to free Jamaicans as rhetorical overreach. Emancipated Jamaicans in his view had not only squandered their own economic mobility by refusing to work but had also harmed the larger colonial economy. In his comments on Cuba, however, he draws on familiar abolitionist tropes to highlight Spanish turpitude in permitting slavery to continue. Although he admits that in the U.S. slave holding persists, he reminds his readers that the *slave trade* "is as illegal there as in England" (134) and argues that while slavery itself would probably continue for a time if Cuba were annexed, the greater evil of the middle passage, with slaves laid like cord wood below decks, "would of necessity come to an end" (135). Fraught with moral ambiguity, the argument resonates with questions asked in many parts of our contemporary world where human rights have been imperiled (e.g., Kosovo, Rwanda): whether there is "some stage in misgovernment which will justify the interference of by-standing nations, in the name of humanity" (135). Beneath lies a complex calculus, pitting moral outrage over violations of human rights against principles of nonintervention and respect for borders. In Trollope's universe, "the horrors of the middle passage, the kidnapping of negroes, the African wars which are waged for the sake of prisoners" (134–35) trump concerns over imperial overreach and the violation of national sovereignty.

DIFFERENTIAL MOBILITIES

Trollope's itinerary, as we now can see, afforded many opportunities to comment on the large, geopolitical concerns at issue in this part of the world. From slavery to filibustering, labor migration to isthmian transit, he trains his keen, frequently jaundiced eye on the abiding problems of the day. Throughout, however, he also focuses on the humble subject of traveling itself, the experiential lens, somatic filter, and authoritative ground of his broader concerns. Filling the page with his own, highly embodied self, he dramatizes his struggles with making his way, a subject that emerges in the text both as a problem of human kinetics and a metaphor for the larger questions of mobility that animate his text. If the question of "how best to get around this world" is "one of the most interesting subjects which men have to consider" (316), Trollope takes pains to show how difficult, and sometimes impossible, it was for him simply to move. Nature erects one obstacle to his mobility after another, with frequently comic results. At sea, he complains that his journey is "progressless" and that his vessel's nauseous bobbing has disturbed the "two sardines which [he had] economically eaten" (6). In Jamaica, he labors to the top of Blue Mountain peak, a herculean struggle against gravity he promises never to repeat, especially after thick fog ruins the longed-for Humboldtian view from the summit. In Costa Rica, he learns the hard way that "a continued seat of five hours on a mule, under a burning sun, is not refreshing to a man who is not accustomed to such exercise" (252). Yet "splash, splash, splosh, splosh" he goes, all "fifteen stone" of him (210 pounds), astride a poor mule that labors through the muddy tracks of Central America in a way reminiscent of the prerailroad passage across the isthmus (304–5).

Expressed as problems of his own fleshly embodiment, these struggles between one man's mortal coil and a geography that appears to oppress it nevertheless connect to his larger belief that Central America was ultimately at odds with the Anglo-Saxon sensibility and hostile to the logic of modernity it reflected. Like the railway promoters and gold rushers of the previous decade, he defines the Western traveler as the master of time and speed. Evoking the customary foil of the laggardly Spaniard, he reminds the reader that in "any country that is or has been connected with Spain," "men have no idea of time." His mule driver's assurances—"'Yes, señor; you said twelve, and it is now only two! Well, three. The day is long, señor; there is plenty of time. . . .'" (277)—only reinforce his belief that the local people lack the energy and drive necessary to succeed in the coming world of mobility, speed, and transport. His own difficulties with movement across space function textually as an admonitory sign of the larger challenges facing the Spanish Main's modernization and suggest his view that Central America could not be left to the Central Americans.

Trollope's stance toward the transformation occurring on the isthmus demonstrates the ambivalence at the heart of his critical enterprise. Like other Britons such as Mary Seacole, he was annoyed at U.S. excesses on the isthmus. He deplores the Yankee insistence that Colón (the Atlantic terminus of the railroad) be known as Aspinwall (after the U.S. tycoon who founded the railroad), remarking that "our friends from Yankee-land," despite the "disgust" of the Nueva Granadians, "like to carry things with a high hand, and to have a nomenclature of their own" (236). He grasps, in ways suggested by the map of a territorially expanded United States, that the power to fix the identity of places was itself an expression of imperial power. He knew, of course, that Aspinwall was no mere name, but a stark reminder of how U.S. capital had forever transformed the isthmus into a link in a global system of transport, one that in privileging the traveler's mobility increased immobility for the locals, whose livelihoods as guides across the isthmus were decimated by the arrival of industrialized machines.

Yet if he remains wary of advancing of U.S. power, Trollope also echoes the railway promoters in characterizing dark-skinned locals as obstacles to the mobility of goods, persons, and mail. His theme of cultural decline would have resonated with British readers accustomed to travelers' accounts representing Spanish American civilization as inimical to modernity. Describing Nueva Granada, and sounding very much like Stephens, Trollope claims that "civilization here is retrograding" and "making no progress." Time itself appeared to have rolled backward, and with it the fruits of a progressive society: "Land that was cultivated is receding from cultivation; cities that were populous are falling into ruins; and men are going back to animals" (231). Dickens's *Household Words,* similarly, had described the local population as "poor and ignorant aboriginals and mixed races, [trapped] in a state of scarcely demi-civilisation."[57] And Otis's *History of the Panama Railroad Company* (1861) blamed the failure of Spanish Americans to build a useable road or rail on "the native population, composed of a mongrel race of Spaniards, Indians, and Negroes," who "were too indolent and unaccustomed to labor to be depended on to any great extent."[58] Even in their hyperbolic form, these characterizations mesh with the orthodox British view that Latin America would have been better served had it been colonized by Anglo-Saxons, not Spaniards. In Argentina thirty years before, Darwin wondered "how different would have been the aspect of this river if English colonists had by good fortune first sailed up the Plata! What noble towns would now have occupied its shores!"[59] In these accounts, a critique of Spanish civilization's failings—its bondage to Catholic superstition, its hostility to modernity—is admixed with a strong dose of regret, a recognition that Great Britain had missed a grand imperial opportunity.[60] By the time of Trollope's writing, the realization of having lost out to the Spanish in the sixteenth century was joined by the more pressing and present concern of losing out to the United States in the nineteenth.

A staunch proponent of Britain's "noble mission" to preserve the "welfare of the coming world," Trollope finally came down on the side of viewing the local population of Central America as a hindrance to the schemes of development and increased commerce that arose from the energy and drive of the "Anglo-Saxon race" (83). Disparaging mestizo Costa Ricans as a "humdrum, contented, quiet, orderly race of men" with "no enthusiasm, no ardent desires, no aspirations," he claims that they simply "vegetate" under the hot tropical sun (264–65). Like Carlyle, he links what he sees as low human productivity to an overly hot and fecund climate, arguing that "it seems God's will that highly fertile countries should not really prosper" (263). Yet he reserves his most damning comments for Nueva Granada's black residents, who in the years before Trollope's visit were the principal beneficiaries of the final abolition of slavery (1852) and the establishment of universal manhood suffrage (1853), this last the result of what Aims McGuinness calls "the most radical constitution in the world."[61] Reverting to a Carlylean perspective, Trollope recoils at the latter development, praising abolition as a "good deed" (231) but criticizing suffrage for allowing every man, whether an "industrial occupier of land" or an "idle occupier of nothing" to have an equal vote (231). Tellingly, he argues that the prospect of all men being "equal for all state purposes" was "not gratifying." Indeed, for Trollope, universal male suffrage implied the unimaginable, that a white man might be represented by a black one. He makes clear that his reasons are explicitly racial by invoking Carlyle's ugly phrase, the "unfortunate nigger gone masterless," employed here to argue that black people have no "strong ideas of the duties even of self-government, much less the government of others" (232).[62]

Mary Seacole's *Wonderful Adventures,* published in London just two years before Trollope's work, offers an important counterweight to these disparaging views of black self-government. Given that Trollope mentions having lodged in Kingston "with a sister of good Mrs. Seacole" (23), it seems likely he had read her narrative and was familiar with her sojourn in Panama. It's also likely he disapproved of her radical opinions, especially her opposing view of sovereignty on the isthmus, a major preoccupation of both works. Among many other examples, Seacole's account of the arrest of an "American by the New Granada authorities" stands out for detailing, from the other side as it were, exactly the issue to which Trollope objects above—the political and juridical power of emancipated black citizens in Nueva Granada over white Anglo-Americans.[63] Providing a level of eyewitness specificity only one who has endured similar slights could offer, Seacole briskly narrates the arrest of a U.S. citizen for "highway robbery." At the start of her brief account, she uses an objective third-person viewpoint to describe an "angry crowd of brother Americans" surrounding the frightened soldiers who had made the arrest, "abusing and threatening the authorities in no measured terms, all of

them indignant that a *nigger should presume to judge one of their countrymen*"
(emphasis mine). The crux of the matter, of course, is who has the authority to
judge, or rather, whether a black man has the authority to judge a white one.
Seacole then goes on to remark that the ruckus "roused the sleepy alcalde,"
or mayor, who charges his soldiers to quell the disturbance before delivering a speech to the unruly crowd. Through Seacole's narration, we now see
the incident through the attributed words of the local official. The content of
the speech, like so many representations from this period, is filtered through
a more literate narrator. The alcalde himself does not speak, but is spoken
for, albeit by a subject who herself has known the slings and arrows of being
black in Panama. Importantly, however, the speech's content corroborates
other accounts we have seen of lawlessness and disrespect among the new
arrivals: "He addressed the crowd, declaring that since the Americans came
the country had known no peace, that robberies and crimes of every sort had
increased, and ending in his determination to make strangers respect the laws
of the Republic." Notably, like others such as Arosemena and José Manuel
Luna, the Panamanian fruit seller, the alcalde reinforces the crucial idea of
sovereignty by reminding the mob that they are not in the United States but in
another country, whose laws they must respect. Yet to ensure that the reader
grasps not only *what* was said but *who* said it, Seacole again switches perspective, voicing the thoughts of the bewildered white U.S. citizens: "The Americans seemed too astonished at the audacity of the black man, who dared thus
to beard them, to offer any resistance." As historians have documented, many
of the local mayors or "alcaldes" in Nueva Granada were black, a reflection
of the liberal policies toward suffrage and abolition noted previously. Their
power—here on display both in the ability to order the soldiers and to quell a
disturbance caused by white men from the United States—was indisputable,
giving the lie to, and perhaps the rationale for, Trollope's mistaken ideas about
black self-government.[64]

It is therefore not surprising that Trollope dismissed the ability of Nueva
Granadians to conduct their own affairs, or, in the terms derived from theorists of mobility, to define place as a coherent center of meaning independent
of its function as a connecting point. For Trollope famously concluded that
Central America could only be "great in the world" by serving as a "passage
between other parts of the world which are in themselves great" (339). He thus
defined the region as a nodal point in a large network that facilitated, organized, and enhanced the flow of mobilities across the world. That he saw the
region this way is clear from "The Journey to Panama," one of the short fictions inspired by his West Indian and Spanish American travels. His narrator,
echoing Trollope, argues that the West Indian route is great

not on account of our poor West Indian islands which cannot at the present moment make anything great, but because it spreads itself out from thence to Mexico and Cuba, to Guiana and the republics of New Granada and Venezuela, to Central America, the Isthmus of Panamá, and from thence to California, Vancouver's Island, Peru, and Chili.[65]

Defined as a network node, a connection point, the West Indies and Central America dissolve as places with intrinsic value in themselves. Absorbed into a global system of travel, they become places between, interstices. Trollope's English analogue for this state of affairs is telling—Crewe, the famous railway station which, in the years after its founding in 1837, became a key junction in Britain's expanding rail system. Crisscrossed by lines, the town was all but eclipsed by its functional role in transport: "Men must reach Crewe and leave Crewe continually" (339). It became a nonplace, dominated by machines that whizzed people and goods through it on the way to other places.[66] In Central America, the disruptive technology that changed the landscape was the "great fact" (237) of the Panama Railway, which similarly served larger economic and geopolitical imperatives, both for the British Empire, which Trollope represented, and the United States, the hemisphere's dominant power. As a traveler along, and a colonial administrator of, this larger network of mobilities, Trollope was well placed to understand its reach and power, its limitations and exclusions. Far more than a bald catalogue of racial oppositions, his travel narrative vividly captures the tensions of a rapidly modernizing world.

CHAPTER 3

~

Photographing Panama

Eadweard Muybridge and
Trans-Hemispheric Modernity

AFTER THE railroad and steamship, the most important machine to come to nineteenth-century Panama was the camera. Like its counterparts, the camera was an instrument of mobility, enabling the circulation of images that transported their viewers to other worlds. Just as the steamship and railroad made Panama accessible to Anglo-American travelers, so the camera made it available for visual consumption by a global viewership, most of whom would never set foot on the isthmus. These technologies, moreover, were mutually supporting. Photographic images spread around the world by steamship and rail, reaching ever-wider publics. In turn they depicted the vessels, ports, locomotives, and track that embodied the brave new world of transport (fig. 3.1). Images of technological might affirmed the Victorians' view of themselves as industrious masters of space and time. New horizons of speed—in both transport and photographic representation—redefined the limits of human mobility and visual apprehension, which in turn shaped the present era of global modernity.

Eadweard Muybridge's 1875 photographic journey to Panama unites these concerns in a particularly compelling way. The famed British photographer traveled to Panama at the bidding of the Pacific Mail Steamship Company, which hoped that alluring illustrations of the region's transport infrastructure and docile workforce would increase tourism and trade, benefiting both investors and the company itself. The *Panama Star*, closely associated with U.S.

FIGURE 3.1. Eadweard Muybridge, "Long Ravine Trestle and Bridge, 113 feet high—878 feet long—looking East." Lone Mountain College Collection of Stereographs. Courtesy of the Bancroft Library, University of California, Berkeley.

interests in the region, stated that Muybridge was sent "to illustrate by views all the curious places that a traveller by Railroad and the Pacific Mail Company's ships can see or be within reach of in a journey from New York to San Francisco via the Isthmus," but also, and more crucially for my purposes here, to mediate Panama for viewers at a far remove. Muybridge, the *Star* asserted, would do for Panama what "has never been so well done for it before, either by pen or pencil, in making its beauties known especially to those will never see them otherwise."[1] As we have seen in previous chapters, the steamship company was established in the 1840s to capitalize on U.S. territorial expansion along the West Coast and played a crucial role in the patterns of mobility that made Panama important to U.S. Manifest Destiny. Yet during the 1860s and early 1870s, slowing gold rush traffic and the transcontinental railroad, which opened in 1869, damaged the company's fortunes. According to Tracy Robinson, a long-time U.S. resident of Panama, "The best of the California business of the Panama route was over, and the Parent Company never again pretended to skim the cream of *that* great traffic."[2] That Muybridge was sent to Panama to help reverse this trend is an important acknowledgment of his artistic stature, and more generally of the camera's role in bringing Central America into the fold of U.S. imperialism.

Muybridge's journey, however, has been overshadowed by the lurid and catastrophic events that immediately preceded it. In October 1874, having learned of his wife's infidelity, he killed her lover by shooting him point blank in the chest. He was indicted for murder and appeared destined for the hangman's noose, but a San Francisco jury ignored the judge's instructions and acquitted him on grounds of justifiable homicide. Within days he had departed for Panama, seeking, as Robert Hass has argued, to "regulate his life again and return to the demonstration of his abilities as a pictorial photographer . . . freed from the disharmonies that he brought with him from San Francisco."[3] Hass's psychological reading of the journey is not without merit. Born in Kingston-upon-Thames as Edward Muggeridge, Muybridge changed course several times over his career, taking on new identities as he went: book dealer, "artist-photographer," and most grandly "Helios," after the solar deity who drove his chariot daily across the skies.[4] A tropical excursion to a distant Central American republic fits his lifelong pattern of movement and reinvention especially well.

Yet to read the Panamanian journey simply as an episode in the artist's development diminishes the images themselves, both as aesthetic objects in their own right and representations of the isthmus during a key moment in its history—subjects that critics have overlooked despite much attention to Muybridge in recent years. Situated in Muybridge's career between his magisterial American landscapes of the 1860s and 1870s and his innovative studies of human mobility in the 1880s, the approximately sixty-five stereographs and an equal number of large-plate prints speak to his interest in the technological changes that were transforming the American West. By extending this *West* beyond the nation to Panama, Muybridge's work anticipates contemporary arguments about the importance of hemispheric cultural formations. In his work, the American West includes Panama, even as Panama shapes distant places such as San Francisco. Muybridge, moreover, found in his Panamanian subjects rich material for his later studies of human movement, published as *Animal Locomotion*. The powerful, often disturbing Panama images suggest an important though heretofore unexamined colonial context for the work on motion, one that brings into focus transregional dimensions of mobility, technology, sexuality, and racial difference. Taken together, the Panama images yield an ambivalent portrayal that unsettles the narrative of economic development and U.S. hegemony that enfolded the region from the 1840s onward. Amidst the widespread boosterism of his era, Muybridge sounds a dissenting note, imaging a Panama riven with contradictions, caught between traditional ways and a new technological era that had altered but not utterly transformed the region.

MUYBRIDGE, MOBILITY, AND MODERNITY

The 1855 completion of the Panama Railway redefined the isthmus as a zone of mobility, a place through which people and things passed rapidly on their way elsewhere. A new infrastructure of track, ties, stations, buildings, bridges, and telegraph wires remade the landscape.[5] Rivers were spanned, earth graded, pylons driven. Locomotives belched smoke and shook the earth. New towns sprung up, as if overnight, serving legions of foreign travelers who arrived with each steamship. These outward, visible signs of the new, postrailroad reality spawned changes in language, symbolism, and social relations. Maps were redrawn and names changed, shifting conceptions of sovereignty and self-determination. The era of telegraph lines and locomotives produced new ways of being in the world, defined by speed, transport, communication, mobility, and global interconnection. The pace of life quickened. The rush that began with the discovery of gold in California lingered long after.

The new watchwords were speed and mobility. Early travelers across the Panama isthmus slogged days or even weeks along muddy trails and swollen rivers, but by 1855, the year Muybridge arrived in California, the newly built railroad whisked them across in three to four hours. It is likely Muybridge himself rode the train across Panama on his initial journey from New York to San Francisco, rather than sailing around the Horn or crossing overland by coach, for he was fascinated by new technologies wherever he went. In 1857, in his role of bookseller and operating under the name E. J. Muygridge, he published an illustrated pamphlet celebrating Isambard Brunel's *Great Eastern*. At 680 feet in length, it was the largest steamship of its time and a symbol of a newly interconnected world where it was possible to steam from Britain to India in thirty days. The pamphlet presents images of massive furnaces, boilers, engines, and smokestacks along with hyperbolic testimonials to the ship itself, which it calls "the most stupendous project of modern times in steam navigation."[6] It is tempting, from the perspective both of photographic and industrial history, to speculate whether Muybridge had seen the most famous representation of the SS *Great Eastern*—Robert Howlett's 1857 photograph of a top-hatted and watch-fobbed Brunel posing triumphantly against a massive bank of iron chains. Although it doesn't show the ship at all, but rather the chains used to launch it, Howlett's portrait is the kind of image Muybridge would have appreciated, suggesting as it does the uncertain place of human beings in an increasingly interlinked and transit-oriented world. In his own photographic work, Muybridge would attempt to capture something of this new world of speed, in which decreases in travel time paralleled advances in the rapidity of communication and representation. In an era when messages zipped along telegraph wires and photography rendered fully realized landscapes faster than any sketch artist or painter, Muybridge would later train his lenses on trotting horses and flying birds, opening a reality previously too fast for the human eye to capture. The perfection of steam-powered printing presses in the 1840s hastened the era of mechanical reproduction. In turn, words and images, repackaged in various forms (books, newspapers, magazines), sped across the globe on ever-faster steam vessels and trains. Communication and mobility had entered a new era.

Technologies of speed, transport, and communication combined to produce hybrid cultural forms in which visual images were central. On May 10, 1869, Leland Stanford drove the final spike of the transcontinental railroad in Promontory, Utah, uniting the Central Pacific and Union Pacific Railroads—and the nation. By means of wires attached to his maul and the spike, he also closed a circuit that in turn sent a telegraph message around the country: "dot, dot done." At the same time, Andrew Russell commemorated the event in a now-celebrated photograph, "Meeting of the Rails."[7] Thus did the final stage of a construction project become, by a familiar logic, a nationwide media event, a spectacle created by the same combination of collective participation, shared affect, visual memorialization, and instantaneousness we are accustomed to today. Muybridge's camera was both witness to and product of this new technological era, a machine not unlike the other machines he imaged in his quest to document the newness of his age. Muybridge's *Photographic Views* (1873), a work of towering ambition, lists over 150 images of the Central Pacific, Union Pacific, and California Pacific Railroads. Exhaustively, even obsessively, Muybridge recorded the world of transport infrastructure—even as that infrastructure and its technologies enabled his own mobility—the photographs he was able to take, and their global circulation. Arthur Brown, who worked for the Central and Pacific as a superintendent of bridges, helped Muybridge refine the mechanically tripped shutters used to photograph Stanford's trotting horses, whose motions, in turn, have a suggestively mechanical quality about them. And along with photographs of other machines, Muybridge captured the apparatuses of his "flying studio," which in its extent—chemicals, glass, paper, various cameras—also foregrounds the status of photography as technology.[8] For Muybridge the camera formed part of a broader range of technological developments such as steamships, lighthouses, railway locomotives, track, and bridges that were redefining older conceptions of space and time.

Yet Muybridge was not an unabashed booster of mechanized modernity. In ways that anticipate his Panama work, several photographs from the 1860s and 1870s strike an ambivalent pose toward the pace and scale of industrial change. His celebrated 1868 photograph of the Pacific Mail Steamship *Colorado*, then in dry dock at Hunter's Point, San Francisco, is a case in point (fig. 3.2). The *Colorado* played a key role in the shipping network that joined San Francisco, via Panama, to the global circuitry of trade and transport. Built in 1865 at a cost of one million dollars, and weighing nearly 4,000 tons, it measured 363 feet in length, 45 feet in width, and 31 feet in depth. To capture its great size, Muybridge positions himself obliquely to the prow, with the ship's length receding into the distance. Just as this camera placement exaggerates the ship's length, so also does the dry dock exaggerate its height, revealing what would normally lie unseen below the water line. Muybridge also times his picture to include two workmen. Nearly invisible by their low, off-center placement, they stand on a scaffold, dwarfed by the hull itself, which towers over them. Like the tiny human figures found in nineteenth-century landscape paintings by Bierstadt (whom Muybridge photographed), Cole, Church, and other practitioners of the American sublime, the men function as visual markers to illustrate scale. Yet their puny size also suggests the ship's grotesque monstrosity, and thus, the implicit threat posed by ever more powerful regimes of industrialization.

FIGURE 3.2. Eadweard Muybridge, "California Dry Dock, and Steamer Colorado." Lone
Mountain College Collection of Stereographs. Courtesy of the Bancroft Library, University of
California, Berkeley.

The potentially dehumanizing effects of a newly industrialized world are
clearer still in Muybridge's photographs of indigenous peoples, whose traditional ways of life were imperiled by the United States' westward expansion.
Muybridge vividly recorded these clashing cultures in his earliest expeditionary work, his 1868 series of Alaskan views, which were among the first photographs ever taken of Alaska.[9] Under the direction of General Henry Halleck,
commander of the Military Division of the Pacific, Muybridge sailed up the
Pacific Coast, past Vancouver Island, to the newly acquired territory, which
the U.S. government had purchased from Russia. His mission was to create a
photographic archive to help justify the $7.2 million price to a skeptical public.[10]
In this role, he took approximately fifty views of steamships, harbors, military
forts, gunnery stations, settlements, and local inhabitants. These subjects conform to his subsequent account of the work: "to accompany General Halleck
for the purpose of illustrating the Military Posts and Harbours of Alaska."[11]
Indeed, many of the pictures can be read as straightforward illustrations of

FIGURE 3.3. Eadweard Muybridge, "Fort Tongas, a View from the Fort" (half stereo). Lone Mountain College Collection of Stereographs. Courtesy of the Bancroft Library, University of California, Berkeley.

Alaska's commercial and strategic value as a territory and, therefore, the wisdom of the purchase itself. In "Fort Tongass, View from the Fort" (fig. 3.3), the camera looks down the barrel of a cannon at the harbor below, suggesting an equivalence between gun and lens, military and aesthetic understandings of an "overview," an identification further enhanced by Muybridge's inscription of his photographic nom de plume, "Helios," on the plank supporting the gun's left wheel. Images such as these led Halleck to praise the artist's ability to provide "a more correct idea of Alaska, its scenery and vegetation than can be obtained from any written description of that country."[12]

Muybridge's work, however, is never one dimensional, and among pictures of military advancement he depicted the indigenous people who had endured successive waves of European contact and colonization. Like his images of Russian orthodox priests, who witnessed fealty shift under their feet at the

FIGURE 3.4. Eadweard Muybridge, "Fort Wrangle, from Rock Cod" (half stereo). Lone Mountain College Collection of Stereographs. Courtesy of the Bancroft Library, University of California, Berkeley.

signing of a document, these photos—of groups of individuals, totem poles, lodges, and villages—disrupt the government's official narrative by implicitly drawing attention to the violence of colonial domination, which threatened the vividly realized culture represented everywhere in these images. In "Fort Wrangle, from Rock Cod" (fig. 3.4), Muybridge places his camera across from a small group of local people, probably Tlingit, the indigenous group that for thousands of years had lived in the region. Like many of Muybridge's group shots, the scene is carefully posed, requiring the Tlingit to hold still while the photographer went through the laborious process of taking then developing the image.[13] Seated near the shore on a rocky incline that slices from left to right across the image, placed so each is visible to the camera's eye and receding into the depth of the image, Muybridge's subjects look toward him or off into the distance. Their backs are turned to the sound and the newly established fort on the far shore. They have also turned away from the steamship anchored behind them, which occupies the center of Muybridge's composition, fixing their gaze instead on the other machine, the camera, and at the stranger operating it. The visual arrangement suggests Muybridge's self-consciousness about the material economy of his own medium, as the photograph is both an image of otherness and the modern systems of transport that made its circulation possible in a larger visual economy.

Although the named photographic subject is Fort Wrangell, an important military asset acquired from the Russians and thus an official subject in the catalogue of Alaska's views, Muybridge's composition reduces it to only one of several competing elements—ship, native people, fort, reflective water, rocky foreground, and finally his own subjectivity. In a strategy accentuated in the stereographic technique of creating depth and fractured visual planes, the composition of these elements subverts rather than reinforces a dominant perspective.[14] The fort itself is literally and figuratively decentered, placed to the far right of the image and captured from a great distance, seemingly an afterthought. Muybridge further complicates the picture's meaning by again concealing his trademark, "Helios," in the image, here among the rocks and grass just in front of the seated woman on the right. Apparently inscribed with a stylus on the negative itself, the signature is only fully legible when seen through a stereographic viewer, and even then only if the image is focused just so. This flickering trace of the photographic signature, aside from protecting Muybridge's brand, echoes the larger self-reflexivity about image-making everywhere in his corpus.[15] The hidden Helios signature gestures toward a tradition of European easel painting in which artists such as Caravaggio playfully concealed images of themselves in their work and signals Muybridge's ambition, already suggested in the name itself, to elevate photography to a high art. To look for the name and focus on it in the depths of the stereograph is necessarily to draw one's attention away from the photograph's putative subject toward Muybridge and his coyly figured displacement, Helios.

We know from Muybridge's Yosemite views that he took great pains to find just the right spot to locate his camera, engaging in what became another attempt at self-inscription, of making a corpus of pictures that could only be his own. He scrambled down perilous trails, perched himself on rocky outcrops, dangled from ropes, and stood in icy rivers, all in an effort to achieve a signature style by expanding the limits of representation beyond what his competitors had already attained. "The artist," he wrote self-aggrandizingly, "has gone to points where his packers refused to follow him, and has carried his apparatus himself rather than forgo the picture on which he had set his mind."[16] In "Fort Wrangle," this pursuit of a novel camera placement, a reflec-

tion of his singular vision, as well as the careful composition and personaliza-
tion of the images, transforms a stock anthropological portrait into a deeply
subjective and ultimately self-reflexive story of an imperiled indigenous world
caught between steamship and camera, and the new regimes of mobility and
representation they signal. By thus recording ways of life threatened by U.S.
territorial and economic claims to ownership, and making this recordation a
project of the artist's own ambition, the photos work against the logic of the
mission Muybridge was sent to perform, providing a "correct idea of Alaska."

PANAMA THROUGH THE LENS

Muybridge produced his Panama images in three photographic formats—
glass lantern slides, large-plate photographs, and stereographs in standard and
cabinet-size format. Although these formats overlap in some ways, there are
key differences in content, form, as well as intended audience. A master show-
man, Muybridge used the lantern slides for public presentations at learned
societies, where he was quite active. He issued the large-plate photographs
(approximately 14 x 24 cm) in a small run of bound volumes entitled *The
Pacific Coast of Central America and Mexico; The Isthmus of Panama; Guatemala; and the Cultivation and Shipment of Coffee* (1876). He clearly intended
these volumes, containing from 120 to 264 prints, for a select group of viewers:
wealthy patrons, institutions, close friends, and collectors. Each was unique,
differing in the number of prints, sequencing, and techniques of development. As Byron Wolfe has documented, Muybridge experimented with multiple versions of the same photograph, making combination prints by adding
previously photographed details such as clouds and mountain scenery.[17] These
carefully constructed, highly intentional works show Muybridge's skills not
only in the field but also in the process of development, where he continued
to modify his images.

The most widely disseminated of Muybridge's formats, and the one I focus
on here, were the sixty-five stereoscopic views issued as *Isthmus of Panama
and Central America, Illustrated by Muybridge*, which were available individ-
ually and as a set.[18] Ubiquitous by the 1870s, stereographs consisted of two
slightly different images which, when examined through a special viewer
called a stereoscope, combined to give the illusion of seeing in three dimensions (fig. 3.5). When the two nearly identical photographs, mounted side by
side on a card, are properly adjusted, they resolve into a single image that
gives a powerful illusion of three-dimensionality, seeming to locate the viewer
in the middle of the landscape. To see the image correctly, viewers slid the

FIGURE 3.5. Stereoscope. Library of Congress.

card back and forth along its special track until it resolved into focus. Once positioned, the card allowed the viewer to range over the image's visual sectors—foreground, middle ground, and far distance—producing what Jonathan Crary has called a "planar" effect.[19] Sold inexpensively in the consumer marketplace through concerns such as the London Stereoscope Company, founded in 1854, stereographs were widely collected and exchanged. A portable stereoscopic viewer became a common feature in the Victorian home, a window to foreign and domestic landscapes, portraits, architectural sights, sculpture, and easel paintings—whatever could be represented in an image. Never considered examples of high art, but rather mass-produced consumer articles, stereographs functioned as vehicles for education and entertainment, cultivating spectatorship itself as a middle-class practice. Their wide circulation helped create what Deborah Poole, writing in a different context, has called an "image world," comprised of "relationships of referral and exchange among images themselves, and the social and discursive relations connecting image-makers and consumers."[20] Although easily dismissed as visual toys that encouraged "familiarity rather than informed understanding," stereographs were as important to visual culture as large-format photographs, if not more so.[21] They reached a wider audience, and perhaps more deeply, for viewing them was an interactive experience, engaging eyes and hands.

The aesthetic ambition of Muybridge's stereo series becomes clear when compared to the Central American work of two contemporary photographers. In 1870, five years prior to Muybridge's Panama journey, Timothy O'Sullivan (c. 1840–82) signed on as official photographer for Commander Thomas Oliver Selfridge's Darien Expedition, which was commissioned to explore a canal route across this particularly remote part of Central America.[22] Like Muybridge, O'Sullivan was a figure of enormous talent, honed during his apprenticeship to the civil war photographer Matthew Brady. He also played a key role in the photographic documentation of postbellum America, serving as the official photographer for Clarence King's Geological Exploration of the Fortieth Parallel, one of many large-scale U.S. governmental surveys that lent visual support to the project of national expansion.[23] O'Sullivan's Darien photographs depict jungle growth so thick it crowds out the nineteenth-century photographer's sine qua non, natural light, and the traveler's knowledge it metaphorically represents. Even at the coast, O'Sullivan reminds the viewer of the ever-creeping forest. In one image thatched-roof huts cling to a narrow beach, pressed from behind by encroaching jungle (fig. 3.6). In another, O'Sullivan captures the visibly fatigued members of the expedition with their backs against a wall of palms, again rejecting the visual relief offered by the sea's horizon (fig. 3.7). Drawing on a conventional rhetoric of the heroic explorer, Sullivan represents the jungle as fecund and oppressive, and Darien as a place hostile to schemes of Western development.[24]

Closer to Muybridge's subject but different in sensibility is the 1870 photographic album entitled *Views on the Isthmus*.[25] Comprised of twenty-one, large-albumen prints (28 x 39 cm), the anonymous volume offers an official perspective on the Panama Railroad journey. It begins with respectful scenes of economic development in Aspinwall, headquarters of the Company and sign of U.S. imperial sway. These images support the grand narrative of the benefits of American development by depicting its solid, institutional forms: commercial buildings, Protestant churches, memorials to heroic figures, the official residence of the Superintendent of the Panama Railway Company. "Church and Monument, Aspinwall" (fig. 3.8) depicts a triangular pillar commemorating John Lloyd Stephens, Henry Chauncey, and William H. Aspinwall, the railroad's founding fathers. The view is taken from the side that honors Stephens, which places the monument against a large Episcopal church built by the Railroad Company in 1865.[26] The image affirms the isthmus's dual

FIGURE 3.6. Timothy O'Sullivan, "Huts, Palm Trees and Beach, Isthmus of Darién, 1870." Albumen Silver Print, 22.1 x 28.9 cm. The J. Paul Getty Museum, Los Angeles.

FIGURE 3.7. Timothy O'Sullivan, "Lt. Commander Thomas O. Selfridge and Members of the Darién Expedition, 1870." Albumen Silver Print, 21.7 x 28.7 cm. The J. Paul Getty Museum, Los Angeles.

FIGURE 3.8. Anonymous, "Church and Monument, Aspinwall," c. 1870. Getty Research Institute, Los Angeles.

transformation under the aegis of Protestant religion and American capital investment.[27] In other images, local people are positioned marginally to accentuate the isthmus's commercial thrust. In the opening view, "Main Street, Aspinwall" (fig. 3.9), four sets of railroad tracks slice across the frame's lower right-hand side, occupying the foreground and dividing the visual field from the Main Street buildings. The tracks' foreground position suggests their centrality as the force that has reshaped the region into a global transportation hub. The two groups of men in the photograph stand off to the far side, visually minimized by the photograph's composition. By contrast, a surviving Muybridge glass lantern slide of the same scene tells a more complex human story by focusing on local Panamanians and their interface with the railroad (fig. 3.10). His image places them in the center foreground and by means of contrasting machines—wheelbarrow and railway car—suggests the technological changes that were sweeping the region.[28]

Muybridge's Panama stereographs begin on a note of imperial decline, with depictions of Panama's historic battlements and sea walls, remnants

FIGURE 3.9. Anonymous, "Main Street, Aspinwall," c. 1870. Getty Research Institute, Los
Angeles.

of the once-proud Spanish city that by 1875 had fallen on hard times. These
images of the *Casco viejo* (Panama's Old Town) seem hardly designed to foster
increased commerce. There are no pictures of Pacific Mail steamships moored
in the harbor or taking on passengers and cargo, and little sign of other economic activity. One would be hard pressed to identify this Panama as the
gateway to the Pacific, an important hub in a global transportation network
connecting Europe to Asia and North America. In place of the fast-paced
modernity Muybridge everywhere else celebrated, there are desolate beaches,
battered skiffs, crumbling sea walls, and general poverty and disrepair. The
landscapes are eerily depopulated, as if a tsunami had swept the townspeople
away. The ones that remain occupy subjective positions of deep solitude and
alienation. In one image, "From the Water Gate," a lone figure stares abstractedly out to sea (fig. 3.11; #1851); in another, a man holds a basket near a small
boat, his expression similarly detached (fig. 3.12; #1852).[29] The nature of their
employment remains opaque and hardly seems urgent. These images of industrial dereliction form a striking contrast to Muybridge's depictions of Western
railway development, which vividly evoke a world of dynamic energy.

FIGURE 3.10. Eadweard Muybridge, "Aspinwall." Lantern slide. Kingston Museum. Courtesy Royal Borough of Kingston Upon Thames.

Capitalizing on the conceit of the photographer's initial survey—"a walk around the walls"—Muybridge presents his urban subject from several, competing standpoints. In one image, a lone turret facing the sea suggests a battlement, but the larger building to which it belongs appears only as a fragment. The camera lingers on other buildings that have been reduced to mere shells, their purpose as opaque as the labor of the men standing on the beach. Some images are given in tight focus and others from a great distance. We see the fruits of what Muybridge learned at Yosemite about scrambling for just the right vantage point and perhaps as well a glimpse of his interest in panoramic photography, at which he became an acknowledged master. The panoramic carries implications of epistemological mastery, which derive from the subjective consequences of occupying the visual high ground, a privileged standpoint that imposes conceptual order on the world's jumbled forms. Muybridge's multiplicity of views, by contrast, refuses the stabilizing comforts of unitary vision in favor of partial knowledge and fragments.[30]

FIGURE 3.11. Eadweard Muybridge, "From the Water Gate" (half stereo). Lone
Mountain College Collection of Stereographs. Courtesy of the Bancroft Library,
University of California, Berkeley.

Muybridge's sixteen photographs of ruined colonial-era churches, the broken architectural fragments to which he turns next, thematically intensify his
fractured visual portrait. These haunting photographs—of Santo Domingo,
San Miguel, San Juan de Dios, and several others—belong in a visual tradition
of representing Latin American ruins going back to John Lloyd Stephens's
and Frederick Catherwood's best-selling volumes, discussed in chapter 1. The
New York Muybridge emigrated to in 1850 was abuzz with their work, and
Muybridge reported that his bookshop in San Francisco had a "larger assort-
ment of handsomely gotten up Illustrated Works than any other house in
California," a description that would aptly characterize Catherwood's lavishly

FIGURE 3.12. Eadweard Muybridge, "A Walk around the Walls" (half stereo). Lone
Mountain College Collection of Stereographs. Courtesy of the Bancroft Library,
University of California, Berkeley.

illustrated volume, *Views of Ancient Monuments* (1844), which Muybridge
may well have stocked.[31] Muybridge was likely familiar with Claude Désiré
Charnay, the pioneer photographer who followed Stephens and Catherwood
to produce some of the earliest and most powerful photographic images of
pre-Hispanic sites such as Chichén-Itzá, Uxmal, Mitla, and Palenque. Appearing in two lavishly illustrated volumes, *Album fotográfico Mexicano* (Mexico,
1860) and *Cités et ruines Américaines* (Paris, 1862), Charnay's large-format photographs refer explicitly to Catherwood's *Views of Ancient Monuments,* depicting many of the same monuments from the same angles.[32] Like Catherwood
and Charnay, and indeed Piranesi before them, Muybridge perceived ruined
architecture through the lens of a culture obsessed with picturesque rot and
crumbling grandeur. For example, the British architect Sir John Soane, who
was among Catherwood's teachers at the Royal Academy, instructed the painter
Joseph Gandy to illustrate his recently completed Bank of England as if in ruins,
and filled his house at No. 12–14 Lincoln's Inn Fields with antiquities and representations of antiquities, even building within it a simulated "Monk's Yard"
whose "gloomy scenery" was designed to "produce the most powerful sensa-
tions in the minds of the admirers."[33]

In Muybridge's work, pictured ruins serve as crucial temporal markers
of modernity itself. For if they point backward by evoking "past genius, the
ravages of time, and the frailty of man,"[34] they also stand in uneasy tension
with the forward-moving, seemingly progressive forces of the age. It is no
accident that the same cultures that venerated them also sung the gospel of
rising economic development, and that representations of pre-Hispanic ruins
were featured at several international exhibitions and world's fairs, notably
Paris (1889), Chicago (1893), and San Francisco (1915), where they were con-
trastively displayed alongside the latest mechanical inventions and scientific
breakthroughs.[35] We may recall that in the same 1841 volume that features
Catherwood's moody drawings of jungle-encrusted Mayan remains, Stephens
set forth a detailed proposal for a massive engineering project, a ship canal
across Lake Nicaragua that would connect underdeveloped Central America
to the world's industrialized economies through a vast transportation network. Charnay, whose trip to Mexico was sponsored by the French Ministry
of Public Instruction, employed the most sophisticated photographic technology of his time to represent Mexico's antiquities. And Muybridge, enam-
ored equally of steamship and railway locomotive, spent the years before his
Central American journey perfecting the camera's uncanny ability to capture
motions invisible to the human eye. Antiquity's haunted traces were not in
opposition to modernity, but constitutive of it. As the examples of the world's
fairs suggest, the desire to embrace a future defined ever more exclusively by
speed and technology lay side by side with the retrospective work of finding,

FIGURE 3.13. Eadweard Muybridge, "Ruins of the Church of San Miguel" (half stereo). Lone Mountain College Collection of Stereographs. Courtesy of the Bancroft Library, University of California, Berkeley.

unearthing, and displaying the ruined past. At times romanticized, at others maligned for barbarity and otherness, the material remains of past epochs were as crucial to the project of modernity as any newfangled machine or invention. It is hard to imagine one without the other.

Soane's fabricated "Monk's Yard" as well as the installation of ruins at world's fairs reminds us that artists used cunning production techniques to tune the affective experience of perceiving ruins. This is no less true in Muybridge's photographic documentation of Panama's ruined churches, which are similarly staged to heighten certain desired effects. This accords with his well-known deliberation in constructing images—positioning his subjects just so, searching for the perfect camera placement, cleverly making combination

prints by overlaying clouds and other choice details on his photographic landscapes, and later altering the sequences of photographs in *Animal Locomotion*
for particular aesthetic ends.[36] His views of "old Panama," as the *Panama Star*
revealed on November 1, 1875, "were obtained at the expense of cleaning away
the trees and brushwood that concealed ruins of the highest interest to the
Colombian as well as to the antiquarian." He followed the example of Charnay, who employed large numbers of Indian laborers to clear overgrown brush
from temple façades prior to photographing. Like these images, Muybridge's
"The Ruins of the Church of San Miguel" (fig. 3.13; #1863) features an overgrown ruin, its roof caved in, which has been carefully presented to stimulate
feelings of absence and melancholia. At once monumental and fragile, enduring yet subject to decay, a work of religious culture reclaimed by nature, then
reclaimed again for different cultural uses and pressed into circulation as an
image, this colonial sanctuary invites the viewer to ponder the themes of tran-
sience and loss that have traditionally been associated with ruined structures
at least since Piranesi. Its faded grandeur speaks of a glorious past reduced
to rubble, and of the fragility of monuments themselves. Yet the image also
warns against an overweening confidence in the works of the present and
future, which might similarly crumble or succumb to nature. Indeed, Muybridge's photograph memorializes a structure that is no more. Having once
stood just outside the *Casco viejo*, now a popular tourist site for appreciating
the restored structures of Panama's colonial past, the church was eventually
torn down. The new San Miguel in Panama's Caledonia district, which looks
nothing like the original, was erected in the 1940s.

TIME AND THE OTHER: MUYBRIDGE'S WASHERWOMEN

Muybridge came to Panama fresh from experiments in stopping time. By capturing motions too rapid for the eye to see, he probed the millisecond, slicing time into ever-smaller increments of perception. His advanced cameras
and novel ways of sequencing them revealed a vast new world, as invisible to
the eye as swarms in a water drop before the invention of microscopes. He
unlocked what Walter Benjamin, writing in 1936, would describe as the hidden universe of "unconscious optics":

> The act of reaching for a lighter or a spoon is a familiar routine, yet we
> hardly know what really goes on between hand and metal, not to mention
> how this fluctuates with our moods. Here the camera intervenes with the
> resources of its lowerings and liftings, its interruptions and isolations, its

extensions and accelerations, its enlargements and reductions. The camera introduces us to unconscious optics as does psychoanalysis to unconscious impulses.[37]

He combined this interest in Benjamin's "fractional second" with a passion for imaging long durations, the rise and fall of epochs, and history's grand sweep. By 1875, Panama had become defined as a site of transport modernization, rising to prominence as a geographical shortcut that reduced the New York–San Francisco journey from several months to a few weeks. Yet as the ruined churches and other monuments suggest, it was also a site of deep antiquity. A modernity defined by speed lay side by side with visible signs of centuries-old structures and ways of life.

The camera's gaze on the anachronistic site of colonial ruins parallels the anthropological conceit that locates colonial peoples in a time anterior to the modern time of the Western subject. Indeed, U.S. and British travelers to Latin America had long engaged in a culturally inflected version of the Black Legend, blaming Spanish culture for what they perceived as the local populace's gross ignorance and superstition, while also using the traveler's empirical authority to uphold theories of European racial superiority. Charles Merewether points out that Charnay believed "Mexicans to be an inferior indigenous race and a people of the past," a view Charnay reinscribed by comparing ethnological drawings of various contemporary "types" such as Maya and Lacandon to profiles of ancient Maya found on the façades of ruined temples.[38] As Charnay wrote, the native encountered in modern Mexico was "pretty much what he was three or four hundred years ago."[39] This attitude of cultural chauvinism also extended to colonial-era architecture. Anne Cary Maudslay, a late nineteenth-century U.S. traveler to Guatemala, argued that Spain had not enjoyed an authentic Renaissance, and that the aesthetic and intellectual culture it imposed on its New World colonies was debased. "Such art as the Spaniards brought with them," she wrote, "was a degraded form of the renaissance, and the innumerable churches which they built are without any architectural merit but mass."[40] In this light, Muybridge's stereographs of Spanish colonial ruins carry an additional charge. Whereas Latin America's pre-Hispanic ruins, as relics of a bygone civilization, were centuries distant from the modern observer, Spanish colonial culture lived on in the present. To associate it with ruination reinforces the anthropological point that although it is *historically* contemporaneous with the present, forward-moving modernity of photographer and viewer, it occupies a different time and an inferior stage in civilization.

FIGURE 3.14. Eadweard Muybridge, "Suburbs of Panama" (half stereo). Lone
Mountain College Collection of Stereographs. Courtesy of the Bancroft Library,
University of California, Berkeley.

The "Suburbs of Panama" (fig. 3.14) illustrates the ideological differentials
of temporality particularly well. On the surface, this is a relatively straightforward image, capturing a stretch of railroad track curving into the distance.
Especially when seen through a stereoscopic viewer, with its illusion of three-
dimensional space, the swooping line of track emerges from the picture's far
depths, suggesting the inexorable, progressive forces of technology, as well as
the latent narrative logic of the entire Panama sequence, which unfolds as a
segmented visual journey across the isthmian landscape, from Panama City
on the Pacific to Chagres on the Atlantic. Given Muybridge's enthusiasm for
Western railway development, as well as his Pacific Mail Steamship Company
commission to promote industry and trade, we might expect him to valorize

FIGURE 3.15. Eadweard Muybridge, "The Principal Street, Chagres" (half stereo).
Lone Mountain College Collection of Stereographs. Courtesy of the Bancroft
Library, University of California, Berkeley.

the railroad as a symbol of technology's ameliorative power. Yet like several
other images in the stereograph sequence, such as "The Principal Street, Chagres," the title is ironic. Just as the "principal street" depicts a squalid, muddy
lane (fig. 3.15), the "suburbs" turn out to be a few grass-roofed huts standing
alongside the tracks. There is no locomotive, which might signify the railroad's
link to a larger system of transport and trade, and therefore to his sponsor,
the Pacific Mail Steamship Company. There is only the track and a lone figure
staring abstractedly across it at the aforementioned huts, the entire picture an
assemblage of parts rather than a unified whole. Compositionally, the slicing
track divides the lone figure from the suburbs on the other side, a spatial division that implies a temporal one. Although railway and lone figure occupy

FIGURE 3.16. Eadweard Muybridge, "Modoc Brave on the War Path" (half stereo). Lone Mountain College Collection of Stereographs. Courtesy of the Bancroft Library, University of California, Berkeley.

the same moment in history, they symbolize radically different conceptions of time. The grass huts of traditional Panamanian life represent both what the railway has come to abolish, and modernization's slender hold on postrailway Panama.[41]

The clash between temporal orders takes on greater urgency as the series moves from a preoccupation with infrastructure—sea walls, ruined churches, and official buildings—to a focus on stark, frequently disturbing images of Panama's poor, whom Muybridge encounters farther along the railway journey. Muybridge, it is said, was uninterested in the genre of the portrait.[42] Certainly his most celebrated photographic work, which breaks down motion into com-

FIGURE 3.17. Eadweard Muybridge, "Making Bread in the Yosemite" (half stereo). Lone Mountain College Collection of Stereographs. Courtesy of the Bancroft Library, University of California, Berkeley.

ponent parts and employs mammoth-plate techniques to capture monumental geology, points to a craftsman's concern with technique, not personality. Yet if studies of faces left him cold, he demonstrated a strong interest in the racialized body and photographed indigenous people throughout the West: the Tlinglit of Alaska, Modoc warriors fighting their last stand in California (fig. 3.16), and the tribes of Yosemite Valley (fig. 3.17).[43] Despite their status as representatives of conquered or subdued populations, these figures remind us of that which cannot easily be assimilated into dominant narratives of smooth, progressive development. Their ways of life implicitly challenge a modernity defined by rapid technological change, their racial differences the universality

FIGURE 3.18. Eadweard Muybridge, "Ruins of the Church of San Miguel." Courtesy of the California History Room, California State Library, Sacramento, California.

of the Anglo-Saxon ideal. Panama's dark-skinned inhabitants, who labor as if the industrial revolution never occurred, belie the official image of the isthmus as a bustling, forward-looking center of hemispheric trade and commerce. Like the colonial ruins in Old Panama, they seem to inhabit a time anterior to the photographer and the image-making mechanisms he carries with him.

Once beyond the ruins of Old Panama, Muybridge turns his lens directly toward the figure of the dark-skinned and sexualized woman, imaged both as an instance of premodern Panama, a temporal and cultural marker, and an object of visual desire. Presenting eight consecutive images of what he calls "native women," Muybridge detours from the themes explored in his opening images, offering little guidance for what comes next. A comparison of the stereographic and the large-plate print of "Ruins of the Church of San Miguel" reveals that in the latter Muybridge replaced the lone male figure of the stereo with a black woman (clothed) and her child, who sit enigmatically on the steps (fig. 3.18), but the expense of the large-plate photographs meant only a select few could make this connection. The stereographs, by contrast, were affordable, and a sequential viewing of them suggests a pattern whereby civilization and economic development recede the farther one travels into Panama's interior. Indeed, in the images titled "Native Hut," "Laundry," and "Native Women" all signs of religiosity and industrialized economic activity disappear, leaving the pictorial canvas bare for the display of female sexuality itself, which comes as a shocking visual break after photographs of portside infrastructure and ruined churches. These images put on view a specific colonial and anthropological context of the male desiring gaze, even as they foreshadow preoccupations about female labor and sexuality Muybridge would explore at greater length in his work on human and animal locomotion.

"Native Hut" (1885; fig. 3.19), which opens the series, is an apparently direct image of a Panamanian family: husband, wife, and infant, standing before their humble dwelling, which is given the all-purpose descriptor, "native," even though the term does not accurately describe its inhabitants.[44] This conflation into "native" of nonwhite peoples, whether black, indigenous, or mixed, is one sign of these photographs' anthropological dimension. Another is the genre of the group shot itself, in which individuals are subsumed into types and portrayed as representatives of a larger phenomenon—here, "the native."[45] These particular residents have been summoned for what appears to be a family portrait, but their rigid stance indicates staged artificiality, the only blur caused by the infant who cannot remain still for the long exposure. The father, shirtless, cradles the infant in his arm, a reassuring sign of strong family bonds. Yet economic discord disturbs the comforting image of familial accord. The hut is a ramshackle affair with a thatched roof. Dilapidated

FIGURE 3.19. Eadweard Muybridge, "Native Hut" (half stereo). Lone Mountain
College Collection of Stereographs. Courtesy of the Bancroft Library, University of
California, Berkeley.

furniture and crude household wares are strewn about the yard. The woman
stands barefoot on the dirt, a bowl balanced on her head (woman and bowl
will reappear later in image #1888). Their poverty is writ large in the few,
small possessions gathered around them. More troubling than the privation
is what emerges from the margin, a leering male figure standing to the left of
the hut itself, dressed like the stranger he most certainly is. In, but not of, the
scene, he complicates the picture's relationship of gazes. Although the grainy
production values prevent a clear identification, the figure may be Muybridge
himself, who appears slyly in several photographs throughout his career and
became the overt subject in many sequences from *Animal Locomotion*. In any

case, this troubling and indeterminate male figure stands as a proxy for the image's North American or European consumer, a sign of how the image itself would be transformed into a commodity for sale elsewhere.

That putative consumer is crucial to understanding the move from scenes of ruined churches to depictions of partially dressed native women that highlight labor, race, and sexuality. Europeans and North Americans had an insatiable appetite for sexualized images of dark-skinned, colonial women, and the advent of cheap and readily available photographic forms such as stereographs, and later postcards, meant it could be endlessly stimulated. Muybridge's photographs of the Modoc war, the indigenous of Alaska and Yosemite, and San Francisco's Chinese immigrants show his willingness to capitalize on the demand for exotic subjects. Yet although these images traffic in familiar stereotypes (the dignified "Indian," the stoic Chinese), they are not overtly prurient or exploitative. Muybridge's stereographs of semi-clothed Central American women, by contrast, play on disturbing fantasies of male desire, which are hinted at in the leering figure emerging from the margins of the "Native Hut" but made manifest in the stereographs that follow. As opposed to his images of ruined architecture, or for that matter his large-plate photographs of partially clothed Guatemalan women, there is little that is especially artful or appealing in these images. Several have a rough, unfinished, almost cheap pornographic quality, as if what mattered were only bare, anatomical facts. Whether clothed or partially dressed, the women in these pictures gaze directly at the camera. That they stand for the camera's consuming eye and the male photographer who wields it may suggest consent, but we cannot know whether Muybridge's photographic subjects were paid or compelled to pose. Both "Native Hut" and "Laundry" (fig. 3.20; #1887) show white males in the background who may have been overseers with the authority to command photographic cooperation. Moreover, it is also quite unlikely that these women would have understood how their performances might enter the global circulation of images via the market in inexpensive stereographs and postcards. Whatever consent they have given must be understood within colonial and economic conditions that render their agency suspect, if not curtailed altogether. These stereographs also involve highly specific photographic conventions that emerged from within the discipline's entanglement with colonial anthropology, which give them an additional racial and temporal charge.

In "Native Women" (fig. 3.21; #1890), a dark-skinned Panamanian woman poses for the camera with a young boy, perhaps her son. She stands bare breasted, holding a bowl on her head with one hand, while he sits, unclothed except for the broad-brimmed hat resting on his head, a visual parallel to her bowl. In this makeshift outdoor studio, Muybridge has suspended a large

FIGURE 3.20. Eadweard Muybridge, "Laundry" (half stereo). Lone Mountain College Collection of Stereographs. Courtesy of the Bancroft Library, University of California, Berkeley.

FIGURE 3.21. Eadweard Muybridge, "Native Women" (half stereo). Lone Mountain College Collection of Stereographs. Courtesy of the Bancroft Library, University of California, Berkeley.

white cloth between two trees, forming a crude backdrop for the display of his subject's blackness and nudity.[46] He stages the scene so that the sun's rays, projected from over his right shoulder, cast her shadow against the screen, like light against a piece of chemically treated paper to make a photographic image. This deft, nearly textbook composition illustrates Nancy Stepan's claim that nineteenth-century racial discriminations were a "contrastive concept," in which "any representation of one race could only be understood in explicit or implicit relation to the representation of another, through a process that highlighted the signs of difference."[47] Like a negative to a positive, or a light switching on and off, the binaries implicate each other, accentuating the subject's blackness even as they gesture toward the origins of the photographic process in light and paper.

The suspended sheet, however, also alludes more disturbingly to photography's role in anthropological measurement and the project to collect data of "vanishing races" presumed to be imperiled by the onslaught of industrialism and modernity. As early as 1854, leading institutions in the nascent science of anthropology called for obtaining "individual likenesses [of colonial subjects] by means of some photographic process."[48] By 1869, J. H. Lamprey, assistant secretary of the Ethnological Society of London, was proposing specific refinements to photographic technique in order to assemble a *standardized* photographic archive of colonial peoples. As opposed to the variable records then extant, which conformed to no compositional norms and thus were of limited utility to the anthropologist, Lamprey advocated that travelers and colonial officials photograph their subjects against a grid comprised of uniform, white twine squares, which was to be carried into the field along with the other necessaries of outdoor photography (fig. 3.22). The neatly regular grid, which resembles our modern graph paper, was imagined to facilitate precise anthropometric measurement of such features as height, facial angle, and skull contour.[49] Its compact size was crucial to the creation of a mobile clinical space, able to generate raw ethnological data from anywhere in the world for analysis in metropolitan centers of calculation such as London, Paris, New York, and Philadelphia. In the same year, Thomas Henry Huxley, then president of the Ethnological Society, advocated a similar project, urging that native subjects be posed nude with measuring sticks; the belief at the time was that "women's breasts not be concealed," since "they had characteristic sizes and shapes in different races."[50] Neither project resulted in the authoritative data sought by anthropologists, as there was no system or database to catalogue the images. However, the work established a strong disciplinary interdependence between the fields, leaving the traces of anthropological thinking in photographers such as Muybridge, who improvises here with a white sheet but would later

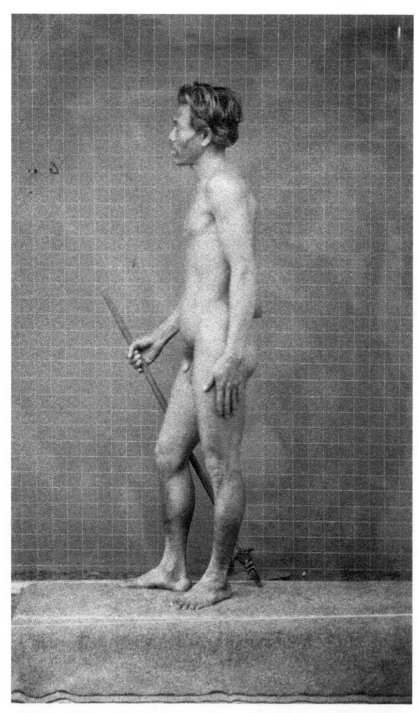

FIGURE 3.22. Anthropometric Grid. RAI 2117 Ternate, Malagasy man; full length; profile illustrating method of anthropometric photography devised by John Lamprey. Photographed Adamo Pedroletti or Henry Evans, c. 1868–69. © RAI.

execute thousands of images in his Philadelphia studio, some of them racial, against just such a grid.[51]

These images from Panama's interior also represent the earliest examples of Muybridge's overt interest in representing the female nude, a concern that would become central in the next decade with *Animal Locomotion*. Scholars examining the locomotion studies have shown how a set of voyeuristic fantasies and quasi-pornographic concerns interrupts the project's ostensibly scientific aims, with important consequences for gender and visual representation in the period. This scholarship is extensive and deep, and I will not retrace it here.[52] Instead, I want to focus on what has thus far escaped notice—areas of anticipation between the Panama work and the later motion studies, especially as pertains to overlapping domains of race, gender, and work.

Muybridge thematized the entwinement of labor and gender throughout his oeuvre. In one sequence from *Attitudes of Animals in Motion* (1881), he poses himself nude and muscular, swinging a pickaxe, his toil a self-reflexive comment connecting the labor of photography with the masculine work of settling the West, building its railroads, and mining its ore (fig. 3.23). Here, manliness is embodied both in the subject and object of the gaze, with photography coded as a masculine enterprise. The pages of *Animal Locomotion*, similarly, are filled with virile men in action. Muscles rippling and tendons taut, they leap, sprint, lift, and tumble across the photographic page, their athleticism demonstrating ideals of Anglo-Saxon vigor and masculinity. Muybridge's female sequences, by contrast, present highly idealized, frequently classical or pastoral images of labor, invariably featuring alabaster-skinned models, some nude and others in white, flowing drapery. Urns, goblets, and other anachronistic objects, along with the minute rituals of bathing and the toilette, receive extensive attention, mirroring well-established traditions of visual erotica. In July 1885, Muybridge employed one of his female models, Catherine Aimer, to perform a sequence of behaviors for the camera. Working over the space of two days, she received five hours' worth of wages. The extant photographs show her undressing, pouring water over herself from a basin, bathing, drying, turning, covering her face with her hand, and running away.[53] Muybridge went to great lengths to aestheticize these actions, for instance habitually referring to undressing with the oddly stylized phrase, "Relinquishing drapery for Nature's garb."[54] He also framed his photographic sequences with elaborate, narrative scenarios: "Crossing Brook on Step-Stones with fishing-pole and basket" (pl. 176); "Getting out of bed and preparing to kneel" (pl. 264). No amount of mystification, however, can conceal the images' prurient viewpoint, which both infantilizes and eroticizes Muybridge's female models.

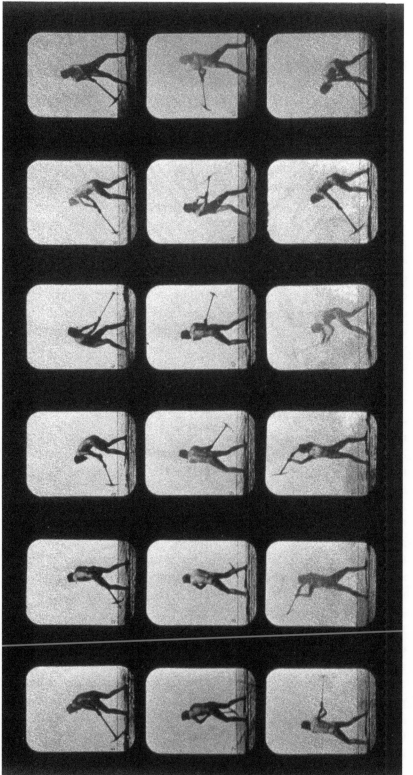

FIGURE 3.23. Eadweard Muybridge, "Athletes. Swinging Pick." From *Attitudes of Animals in Motion.* Library of Congress.

Muybridge's photographs of laundering explicitly connect the Panama work with the later motion studies. Traditionally associated with domesticity and working-class women's labor, laundering is on one level so familiar it hardly seems worth the trouble to photograph. Yet Muybridge, as we have seen, specialized in representing the unseeable. Here, it is not rapidity of motion that veils the subject, but the concealing power of ordinariness itself. To trouble this familiarity, Muybridge creates deeply aestheticized and erotic routines in *Animal Locomotion* that break the humble act of laundering down into ever-smaller increments. The fractured views heighten our visual attention to commonplace but also luminescent moments such as the pleasing splash of water falling on a floor or the curve of a billowing sheet suspended above a bed. Set against the ever-present grid lines, these sequences are enlisted in the service of narrative, unfolding both in space and time (fig. 3.24). The captions, always written in gerund form, signal movement elongated into an open future: "Emptying Bucket of Water"; "Emptying Basin of Water"; "Wringing Clothes"; "Hanging Clothes on Line"; "Ironing Clothes"; and "Making up Bed." We might also add, from a different section of the work, "Carrying a Bucket of Water in Each Hand" and "Walking, Carrying a 15-lb. Basket on Head, hands raised."[55] Laundering exists here as a trace, an activity quite distant from work itself and closer in fact to dance.[56]

These images of balletic movement, fascinating in themselves, take on additional significance when viewed from the perspective of the Panama stereographs, where laundering first appears as a thematic focus in Muybridge's oeuvre. From this vantage point, we can see the Philadelphia pictures as realized examples of poses and situations Muybridge conceived much earlier, and in quite a different cultural and racial surround. Recall that in one of the Panama stereographs a semi-nude woman delicately balances a bowl on her head. In another, a woman holds the upper half of her garment in her hand, apparently having complied with the photographer's request to relinquish it for "nature's garb" (fig. 3.25; #1891); several are titled, simply, "Laundry," a word notably absent from the choreographed sequences executed in *Animal Locomotion*. The Panama stereographs, more clinical and anthropological than erotic, reveal no attempt to situate laundering in a larger narrative, or to call forth its inner visual poetry through photographic serialization. As opposed to painstaking studies of elegant individuals in motion, the Panama stereographs focus on still groups of women, a compositional choice that marks them out as representatives of a category. Stark and austere, they represent not so much laundering—a choreographed movement of limbs unfolding in space and time—but *the* laundry, a worksite, a squalid outdoor place for toiling in oppressive heat, where individuality succumbs to one's occupation as washerwoman, or *lavandera* in Spanish.[57] Muybridge's Philadelphia sequences

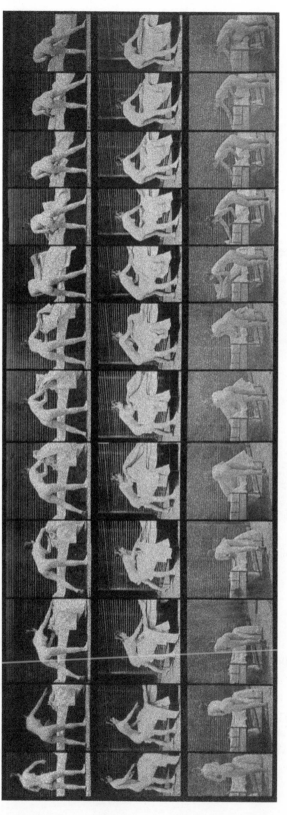

FIGURE 3.24. Eadweard Muybridge, "Making up Bed." From *Animal Locomotion: An Electro-photographic Investigation of Consecutive Phases of Animal Movements* (1872–74). USC Digital Library.

FIGURE 3.25. Eadweard Muybridge, "Native Women" (half stereo). Lone Mountain College Collection of Stereographs. Courtesy of the Bancroft Library, University of California, Berkeley.

suggest that white women enjoy the privilege of participation in visual narrative, signaled by the gerund always applied to their actions. Captured in a studio and photographed under the auspices of a great university, these graceful and balletic figures transform mere mobility—Muybridge's term is "locomotion"—into art itself. The subaltern black woman, by contrast, is represented as a static type, a figure of profound immobility trapped in an anthropological time anterior to the present and denied a larger story to make sense of her existence. Without a narrative, she cannot participate in the onrushing, speed-

FIGURE 3.26. Eadweard Muybridge, untitled. Lantern slide. Kingston Museum. Courtesy Royal Borough of Kingston Upon Thames.

driven new age that was the dream of the isthmian crossing from its earliest inception. Time here is political.

A final image from the Panama work serves to sum up the argument I have been making (fig. 3.26). The image is a glass lantern slide in stereographic form, which Muybridge may have projected at one of his lectures on Central America. To my knowledge, a print of the image has never been published. It does not appear in any of the lists Muybridge issued with his stereographs, and was discovered by the author among over two thousand well-documented lantern slides at the Kingston Museum. Muybridge took care to preserve it, carting it along with all the others back from the United States at the end of his career. The composition, taken in Aspinwall at the Pacific Mail Steamship Wharf, shares many classic elements with his Central American oeuvre: the swaying tropical palms; the derelict buildings in the background; the smooth, highly reflective water, a figurative mirror for the photographic process itself; figures standing in it, familiar from the Guatemala photographs, where *lavanderas* do their work half immersed in streams. The photographer, aloof from his subjects, here positioned on the raised ground of the railroad tracks, is invisible in the image, signifying the ever-present disjunction between the mobility of the photographer and the frozen immobility of his subjects. What is different, of course, is the visual spectacle of the unclothed black male body, wearing only the most meager of loincloths, penises exposed and caught in profile. The five young men in the foreground occupy the photographer's attention, not the anonymous buildings or generic scenery. Their pose is defiant, hands on hips and, in one case, on genitals. They gaze directly at the camera, their watery immersion a sign of their stubborn difference, their nakedness a sign of their location outside the forward-moving, mobility-driven logic of Panama's modernity, their detachment from the ideal of the heterosexual family group a visual comment on the problem of unchanneled, and perhaps ungovernable, subaltern identities. The photographer, too, stands apart and at a distance, creating an image at once revealing and aloof, intimate and distant, homoerotic yet clinical. As in all the Panama photographs, time looms.

Muybridge's Panama photographs belong in a nineteenth-century tradition of visual representation that juxtaposes black and native people with the machines that were changing their way of life. Frequently, as in his series, "Native Women," the images represent local Panamanians as standing apart from the technological revolution sweeping the isthmus, as if their lives were utterly incompatible with mechanized modernity. This was, of course, an illusion, as other photographs such as "Suburbs of Panama" reveal, with its railroad track slicing through the center of a village. After the railroad, and continuing apace through the construction of the canal, there was no place apart. The railroad was built by and shared the land with the very people the images represent as inimical to its status as a sign of a progressively defined modernity. In a subsequent period, the same would be true of the canal. Yet in other ways, as I have tried to the show, the Panama imaged in these pictures indicts rather than supports an ameliorative view of U.S. capital investment, unsettling the commercial narrative that would present the isthmus as ripe for economic development and increased tourism. From its battered seawalls and ruined churches on the Pacific, to the squalid "principal streets" of Chagres on the Atlantic, the isthmus appears in these images as stubbornly out of joint, unevenly developed by a capitalist modernity that was supposed to sweep it forward into a brighter economic future. The railroad, celebrated just two decades before as the transforming agent of modernization, occupies an ambivalent position, its economic benefit to the region negligible at best, perhaps already marked as a remnant of an earlier technology doomed to be replaced by a more efficient and technologically sophisticated one, the canal. Offering a deeply troubling visual commentary, Muybridge's images suggest not only that the railroad's potential for modernizing Panama was vastly oversold but also that attempts to represent this jagged edge of tropical modernity were far more difficult than imagined.

CHAPTER 4

∾

The Dissonant Lyre

The Panama Poetry of J. S. Gilbert, "Kipling of the Isthmus"

Ten years from date he'll amputate
The Western Hemisphere,
And siamese the mighty seas
To bring the distant near!

—GILBERT, "OUR UNCLE SAM"

THE ESTABLISHMENT of the printing press in the early 1820s spurred a rich, Panamanian print culture, with literary production in many forms and genres. Essayists wrote political and ideological commentary, poets published regularly in magazines and newspapers, and writers of fictional prose brought forth stories of Panamanian and foreign life.[1] The fashioning of the Yankee Strip spurred a parallel world of English-language print. The first English newspaper, *The Panama Star*, began publishing in February 1849 and became essential reading not only for the California-bound travelers but also for policymakers in Britain and the United States, where its columns were reprinted in leading newspapers.[2] Presses in the United States and Britain issued myriad travel accounts and guides, railway and steamship schedules, and detailed maps. Anglo-American writers also produced a varied imaginative literature, mainly in the genres of lyric and historical poetry. In the period before the canal, James Stanley Gilbert (1855–1906) and Tracy Robinson (1833–1915) each published acclaimed volumes of poetry, as well as many occasional pieces for newspapers and magazines. Michael Delevante (fl. 1907) issued his work early in the next century.[3] If, during the 1880s and 1890s, as Joseph Bristow argues, "an explicitly spatial understanding of 'Victorian' would lend the term expressly global range," the same is true for these U.S. poets who wrote at a crucial juncture in U.S., Panamanian, and hemispheric history, when Manifest Destiny was reaching southward across the seas, and the long-anticipated canal was in the offing.[4]

Of these writers, Gilbert achieved the most fame—and deservedly so. Known as the "Kipling of the Isthmus," he published three collections of verse about isthmian life: *Gilbertianae* (1891), *The Fall of Panama* (1894), and his most successful work, *Panama Patchwork*, which first appeared in 1901 and was reissued many times over the next two decades.[5] Forgotten by literary history and utterly ignored by critics, his name was for many years synonymous with Panama, his verses quoted with near biblical reverence.[6] In Anglo-American literature on the isthmus, when one reads "as the poet says," or "according to the bard," this always means Gilbert. To be sure, he had enthusiastic and well-placed champions. Robinson, who made his name with *Song of the Palm* (1889), styled himself the "godfather to Mr. Gilbert's muse" and authored a glowing biographical notice praising Gilbert for his authenticity and "spontaneity of feeling."[7] Edmund Clarence Steadman, the noted poet, critic, and anthologist, urged the *New York Times Saturday Review of Books* to review Gilbert's work, which lauded him for providing a true "document" of isthmian life.[8]

The biographical Gilbert remains obscure. He was born July 20, 1855, at Middletown, Connecticut, and educated at Skinner School, Chicago. He went to Panama in 1886 to work for the Panama Railroad Company and was later employed by one of the many steamship companies. He died August 15, 1906, from complications related to malaria and was buried at Mt. Hope cemetery in Colón. A surviving photographic portrait (fig. 4.1) shows him reclining in a chair dressed in tropical whites, a figure of evident prosperity and comfort. The portrait, however, reveals little of the carefully imaged worlds found in the poems. Although the poems reveal few autobiographical details—no love interest, no professional success or disappointment—they communicate a sensibility and way of looking that resonated with readers near and far. They speak as well to key themes in the Anglo-American discourse of Panama in the run up to the canal. First, like his mentor Robinson, who enjoyed a diplomatic post in Panama, Gilbert wrote several enthusiastically patriotic poems that convey great pride in the transformation of the isthmus, which Gilbert viewed as proof of the United States' growing hemispheric sway. These poems, while reinforcing collective bonds among the isthmian expatriate community, define Panama as a crucial component of the U.S. trans-hemispheric empire. Second, Gilbert captured the world-weariness and philosophical detachment of an American expatriate community blessed, but also confined, by a life of tropical ease. This strain, with its morose meditations on colonial disease,

(DIED AUGUST, 1906)

FIGURE 4.1. Portrait of James Stanley Gilbert, from J. S. Gilbert, *Panama Patchwork*.

death, and immorality, questions the idea of Panama as a carefree tropical paradise by revealing the high human cost of its transformation. Finally, Gilbert displayed a powerful understanding of the unequal quality of social life at this global crossroads. His poetic portraits combine the skilled observer's command of telling details with attention to the larger social questions about rank, class, and race that, as we have seen, structured the Anglo-American experience of the isthmus from the 1840s onward. These three strains—the patriotic, the melancholic, and the ethnographic—combine to produce a lyrical portrait of isthmian life in the crucial years after the railroad but before the canal, which began in 1907 with the construction of the Gatun Dam.

OUR UNCLE SAM

Like many expatriate writers, Gilbert viewed the canal as both a project of U.S. nation building and a world-historical event that would knit the family of nations together. Shaped by the work of the ultra-patriotic Robinson, Gilbert's poems parallel the arc of his own historical experience in the region, which coincided with a period of growing U.S. power. He witnessed the disastrous French attempt at opening an interoceanic passage,[9] the celebrations marking the four hundredth anniversary of Columbus's landfall, the advent of muscular U.S. expansionism in the Spanish-American War, the secession of Panama from Colombia (achieved with U.S. support), and the signing of the 1903 Hay-Bunau-Varilla Treaty, which granted the United States exclusive rights to the canal and formalized a hegemony that had begun with the creation of the Yankee Strip in the 1850s. His verses reflect this broad sweep of geopolitical history, at once Atlantic (Colón as gateway to European shipping), and hemispheric (the isthmus as prosthetic extension of U.S. power and policy in the Americas). The poems extend an ideological narrative that minimizes Panamanian history to accentuate instead a long process of foreign domination that began with the Spanish conquest and would be completed by a new empire, the United States.

"Hail Panama" exemplifies this patriotic theme by characterizing Panama in the familiar language of U.S. exceptionalism:

> Freedom is thine by Right,
> In honor lies thy Might,
> Hail, Panama!
> Justice and Verity,
> Wisdom, Sincerity,
> Bring thee prosperity,

Hail, Panama!
(15–21)

These lines collapse the distinction between the United States and Panama, erasing Panamanian history and putting forth ideals from the North as if they were universal. In hailing Panama as the site of justice, freedom, and truth, Gilbert also defines it in stark economic terms as a crucial locus for the production of wealth. Like the early champions of railway and canal schemes, he proclaims these values as harmonious and unconflicted; verity and sincerity chime with prosperity. For him, the impending canal belongs in a sweeping narrative of economic development in which rising wealth, patriotic ideals, and the southward extension of U.S. hegemony interlock. Although in several other poems, as we shall see, Gilbert represents Panamanian poverty and economic failure, he treats these matters as singular, not structural, phenomena, and therefore as outside the buoyant narratives of the technologically driven modernity he praises.

"Our Uncle Sam," a celebratory lyric of eleven quatrains written on July 4, 1905, places recent Panamanian events within an ameliorative narrative of gradual U.S. hemispheric dominance. This neocolonial narrative casts the U.S. as the hemisphere's civilizing and modernizing power, bringing economic development, social order, and above all technological sophistication to the region's backward zones.[10] This discursive frame reduces local history to a mere foil for U.S. power. Gilbert's mentor Tracy Robinson, in an "oration" delivered at the U.S. Consulate in Colón on July 4, 1866, included in his *Song of the Palm*, described this progressive, U.S.-centric narrative thus: "The frowning barriers of savageism have been swept away by the resistless march of a new, and brave, and free civilization. *American civilization!* Its onward course has been like that of the sweeping, all-compelling storm-wind, save that it has scattered naught but blessings."[11] Similarly, Gilbert's poem looks back 129 years to the nation's founding, and constructs an elaborate, national *bildungsroman* in which Uncle Sam grows from a mere infant—"in the swaddling-cloth of starry flag / Our Uncle Samuel lay" (3–4)—to a terrifying power capable of the "giant's task" of constructing an interoceanic canal, a project at which the Frenchman de Lesseps, of Suez fame, had recently failed:

Ten years from date he'll amputate
The Western Hemisphere,
And siamese the mighty seas
To bring the distant near!
(25–28)

Drawing on masculine and martial metaphors, the poem describes Uncle Sam's growth through various travails, including taming the wilderness, falling into national disunion, flexing imperial muscle in the Spanish American War (figured here as a "neighbor's righteous cause"), and finally assuming his rightful place as the hemispheric colossus.

For the "Panama Poet," this narrative's crowning achievement is of course the canal, whose realization was still a decade away. Yet Gilbert's conceits memorably capture the globalizing terms in which the canal was figured from its inception, as the embodiment of an awesome and quasi-magical power that would "amputate" the hemisphere and "siamese" the ocean waters. These images translate the dull mechanics of a hydraulics project into a frightening and mythic tale of violent dismembering and the imperial reorganization of space. Local ground, the basis of sedentarist accounts of the meaning of place, is emptied of all meaning. It has become simply a stage upon which geopolitical drama is enacted. This version of globalization values abstract ideals of connectivity and speed, and the technological know-how to facilitate the rapid flow of goods, people, and information around the world. The assertion that cleaving Central America will "bring the distant near" recalls earlier claims about the railroad's ability to annihilate time by joining far-flung regions together. Panama is reduced simply to a thoroughfare in a global system of transport and trade. The poem's violent metaphors of cutting and dismembering remind us that behind even the most utopian imperial imaginings lies the ability to marshal and apply coercive force.

An abiding belief in the awesome powers of machines runs throughout the expatriate literature of the late nineteenth century. From the inception of the Panama Railroad, machines symbolized modernity and impending globalization, and were endlessly vaunted in prose and verse. Steamships, bridges, dredges, telegraph wires, and locomotives themselves all received their due in prose, poetry, and visual representation. In this regard, Robinson is again an important precursor for Gilbert. "Among the Dredges," the second poem in *Song of the Palm*, valorizes the machine that would ultimately refashion the isthmian landscape into the long-anticipated canal. "Huge engines of destiny" (8), the dredges are both inanimate tools and otherworldly creatures, swinging "at their work all day, / Like antediluvian monsters, / Devouring the earth in their way" (10–12). Despite the reference to prehistory, it is clear that for Robinson, machine and modernity are one:

> They are toiling for civilization!
> And the world will one day know
> How great is the debt it owes them,

When the tides of the oceans flow
Back and forth, from each other!
(17–21)

The "devouring" machines, however frightening as agents of the imperial power to refashion the natural world, represent civilization in their capacity to accelerate global flows. These flows are not simply intermingled tides, as the poem suggests, but the capital and goods they bear along, which are essential to Robinson's vision of modernity.[12]

Gilbert's "To the Crab," an homage to the humble switch engine, takes up similar themes, but whereas Robinson unreflectingly praises these mighty implements, Gilbert focuses on the machine as an instrument of colonial violence. Although uninspiring in itself, the crab nevertheless represents a technological advance whose result is the displacing of "horse or coach" (21). As Gilbert saw, each new generation of tools destroys its predecessor, as old ways recede before new ones in a relentless and unforgiving process of forced obsolescence. Gilbert's poem also shows the human cost of technological change. In the poem's closing lines, an onrushing train crushes a hapless pedestrian, unnamed in Gilbert's verses, but probably one of Panama's underclass, perhaps a worker:

That's it! Smash him! Grind him fine!
Spread his blood along the line!
Spread it even, spread it thick!
Sand may slip but blood will stick!
(23–26)

In thus measuring the human cost of a mechanized modernity, "To the Crab" reveals the tragedy of disposable bodies that lay just beneath the U.S. transformation of the isthmus. Able to grasp a complex reality, Gilbert shows both the benefits machines created and the violence they wreaked. This understanding of economic development's dark side is Gilbert's hallmark, a moral vision that separates him from the lesser poets with which he is frequently grouped.

TROPICAL MELANCHOLIA

Gilbert could have easily portrayed isthmian life as a long, carefree summer. By his time, the tradition of tropical idylls was already well worn, and Panama, with its natural wonders and plentiful sunshine, would have fit smoothly into it. He rejected this course, however, opting instead to explore the unresolved antinomies of isthmian life, chronicling disease, death, deceit, and myriad other ailments and debilities. Panama emerges in his verse not as a refuge from worry, but a space—at times a condition—that magnified it. Attentive to the imagination's constructive power, he saw how paradise could become a gilt prison. The isthmus was, as he wrote in "Land of the Cocoanut Tree,"

> a land that still with potent charm
> And wondrous, lasting spell
> With mighty thrall enchaineth all
> Who long within it dwell.
> (25–28)

Serving as uncrowned laureate, he captured the expatriate community's persistent melancholia, a sadness that oppressed like the tropical heat, as well as the underlying social and political conditions that created it. As he knew, the strong association between the tropics and escapism made this lingering world-weariness especially poignant.

This sharp melancholia, with its bitter skepticism toward the consoling myths of a tropical Eden, is writ large in "The Paradise of Fools." In five brief stanzas, Gilbert rejects the familiar bromides about life in a sun-drenched paradise, beginning with ease itself, for with "every blessed day the same / Change is nothing but a name" (12–13). To break the tedium, there are only the weary routines of "cards and cocktails" (19), amusements that quickly lose their gloss from dull repetition. The food and drink turn out to be equally unremarkable, nothing more than "old bull-beef" and "logwood wine" (10–11). The only respite, a bittersweet one, comes from gossip, an amusement explored in several other poems throughout the oeuvre, such as "The Busiest Man," in which many-tongued rumor is given anthropomorphic shape as a figure tattling his way around Colón and Panama. In "Paradise of Fools," the speaker defines gossip as the social glue that unites the expatriate community and makes life tolerable amid the dreary sameness of climatic perfection: "Be the subject low or high, / We must gossip—or we *die* / In the Paradise of Fools" (25–27). For despite its role in breeding suspicion and paranoia, gossip introduces a necessary friction into the unchanging routines of paradise, defined here by an aural ellipsis as a condition closer to hell: "We are all content to dwell / In this suburb of—ah, well! / In the Paradise of Fools" (33–35).

"The Land of the Cocoanut-Tree" delineates Panama as a place of contraries, where "'tis eighty-six the year around" and yet "all the insects breed / That live by bite and sting" (5, 9–10). Here, "radiant flowers and orchids thrive" and are "beauteous, yes,—but odorless!" (13, 15). If Panama is rich in gold, as the Spaniards believed, it also smelled of death, as "many a man hath lost his life / That treasure-trove to see" (21–22). For every blessing Panama provides, it compensates with some annoyance or evil. Nothing is unalloyed. In "Sunset," Gilbert builds this binary logic into the formal structure of the poem itself. Each of the six four-line stanzas begins with a two-line description of a paradisal setting *par excellence,* a postcard sunset over a shimmering ocean: "I sit on my lofty piazza, / O'erlooking the restless sea" (1–2). Each concludes with two lines in parentheses that reveal its dark, frequently grotesque opposite and challenge: "(A spider glides over my forehead, / A cockroach runs over my knee!" [3–4]). The effect, to draw a phrase from the poem itself, is to create a "dissonant lyre," a protomodernist break in the traditional association between lyricism and the agreeable. At the same moment "the god of day is preparing / his bed for another night," a "swarm of pestiferous sand-flies / Is obscuring the glorious sight!" (5–8). The insects that appear in cameo roles here receive full billing in other poems such as "The Song of the Mosquito" ("*zim!*") and "The Sand-Fly," in which the tortured speaker earnestly prays that of the "five hundred thousand" kinds of bugs thriving on the isthmus, God will

> at once destroy, annihilate,
> Permit no longer to exist—
> Efface, cut off, rub out, obliterate
> The pesky sand-fly from the list!
> (13–16)

In "Song of the Prickly Heat," Gilbert casts his jaundiced eye on Panama's unrelenting heat, which caused North Americans to perspire "like any old leaky pump," and to "scratch, scratch, scratch, / From forehead down to feet!" (3, 5–6). He satirizes the spectacle of the over-dressed Northerner disrobing in a vain attempt to cool off: "Oh, 'tis off with your coat and vest! / 'Tis off with your shoes and pants!" (19–20). Gilbert understood the thin line that separated pain from pleasure and attractions from oppressions. Here, every stock image of utopian escape is shadowed by an antithesis of one or another kind. Heaven lies close to hell, joy to misery, and death lurks for the unsuspecting around every corner.

Malaria, cholera, and yellow fever were the most feared of all tropical dangers, bringing suffering and death in their wake. In "Beyond the Chagres," Gilbert describes a river abounding with "paths that lead to death— / To the fever's deadly breezes, / To malaria's poisonous breath" (2–4). Before the Panama Railroad, as we have seen, travelers journeyed by canoe up the

Chagres, a river so insalubrious for foreigners it became the namesake for
its own tropical disease, the Chagres Fever. Joseph Fabens, writing in 1853,
two years before the railway's completion, described the fever as the "mean-
est of diseases," which has a "sly, snaky way of making its approaches, and
falls upon one at last like a serpent, enveloping and crushing him."[13] Cholera
outbreaks were particularly deadly. Young Ulysses S. Grant, who saw over 150
men, women, and children succumb to the disease, wrote that "the horrors
of the road, in the rainy season" are "beyond description."[14] In "Yellow Eyes,"
Gilbert vividly describes the stages of the fever itself:

> In about ten days from now
> Iron bands will clamp your brow;
> Your tongue resemble curdled cream,
> A rusty streak the centre seam;
> Your mouth will taste of untold things . . .
> Then you'll sweat until, at length,
> You—won't—have—a—kitten's—strength!
> (2–6, 20–21)

As Gilbert well knew, the remaking of the isthmus caused suffering on an
unimaginable scale. If history is what hurts,[15] the same can be said of Robinson's blithe "civilization," taken all too lightly in his poem but registered as
trauma in Gilbert's verses.

The morbid imagination haunting these poems extends beyond illness and
tropical annoyances to death itself—universal, final, and grim—especially for
Panama's poor and underclass. One of Gilbert's most powerful poems, "The
Funeral Train," tells the story of the ignominious journey of such a person,
her poverty and social invisibility signaled by the Spanish refrain, "pobre de
solemnidad" (a pauper), a common phrase that marks the unnamed woman
as yet another nameless casualty of Panama's uneven economic transformation. Accompanied by anonymous members of the Panamanian demimonde,
the speaker narrates life's closing chapter as a raucous bacchanal, held as the
eponymous funeral train makes its way to an unmarked grave in Monkey Hill,
the local graveyard:

> Thrust her in the dead-car box!
> Jump aboard—let's have a ride!
> Ring the merry engine bell:
> Death has claimed another bride!
> Pass the gin to every one,

Pull the throttle open wide—
Pobre de solemnidad!
(1–7)

As in Emily Dickinson's more famous poem—"Because I could not stop for
Death"—a vehicular journey substitutes metonymically for life's journey. Here,
there is no solemn quiet. The bearers are drunks, as is the lyric speaker himself:

Up the weedy slope we climb:
Billy Black, you're drunk, I swear!
And so are you! and you! and you!
And so am I, I do declare
Now you've dropped her! Pick her up!
Leave the lid—we're almost there
Pobre de solemnidad!
(22–28)

Down and out in Colón, her companions lead lives of quiet desperation, until
they, too, make their final journey aboard the funeral train, an ironic commentary on the U.S. railroad that, in its construction, became associated with
large-scale death. The poem treats these abject travelers, however, not with
condescension but philosophical irony. As the drunken bearers pile earth atop
the body, the speaker enjoins: "No need to make it deep— / No frost here to
nip her feet / *Pobre de solemnidad!*" (39–41). This sly wink at the Northern
reader could be read as reinforcing differences, but perhaps also as a subtle
reminder that death is the ultimate leveler.

The poem also crystallizes the strong dystopian strain in Gilbert's work.
Although patriotic like his teacher Robinson, he demonstrates a broader social
vision, a deeply moral understanding of the universe and his place in it. The
prominence of the abject (insects, suffering, the nameless dead) suggests a
grasp of the tragic sense of life. The poet of the isthmus held no illusions about
Panama. Perhaps he had lived there too long to see it solely through a tourist's
innocent eye. Rooted in a place defined by its stream of passersby, he set his
pen to record a reality few of them would ever know.

LYRIC ETHNOGRAPHY

Gilbert used his long residence on the isthmus to get to know the world
beyond the terminal cities that defined the experience of most travelers.

Poems such as the "Funeral Train" show his skills of social observation and reportage, his interest in scenes of marginal life, and his perfect ear for dialogue, drunken or sober. From the evidence of his oeuvre and the accounts of many travelers, Panama abounded in characters ripe for sketching. The English traveler James A. Froude described the isthmus in 1888 as a rich tapestry of "speculators, adventurers, card sharpers, hell keepers, and doubtful ladies."[16] Gilbert, for his part, rendered the peculiar manners and speech patterns of a modern Panama that was rapidly changing before his eyes. A close observer of human nature, he breathed poetic life into his subjects while placing them in a specific cultural milieu. Examples of this ethnographic work appear in his earliest collections and recur throughout his career. Some editions of *Panama Patchwork* feature photographs that add subtle meanings to the ethnographic lyrics. Like the journalistic sketches of the Victorian social observer Henry Mayhew, the poems and their illustrations focus on marginal figures: servants ("Our Gurl Mary"), washerwomen ("A Frijoles Washer-Girl"), cantina girls ("La Cantinera"), and vagrants ("John Aspinwall" and "Cinco Centavos"). Addressed to white North American or European readers, the poems offer knowing, often intimate, encounters with the isthmian underworld, with the lyric speaker as guide and anthropologist. That intimacy, however, has clear limits. Gripped by the prevailing racial orthodoxies of his day, Gilbert was unable to sympathize fully with his Panamanian subjects, and in most cases, represents them as atavistic, unknowable, and resistant to the modernity the impending canal was bringing to the region. A reading of his ethnographic portraits illuminates the intractable and punishing unevenness of Panamanian modernity, in which massive technological change in the form of railroads and steamships imperiled indigenous, black, and creole ways of life alike.

In "Land of the Cacique," Gilbert celebrates Panama's most storied indigenous group, the Kuna, who were known during the nineteenth century as the San Blas Indians. One of the first English-language treatments of the Kuna, his poem valorizes the indigenous for their stubborn refusal to accept Euro-American ideals of modernization and development. Although exposed for three centuries to European culture, first the Spanish conquistadors and later the European modernizers who poured into the isthmus after 1849, the Kuna had largely managed to preserve their traditional ways in dress, language, and customs. According to their foremost ethnographer, James Howe, the Kuna by 1903 "were finishing a century of relative peace and isolation following two hundred years of war and struggle on the frontier of the Spanish empire."[17] Appearing to occupy a world apart from modernity's forward march, they appealed to the pronounced nostalgia that we find in Gilbert and many other writers of his era, a nostalgia that was however quite at odds with the enthusiastic promotion of sweeping technological change. Fiercely independent in their ways and resistant to outside influence, the Kuna challenged the teleology of the modernizing narrative, even as their customs unwittingly supported certain key aspects of Anglo-American racial theory.

Like the nineteenth-century world fairs, the progress narrative could only achieve its full impact when set against what it was leaving behind. Progress, in other words, was constrastive, not absolute, a function of differences and not essences. Its ideological and rhetorical force hinged on comparison to its other, which was ritually displayed. Thus, in something of a paradox, Gilbert strengthens his affirmation of U.S. capital's modernizing effects by representing a culture that rejected not only capitalism itself but also the established patterns of racial mixing that had defined Latin American history since the conquest. He carefully situates the Kuna within an idealized tropical setting, marked by "soft and tender" skies and clouds that form "wondrous pictures" beneath a "crimson sun." In their forest haunts, nature and culture overlap, as the plants are described in kingly language: the "majestic" palm figured as the "monarch of the forest." Sharing the ground with flourishing almond trees and gorgeous mangos, the regal palm rules over a "kingdom all its own."[18] This monarchial imagery establishes an ideological foundation for Gilbert's overarching idea, the natural aristocracy of the Kuna themselves, and especially of their chief or "cacique."

The poem represents the Kuna as innocents living in splendid isolation, and displaces them from the time and place they currently occupy by writing them into the familiar mythic landscape of the pastoral:

> There, upon the sylvan hillsides
> And within the lovely valleys,
> Nestles many an Indian village
> Of the slender bamboo built.
> (21–24)

To transform these subjects into conventional forms of literary representation, Gilbert turns himself into a rude piper of verses who will sing the Kuna's "customs quaint and curious" with a "a harp uncouth and awkward, / As befits the modest minstrel / Of a lowly race of men" (26, 30–32).

Crucially, Gilbert argues that the Kuna's lowliness is not categorical but relative, a function of cultural perspective. From one angle, they appear primitive, but within their own sphere are as "dignified and haughty / As the proudest of mankind" (37–38). With a careful eye, the poet details marriage practices, domestic architecture, religious beliefs and celebrations, and burial rites: "Each rude hut is sanctuary, / From whence, dying, to the bosom / Of Eternal Rest they go" (68–70). Adopting an ethnographic pose, he presents Kuna beliefs as an organically coherent and reasoned system, tracing Kuna ways to the underlying principles that guide them. Although he describes their religion as primitive, he praises it for its simplicity and beauty: "No need here for costly churches" (67).

Just the same, Gilbert's poem keeps the Kuna carefully at a distance, describing their identity as a group or tribe, but not their individual selves, which remain concealed. Subjectivity is withheld in favor of delineated practices and customs. Yet despite these shortcomings, the poem concludes with a ringing plea to leave the Kuna to their own ways, which is remarkable given the enthusiasm Gilbert otherwise expresses for the transforming effects of modernization:

> Trouble not this gentle people—
> Leave them to their peace and quiet—
> Nor disturb this tropic Eden
> Of the red men of San Blas!
> (166–69)

Particularly striking is Gilbert's admonition to the "pushing missionaries / Of accepted creed and sect" (164–65) to leave the Kuna in peace, an appeal for cultural autonomy and separateness that was remarkable in its time.

However well intentioned, this plea must be contextualized within the poem's larger bias toward racial purity. This bias parallels the polygenetic strain of racial theory that drew raw "data" from many parts of the globe, but found the Americas, with its 300-year history of intermarriage among racial groups, particularly fertile ground for exploring the reputed dangers of racial mingling. Theorists of polygenesis believed that humans derived from multiple, separate, and perdurable racial origins, which were unaffected by change or progress. Joseph Barnard Davis, a strong proponent of these ideas, defined race in 1856 as a "permanent and enduring entity, which . . . exists the same now as it has always done, unchanged and unchangeable," and suggested that the ancient people found in nearly every part of the globe should be looked on "as the venerable and living representatives of nations whose ancestry reaches back perhaps to creation itself."[19] William Bollaert, who rose to become an acknowledged expert in the science of American races, laid out the case against exogamy in his forty-seven-page treatise, "Observations on the Past and Present Populations of the New World" (1863):

Whites, Indians, and Negroes have mixed, producing endless varieties. (I
shall have again to refer to what has for a long time appeared to me that
something detrimental, physically and morally, has been going on by this
mixture of the three species, since about A. D. 1500, producing at times
repugnant varieties among the Zamboes, and especially from the Indian and
negress).[20]

Bollaert's repugnance was widely shared. The U.S. archaeologist, traveler, and
diplomat Ephraim George Squier, who championed a transcontinental route
across Nicaragua, wrote that in Central America, "we find a people not only
demoralized from the unrestrained association of different races, but also the
superior stocks becoming gradually absorbed in the lower, and their institutions disappearing under the relative barbarism of which the latter are the
exponents."[21] According to the naturalist Berthold Seemann, whose writings on
the isthmus we have examined in previous chapters, "the character of the half-
castes is, if possible, worse than that of the negroes. These people have all the
vices and none of the virtues of their parents."[22] It was left to Herbert Spencer to
draw the political moral that "half-castes" were incapable of self-government.
The person of mixed race, having inherited from one side traits adapted to one
set of institutions, and from the other a different set, is a "unit whose nature has
not been moulded by any social type. . . . The South American Republics, with
their perpetual revolutions, show us the result."[23]

The question of hybridity, as Robert J. C. Young has argued, was the central
issue of nineteenth-century anthropological thought.[24] In the novel, the era's
dominant literary form, questions of hybridity and mixing were fundamental to the genre's courtship and marriage plots, and organized more general
questions about the crossing and recrossing of identities. Gilbert's lyric poem
participates in this broader cultural interest in marriage and the merging of
identities, but with a significant difference. In proper anthropological form,
he describes the Kuna male's choice of bride, the building of his sacred boat,
the bride's seclusion from view, the six-day wedding festival, and many other
matters that define the "rites to them peculiar." Crucially, however, these rites
involve no outsiders. The "dignified and haughty" (39) Kuna are strict endoga-
mists. In stark contrast to the widespread practice of intermarriage all around
them, they form an enclosed society: "In their veins no mixed blood cours-
eth" (41). Playing the key role in preserving this genetic isolation is the Kuna
male, a "simple child of nature" whose special mission is to guard his "race
from all admixture" (45). The poem suggests that when the young married cou-
ple reproduce they will also reproduce the endogamous pattern as they "rear
their children / In the ancient superstitions" (146–47), preserving their ways

from cultural and racial contamination. This fierce opposition to racial mixing played neatly into dominant Anglo-American racial logics and fueled the
long romance many writers and cultural observers maintained with the Kuna.

In "A Frijoles Washer-Girl," by contrast, Gilbert draws on a more familiar body of erotic imagery to construct a fantasy of sexual possession, here
centered on the iconographic subject of a young woman washing her clothes
in a stream, which we have seen in Muybridge. The poem offers the putative
reader an ensemble of titillating oppositions: light and shade, concealment and
display, dress and undress. The stream in which the washer-girl works rises
halfway up her legs, and she is both illuminated by natural light and, by way
of association with the startled deer, "half hidden in the distant shade." The
poem's play of description locates visual pleasure in the male beholder's eye,
who appears here as an urbane receptor of ambiguity, tension, and shading.

A dream in living bronze is she
A dusky goddess full revealed;
Clad but in Nature's modesty—
Her wondrous beauty unconcealed.

Half to her knee, the rushing stream
An instant pauses on its way;
The ripples in the sunshine gleam
And tiny rainbows round her play

Lithe as the bamboo growing near
Within the tangle, tropic glade
As graceful as the startled deer
Half hidden in the distant shade.
(1–12)

All the while, the poem conceals the washer-girl's interiority, focusing instead
on her status as a sexualized and racialized object of masculine contemplation.

The poem objectifies the washer-girl both as a part of the natural world
and as a fragmented work of art: "Half to her knee, the rushing stream / An
instant pauses." She is surrounded by "tiny rainbows" and analogized both
to plants and animals, the lithe bamboo and the startled deer of the poem's
imagery. Her rootedness in nature aligns with the view of Anglo-American
writers and visual artists who suggested that Panama's people were trapped in
an anterior time to modernity and doomed by the coming revolution of iron
and steam. Handwashing garments in a stream, she is portrayed as a primitive

clinging to old ways in a rapidly modernizing world. From an initial status
as a "dream in living bronze" the washer-girl moves within a few stanzas to
something rivaling "sculptured marble."

> The limbs, the hips, the swelling bust
> Of famed Olympus' fairest queen
> Ne'er modelled yet on lines more just
> Was ever sculptured marble seen!
>
> Her curl-fringed eyes, now black, now brown,
> Are depths of passion unexplored;
> Her teeth, a glistening, pearly crown
> A Rajah would delight to hoard.
> (13–20)

The poem employs both metaphors to fix her as a passive point of contemplation for the speaker, who catalogs her parts with knowing precision: the half-
revealed legs; "the limbs, the hips, the swelling bust"; "curl-fringed eyes, now
black, now brown"; and "glistening" white teeth. Here, the whole is not greater
than the sum of the parts. As in the Petrarchan tradition of the Early Modern *blazon,* such as we find in the poems of Robert Herrick and other Early
Modern writers, the speaker's careful inventory reduces the female subject to
attractive bits. The effect produces what Herrick calls "a fine distraction" that
kindles "wantonnesse" in the lyric speaker/voyeur.[25] Stripped of her subjectivity, the washer-girl becomes the object of the speaker's possessive fantasy,
signaled by the Orientalized reference to the "Rajah."

The illustrated editions of *Panama Patchwork* complicate the poem's elaborate staging of visual pleasure. The poem describes a single washer-girl, but
the image that accompanies it is a group shot, showing three washer-girls, the
oldest barely a teen (fig. 4.2). The poem suggests a single nude washer-girl,
clothed in nature's modesty, but the picture shows three young girls, all on dry
land, fully clothed. Nevertheless, the image alludes to an important subtext
in the region's popular iconography—representations of *lavanderas,* or washerwomen, which appear repeatedly in books, pamphlets, periodical articles,
stereographs, and postcards. Some, like the image from the French naturalist
Armand Reclus's *Panama et Darien* (fig. 4.3), belong formally to the nineteenth-century genre of scientific travel, with its anthropological interest in
primitive customs and mores. Others, like the Muybridge stereographs examined in the previous chapter, served as promotional material for commerce
and trade. And others, printed on postcards and stereographs, circulated

Frijoles Washer-Girls.

FIGURE 4.2. Washer-Girls, from J. S. Gilbert, *Panama Patchwork*.

FIGURE 4.3. Blanchisseuses, from Armand Reclus, *Panama et Darien*.

as souvenirs, generating meanings by their role in forging homosocial bonds between sender and receiver. A dual language postcard printed in Panama gives the "Gilbert image" in color on one side (fig. 4.4), commemorating a journey to Panama both as a sign of travel and a traveling image that reinforces connectedness between far-flung individuals bound together by shared voyeurism and objectification. That images of women and girls engaged in laundering had such a homosocial function in the circulatory system of travel and tourism is made clear in Gilbert's *Washington Post* obituary. Any traveler going by ship to Panama, the writer observes, would be asked if he had read Gilbert's *Panama Patchwork,* and if not would be presented with the "treasured volume" from the captain's stateroom. To reinforce the appeal of Gilbert's verses, the obituary then quotes several stanzas of "A Frijoles Washer-Girl."[26] Here, a volume of poems that travels, summoned on board a vessel conveying travelers to Panama, forms bonds of intimacy among male travelers and crew. The textual circuit, an imaginative exchange of abstract symbols between writer and reader, is materially embodied in the exchange of books as objects, which in turn serves as a vehicle for the traffic in women.

The images comprising this visual economy make legible entwined themes of sexuality, race, and labor operating in Gilbert's "A Frijoles Washer-Girl" subjects that are central to the Anglo-American discourse of Panama but only gestured at in the lyric. As we have already seen, the poem's language and visual logic creates a strong erotic charge, participating in a tradition of male gazing on female beauty that goes back to Greek and Hebrew legends. But the question of race—what is meant by a *"frijoles* washer-girl"—is not so clear, nor its connection to the labor encoded in the scene. The speaker describes the washer-girl as a "dusky" goddess with eyes "now black, now brown," and the adjective "frijoles," a Panamanian place name, further suggests her otherness. The subject's specific mode of labor is in turn raced and classed by the combination of prurient sexuality and the activity of laundering itself, deeply associated in the visual register with indigenous and black women. The French naturalist Reclus glosses his image of washerwomen by noting that they use large stones to beat clothes in the oppressive heat.[27] In the region's labor hierarchy, such a toilsome activity would only be performed by the most abject, signified by the catch-all term "native" that we have seen in Muybridge's descriptions, used throughout the nineteenth century to signify a range of poor, non-European persons either indigenous or black. To be a washerwoman, in other words, is effectively to be native. Though not all natives are washerwomen, the reverse is almost always true.

Yet just as the poem refers to its visual subtext, it erases all signs of the physical toil to which its thematic subject ostensibly refers. It makes no mention

NIÑAS NATURALES DE PANAMA LAVANDO ROPA, PANAMA, REP. DE PANAMA.

NATIVE GIRLS WASHING CLOTHES, PANAMA, REP. OF PANAMA.

FIGURE 4.4. Native Girls Washing Clothes, postcard, c. 1900.

of clothes or the heavy stones commonly used to beat them. Unlike Reclus, Gilbert's work omits any reference to stifling heat. Indeed, like the statue to which she is compared, the unnamed washer-girl appears motionless. Only the stream remains as a trace of labor, but it is so highly aestheticized as to efface any connection to actual work. The poem detaches the girl from work only to fix her more securely in the category of sexual object. In both referring to and displacing a specific, Panamanian content, "The Frijoles Washer-Girl" plays a key part in Gilbert's poetic catalog of isthmian types. As the *Post* obituary suggests, the poem hints at the region's easy availability of "native" sexual partners, a subject of the Anglo-American discourse from the earliest days of the isthmian route, while at the same time drawing a curtain around the subject for the benefit of modesty. It refers to the region's cheap labor—which built the railroad and would later construct the canal—but obliquely, aestheticizing hard, manual work within a misty haze of sexual fantasy. Functioning both as ethnographic portrait and sexualized *souvenir de voyage*, the poem testifies to literature's role in mediating Panama's otherness for the tourist or armchair traveler back home.

Race, gender, and colonial representation also figure prominently in Gilbert's ethnographic vignette, "Our Gurl Mary," which explores another aspect of Panamanian subaltern life, the confines of upper-class Panamanian households, where master and servant live in tense interaction. The servant here, judging from the illustration that accompanies the verses in Gilbert's volume, is quite likely a black woman (fig. 4.5). The poem is narrated by a North American employer, signified as such by the recollection of the March "rose / That blooms in the snow" (22–23). Now living in Panama as an expatriate, the narrator presents domestic labor not so much as toil for the servant but an exasperating chore for the master, who struggles to manage the help. Quietly willful, the female servant upsets the orderly rhythms of bourgeois life and "always does what she oughtn't to" (3), a form of stubborn resistance to her employer's wishes. The speaker provides a long list of Mary's crimes: rising slowly from her night's sleep, pouring cold coffee, putting cheese in the butter dish, and serving steak *before* fish. In each stanza, the speaker begs Mary to do her assigned work, all to no avail: "Tea-time, Mary! You've been told before, / *Haven't* you, Mary?" (33–34). The poem summons the image of the lazy black worker, familiar from authors such as Carlyle, Trollope, and Froude, here shifted from the plantation to the domestic interior. Like Gilbert's other ethnographic subjects, Mary is described as "fathomless" (47), always spoken to but never speaking. "Our Gurl Mary," despite its female subject, downplays questions of gender to focus on questions of language. The poem represents her relationship to the unnamed master as a verbal contest that is organized

"Our Gurl Mary".

FIGURE 4.5. "Our Gurl Mary," from J. S. Gilbert, *Panama Patchwork*.

by commands on one side and nonverbal resistance on the other. It presents her as the familiar domestic, suffering in silence along with untold numbers of other local women.

Questions of silence, resistance, and racial difference figure prominently in Gilbert's most famous ethnographic vignette, "John Aspinwall," published in the author's first collection of poems (see fig. 4.6). The poem examines the remote interiority of the tattered but dignified Colón resident named in the title (of no relation to the founder of the Panama Railway). As in "Our Gurl Mary," the question of silence is paramount. A historical figure of uncertain lineage, Aspinwall had become by the 1890s a minor celebrity on the isthmus. In a prose remembrance published in 1894, Gilbert called him "one of the most picturesque characters of Colón, if not of the Isthmus" (101), and two decades later, authors commemorating the canal's opening were still singing his name, often in quasi-mythical terms. Willis Abbot, in *Panama and the Canal in Picture and Prose* (1913), referred to him as the "old colored man" who had worked for the Panama Railroad and resided on the isthmus "from the days of the alligators and the monkeys."[28]

In Gilbert's telling, Aspinwall is both familiar and enigmatic, in this world but not of it, placed in history but lacking any knowable past:

A quaint old moke is John Aspinwall,
Who lives by the Dead-House gate,
And quaint are his thoughts, if thoughts at all
Ever lurk in his wooly pate.
For he's old as the hills, is this old black man—
Thrice doubled with age is he;
And the days when his wanderings first began
Are shrouded in mystery.
(1–8)

The racialized terms "moke" and "wooly" immediately establish Aspinwall's blackness, and thus the distance between the white lyric speaker and subject, a gap emphasized throughout several of Gilbert's ethnographic poems. Speaker and subject occupy the same place and time, but utterly incommensurate worlds. The adjective "quaint" translates Aspinwall into the picturesque, no longer a fellow human being but a landscape fixture, a sign of old Panama. His very age ("old as the hills") is measured against a natural feature. If the poem's anthropological register leans on a rhetoric of historical authenticity—a footnote in the second edition of *Panama Patchwork* describes Aspinwall as an "old crazy negro who wandered around Colón for many years"[29]—the

Old John Aspinwall "A quaint old moke was he".

FIGURE 4.6. John Aspinwall, from J. S. Gilbert, *Panama Patchwork*.

poem also refuses the extension of sympathy that an ethic of the individual might reasonably produce and instead retreats safely toward stereotype. That refusal is grounded in the denial of language. His origins shrouded in mystery, Aspinwall's thoughts, too, remain closed to observation. Gilbert's prose sketch, published three years after the poem's first appearance, dwells on Aspinwall's refusal to speak: "Reticent to a degree, no one could ever obtain from him either the name of his native land, or the date of his birth, and his arrival here." A man without a recorded history, Aspinwall is registered in that most classic of colonial tropes—silence—for "no questioning could break his mono-syllabic silence; knowing much he spoke little."[30]

In an exercise of colonial myth making, the next several lines ambivalently locate Aspinwall in what for Gilbert and many isthmian chroniclers were the defining events of Panama's emergence into modernity: the era of English piracy; the California gold rush; and the building of the railroad.

> Perhaps he was living when Morgan's crew
> Came lusting for Spanish gold,
> And drenched the Isthmus with bloody dew
> In the brave, bold days of old.
> Perhaps he was here when the pioneers
> Of the days almost forgot
> Made a trail o'er the land with their bitter tears
> And the bones they left to rot.
>
> Perhaps he was here when Totten came
> And Baldwin and all the rest,
> To build thro' the swamps their pathway to fame
> From Chagres to Ancon's crest.
> And many a night he has lain, no doubt,
> By the side of some comrade ill,
> Whose corpse, in the morn, he has carried out
> To its rest on Monkey Hill.
> (9–24)

Although Gilbert places Aspinwall at these world-historical epochs, the stan-zas diminish rather than enlarge his imaginative role in them, manipulating scales of time to marginalize the historical Aspinwall in favor of a mythic one. They also negate alternate possibilities for Aspinwall's origin: perhaps one of the thousands of black workers who immigrated to the terminal city seeking employment; perhaps an internal migrant who moved to Colón from Panama's interior. The poem refuses the possibility of a subaltern-centered historical narrative in favor of a mythic reading of Panama's history organized by events in which the principal actors are British and U.S. citizens. We see the English pirate Morgan who sacked Porto Bello, the seat of Spanish military strength; the hordes of gold seekers who beat a path through the jungle on their way to California, opening the isthmus to foreign adventurers; and the U.S. engineers (Totten and Baldwin) who tamed the wilderness to build the Panama Railroad, ushering the isthmus into modernity but confining it, as well, as a place between. Gilbert's verses remind us that each exposure to the world-making forces of globalization involved violence and upheaval, the rending, cutting, and wounding that was so much a part of this history. Morgan's crew soaked the isthmus in blood, and the foreign laborers who built the railroad, many of them indentured, perished in droves. At each exposure, Panama's local people recede into historical oblivion. The poem praises Europeans and North Americans for their bravery and "pathway to fame," but relegates Aspinwall to a companion of the nameless souls laid to rest in the cemetery. In Gilbert's Panama, the deeds of tattered black men lay unrecorded.

If, like a blind seer, a sort of Panamanian Tiresias, Aspinwall witnessed the formative events of isthmian history, at least as defined by Anglo-Americans, the poem refuses him the chance to narrate those events:

> Yet never a word will he answer me
> Whenever he passes by,
> Though often a curious light I see
> In his fathomless, coal-black eye.
> Oh, a quaint old moke is John Aspinwall,
> Who lives by the Dead-House gate;
> And quaint are his thoughts, if thoughts at all
> Ever lurk in his wooly pate!
> (33–40)

Aspinwall remains stubbornly silent, giving no answer to the speaker's questions. In a self-canceling paradox, the "curious light," a sign of his intelligence, emanates from a "coal-black eye." After entertaining the possibility of Aspinwall's subjectivity, the poem closes it down, returning to the racialized rhetoric with which it began. In the end, the reader stands no closer to Aspinwall's thoughts—"if thoughts at all"—than at the beginning, and whatever individuality he might possess disappears into the final objectifying phrase: "wooly pate."

Yet if Aspinwall, like the domestic servant Mary, never speaks, we as readers must acknowledge, even if Gilbert does not, the racially inflected trauma that lies behind his reticence. The poem's references to historical wounding open the possibility for sympathetic gestures of readerly understanding only to close them down. For to do so might suggest that which the poem ultimately refuses—the recognition of Aspinwall as a historical actor in his own story, rather than a quaint object of ethnographic curiosity. This unwillingness to enter into Aspinwall's subjectivity, or even to grant that it exists, is part of the larger strategy of Anglo-American representation we have noted throughout this book, a strategy of colonial foreclosing that privileges Anglo-American deeds while marginalizing and silencing subaltern voices. It parallels the process of internalized coloniality Walter Mignolo has examined throughout Latin America, in which "being" itself is colonized by "producing the idea that certain people do not belong to history—that they are non beings."[31] The Yankee Strip was the beginning of that separateness—a zone of U.S. values, laws, and culture laid through the heart of Panama. Gilbert is its bard, casting his jaundiced eye over the late remnants of the strip just before the canal would "siamese" the oceans and mingle their waters. A crucial part of this project was the creation of the Canal Zone, which formalized U.S. legal control over a broad swath of Panama and permitted expatriates to fashion an existence almost entirely separate from local Panamanian culture. As his many subsequent admirers would attest, there was no one better suited to speak for the expatriate way of life than Gilbert, whose dissonant lyre captured both its pleasures and many contradictions.

EPILOGUE

The Isthmus as Tourist Paradise

Today the tourists are coming here by the hundreds and Panama is destined to be as popular as Naples or Nice with her historical background,
foreign charm, great natural beauty and numerous delights that it hos-
pitably offers the passing world.

—JEAN HEALD, *PICTURESQUE PANAMA*

An ugly thing, that is what you are when you become a tourist, an ugly,
empty thing, a stupid thing, a piece of rubbish pausing here and there to
gaze at this and taste that, and it will never occur to you that the people
who inhabit the place in which you have just paused cannot stand you.

—JAMAICA KINCAID, *A SMALL PLACE*

THE OPENING of the canal locks in 1914 released a flood: speeches, proclama-
tions, scientific treatises, government reports, learned histories, maps, postcards, stamps, songs, and poems. In distant San Francisco, tightly wedded to
Panama since the gold rush, civic leaders mounted the Panama-Pacific International Exposition, which celebrated the canal as the century's technological
masterwork.[1] An estimated 18 million visitors came to see the fair. Representations of the canal depicted the transoceanic passageway as a compelling tes-
tament to U.S. ingenuity and imperial power, and supported this claim by
recirculating themes from the pre-canal tradition we have examined in this
book: the collapsing of time and space, the extension of U.S. hegemony to
the Canal Zone, the triumph of heroic engineering over pestilential swamps,
the promise of new markets and increased trade, the vision of a radically
collapsed world that would produce new, more rapid forms of mobility and
movement. Reflecting the confidence born from military ventures such as the
Spanish-American War, these representations hailed the canal as the embodiment of a new American imperialism, capable of rearranging the hemisphere
and uniting the oceans.[2]

In succeeding years, another perspective would emerge, one important for understanding Anglo-American views of Panama today, as well as the larger problematics of mobility in a globalized world: that of the pleasure-seeking and privileged foreign tourist. By definition capricious and fleeting, the tourist comes and goes as he or she wishes, seeking new diversions among familiar places or sites not yet discovered.[3] An entire infrastructure supports the tourist's mobility, from ocean liners (and later airplanes) to hotels, currency exchange to shops and restaurants. In this world, travel may sometimes involve travail but is not defined by it. As Jamaica Kincaid's comments above suggest, the very possibility of the leisured traveler suggests the reality of radically differential mobility, the gap between those who enjoy the means to escape and those for whom movement is either impossible or involuntary. Caren Kaplan has called this the difference between travel as a product of the leisure industry of Western capitalism, and travel—or rather, movement—as displacement, the effect of diasporic migrations that place a question mark over the term "mobility."[4] Nothing suggests this distinction more than the canal itself, an engineering feat whose promise of delivering the traveler quickly from one ocean to another was founded on the economic displacement of the laborers who built it.

Previous chapters have revealed, albeit in disaggregated form, the component parts of the leisure traveler's origins and material conditions. The fantasy of annihilating time appears in John Lloyd Stephens's fanciful notion of taking a morning bath in the Euphrates and his afternoon tea on the Pacific. The provision of desired comforts occurs, similarly, in his wish to erect a hotel for tourists on the Nicaraguan volcano of Masaya, and, in a different form, the creation of the Yankee Strip itself. Coordinated intermodal travel is anticipated by the neatly tabular railway and steamship tables in Otis's *Illustrated History of the Panama Railroad,* the popular guide that defined Panama as a site of connection to other places, and which formed the basis of such later volumes as *The Pocket Guide to the West Indies* (1907) and *Canal Zone Pilot* (1908).[5] A consciousness of travel understood not simply as an instrumental act serving governmental or scientific purposes but as a leisure-time activity lies behind Anthony Trollope's detailed comments on local hotels, meals, and manners. This hope also glimmers in the Pacific Mail Steamship Company's scheme to promote tourism by commissioning beguiling photographic images of Panama and Guatemala's railways and coffee plantations in the 1870s, and in promoting the isthmus as the gateway to Asia toward the end of the century. The power of tropical places to sustain fantasies of escape in a dream world of *dolce far niente* animates many of James Stanley Gilbert's best poems. The touristic subject emerges from an amalgam of the material conditions of mobility (which includes but is not limited to the infrastructure of travel) and a powerful set of myths, fantasies, and selective understandings that derive from the experience of travel.

Few post-canal texts draw these strands together better, nor more fully reveal their entwinement in the Panamanian context, than Jean Sadler Heald's *Picturesque Panama* (1928). The wife of Samuel W. Heald, longtime Superintendent of the Panama Railroad and Steamship Line, Jean Heald spent twenty years on the isthmus, an experience she drew on for her popular book. Parting ways with her (male) contemporaries' "learned and often monumental" publications, she describes her work as "plain and unpretentious," speaking to "short-time visitors" and "merely covering the points of interest."[6] This discursive modesty is reinforced by her adoption of the centripetal pattern of female travel accounts. Instead of a linear, exploratory pattern across geographical space, featuring the masculine traveler as conquering hero or bold scientific genius, she largely follows the example of nineteenth-century women travelers to Latin America such as Maria Graham and Fanny Calderón de la Barca, who took up a fixed residence in the countries they resided in, sallying back and forth from her home in the Canal Zone in short, periodic visits. Partly a response to restrictions on women's mobility and freedom, this structure of centripetal mobility also critiques the imperial stance—exemplified by Alexander von Humboldt and his followers—of epistemological mastery, the "master of all I survey," founded on the homology between seeing and being, between the *eye* and the *I*.[7] Although Heald gives an overview of Panama's geography and history, she also focuses on experiences of intimate social relations that are largely absent from the texts that we have examined thus far in this book. In so doing, she draws attention to alternative affective logics that have the potential to resist and complicate the masculine tradition of travel and discovery. As in the material examined in previous chapters, the resulting view is decidedly mixed.

Like any good Baedeker, Heald offers useful information for the tourist, but focuses particularly on sites that illustrate Panama's modernization under the stimulus of foreign capital and investment, reinforcing an imperial narrative in which U.S. culture and economic power aids Latin American underdevelopment. This bias toward the values of U.S. capitalism is exemplified in her list of a tourist's necessities, which could stand as a brief on the fruits of full integration into the global economy: train service and roads; ocean transportation; the post, telegraph, and currency; hotels; shops; and clothing. Representing Panama as a place for the acquisition of luxury goods, she recommends evening gowns and sports frocks for the tropical climate, the best shops for jewelry, oriental rugs, Japanese silks, and of course a Panama hat, the perfect metonym for the isthmus as crossroads of tourism and trade. Her confiding tone, at once informed and relaxed, is pitched to the wealthy audience she addresses, the newly mobile leisure classes eager to reap the benefits of the roaring twenties. There are photographic plates showing stylish women dressed as if they had stepped from the pages of *The Great Gatsby* and images of upper-class retreats such as the Panama Golf Club. The grounds and gardens of Canal Zone buildings are as neatly manicured as the young flappers pictured in the volume. One can almost hear the syncopated rhythms of the Charleston and the clinking of gin glasses, for Canal Zone residents could easily escape prohibition by going into Panama itself. This is a safe and sanitary Panama, offered up to the white, ruling classes of the United States as an escape from the habits of getting and spending that make leisure possible, but which, paradoxically, necessitate a structure of leisure to counter and mystify. Along with the mobility of capital and military strength, Heald presents the globe-trotting U.S. traveler, whose need is both for transit and recreation. The serious business of economic and military hegemony goes hand in hand with the redefinition of Panama as tropical idyll, geographically proximate, and in many ways, familiarly American.

Yet the light-hearted tone of *Picturesque Panama* barely conceals the darker side of economic development in Panama, which creeps in from the margin like a guilty secret. Everywhere there is troubling evidence of the violence of Panama's history under colonial and neocolonial rule, not least in the work's structure, which narrates Panama's emergence into modernity through three progressively linked phases: Panama under Spanish dominion; Panama during the period of the railroad; and Panama as nexus of global trade via the canal. This structure describes an arc of historical destiny that points to the U.S.-governed Canal Zone as the culmination of an unfurling modernity and southward Manifest Destiny characterized by speed, mobility, and technology.[8] Despite its sunny meliorism, this American version of progressive, Whig history remains haunted by those who have been excluded from the pleasures of global mobility—the slave, the worker, the black and indigenous Panamanians we have seen in Muybridge's photographs and Gilbert's poems. As Kincaid writes, the locals are "too poor to escape the reality of their lives; and they are too poor to live properly in the place where they live, which is the very place you, the tourist want to go."[9] Panama's redefinition as a site of global transit, as we have seen, was never about new mobility for the locals, but quite often the opposite. Heald's text participates in this distinction by celebrating her own upper-class mobility while largely repressing the larger immobilities on which it depends.

TOURIST VISIONS

Heald presents her subject as already aestheticized, enfolded in a literary and symbolic tradition that goes back centuries. Panama, she writes, has "a breath of ancient poetry" about it. She tries to match this effect both in the scope of her work, which dwells on incidents from the most colorful of Panama's epochs, and in the descriptive quality of her own language:

> Southward bound for Panama are words to conjure with, and to the prospective visitor, bring visions of sunshine, flowers, and the song of birds, the radiance of moonlit tropic nights and the lure of the Southern Cross, which hangs low, flooding the sky with its brilliance in "latitude nine." (19)

Heald's aim is to use picturesque description to lure "prospective visitors" southward. By showing that Panama's transformation from rough, inhospitable wilderness to tourist paradise is complete, she argues for the success of U.S. economic development in Latin America. Description here is instrumental. Its aim is to allure. Its intended audience is the "southward bound" visitors encoded in the passage, wealthy U.S. tourists, leisured and leisure-seeking, with time and money to escape from the "snow, sleet and cold winds" to a place where it is always June (19). Here, the emergence of the global South as a place of touristic fantasy has already begun.

That Heald's address is to a particular class stratum is evident from the list of posh shops and fancy hotels, as well as the images of golf links, tarpon fishing, and other elite pursuits. She presents the Canal Zone as an ordered, safe place for relaxation and personal restoration, where wealth, always subdued and mystified, enjoys its privileges, relaxing the energy that makes capital accumulation possible. Giving a literary flavor to the pursuit of idyllic rest, she quotes J. S. Gilbert, here noted in the usual way simply as "the poet":

> O Land of Love and Pleasure,
> Of soft and languorous days,
> Of brilliant flowers and sunny hours,
> How shall I sing thy praise? (19)[10]

She understands that for the well-heeled tourist the crucial commodity is time, mentioned both in the "sunny hours" and the even more expansive "languorous days," the latter adjective a favorite of Heald's throughout the book. From a place defined by its ability to save and shave time, Panama is here revealed as one where the consciousness of time disappears altogether, a place of blissful forgetting where the "feeling of tension and hurry unconsciously

falls" (19). On the eve of the stock market crash, in the midst of an age that
Enda Duffy has rightly described as speed-addicted and Heald as "agitated
and feverish" (23), the fantasy of escaping capitalism's relentless motion holds
a strong allure.[11]

As we have seen, pre-canal Panama was infamous as an insalubrious place,
the location of the death-dealing Chagres fever, the "pest hole of the universe" (22). Sites like Monkey Hill, Colón's cemetery, symbolized the status
of Panama as graveyard. For Panama to succeed as a tourist destination, such
associations had to be countered by a discourse of sanitation, one that gave
indisputable proof that economic development had made the notorious, mos-
quito-ridden swamp safe for visitors. Here, Heald's images combine with her
prose to do the necessary cultural work, employing binary logic to mark the
arrival of U.S. canal builders, and by extension the entire apparatus of U.S.
control, as the decisive break in Panama's narrative of sanitation and health.
"Colon before the Arrival of the Canal Commission" (fig. E.1) shows a mud-
filled urban street, filled with standing water. A horse walks through, suggesting the taint of animal waste. A man tries to rescue his hat from the muck. A
companion image, entitled "Modern Colon—A City Fair to See" (fig. E.2)—
shows the transformational power of modernity. The mud has been replaced
with paving, a wide colonnade protects pedestrians from the elements, and
loiterers have disappeared in favor of well-dressed men in suits and hats—
stand-ins for the tourists such images are designed to address. Further on
in the text, these images are bookended by another pair of images showing
a similar transformation across the isthmus in Panama. Heald reminds us
that both terminal cities, Colón and Panama, "are under the control of the
Health Department of the Panama Canal, which has in the past and is at
present maintaining a high standard of progressive development along the
lines of sanitation" (78). These binary images reinforce the central message of
American economic development: the swamps have been drained, the cities
have been made safe for visitors, and prosperity reigns. In her discussion of
sanitation and health, Heald suggests that standards of hygiene *exceed* those
in the continental United States. "It is not an exaggeration," she writes, "to
say that the Canal Zone is the best governed section of the United States, if
not the world. Certainly it is the cleanest" (22). In the years before the publication of *Picturesque Panama*, malaria rates declined by ninety percent as a
result of William Gorgas's efforts at abating tropical disease; he went so far as
to change the holy water in Panama's cathedral to kill larvae.[12] As Blake Scott
shows, the news of the successful battle against mosquito-borne disease was
widely disseminated in the United States, transforming the isthmus, as Willis
J. Abbott put it in 1913, from a pestilent swamp into a "health resort."[13] With
these improvements, the taming of the tropics, which had begun for the trav-

COLON BEFORE THE ARRIVAL OF THE CANAL COMMISSION IN 1905.

FIGURE E.1. "Colon before the Arrival of the Canal Commission," from Jean Salder Heald, *Picturesque Panama*.

MODERN COLON—A CITY FAIR TO SEE.

FIGURE E.2. "A City Fair to See," from Jean Salder Heald, *Picturesque Panama*.

eler in the 1850s, was now represented as complete, its beneficiary the leisure-seeking tourist.

Heald's narrative of sequentially unfolding modernity begins with Columbus's landfall and leads to the Canal Zone as its logical fulfillment. That narrative, like so many in the literature we have examined, assumes a familiar progressive form, commencing with the Spanish conquest, moving to the Panama Railroad, and concluding with Roosevelt and the establishment of the Canal Zone. Within her largely centripetal structure of personal movement and mobility, Heald reinforces this narrative by taking the reader on a familiar linear journey along the line of the Panama Railroad from the Atlantic to the Pacific, from Colón to Panama. Along the way, she pays homage to the Aspinwall memorials that link the isthmus's modernity to the arrival of Europeans and Americans: one to Columbus, presented by the Empress Eugenie, and the other to the founders of the Panama Railroad (see fig. 3.8). This spatial narrative, inset within the text, parallels the historical narrative in its ideological structure. A journey from the Atlantic to Pacific suggests an advancing modernity instanced by the technological wonder of the canal:

> To have seen Colon and its environs is not to say that one has seen Panama—the part only serves as a foretaste of the whole, and the visitor taking the trip across the Isthmus, via the modern Panama Railroad, whose past history forms a link with the present, finds the fifty-mile ride an ever-varying source of picturesque beauty . . . the interest being chiefly enhanced by charming views of the Panama Canal. (28)

As the passage suggests, Heald's discourse of the picturesque (the "charming" views) reframes the seemingly dry achievements of an engineering project for touristic consumption. The illustrations of locks, spillways, bridges, cranes, and railway locomotives serve a dual purpose: they show the material embodiment of a progressive narrative of historical development while at the same time underscoring the awesome power of American engineering to reshape the land, not only draining swamps and paving roads but remaking vast landscapes to mingle the waters of two great oceans. The illustrations, however, do not show or even register that which was inundated—the towns and villages that were overwhelmed by the rising waters.

In Heald's narrative, mechanized modernity stands in tension with the awesome force of a tropical fecundity that both inspires wonderment and threatens civilization. In her descriptions and images, climbing vines encrust the ruined towers and bridges of Old Panama, and tropical forest stretches for miles beyond the watery lane of the canal, despite its breadth reduced to a slender thread in a vast fabric of vegetation (fig. E.3). The artist Joseph Pennell, whose celebrated drawings of the isthmus Heald knew well, captured the overwhelming power of massed tropical vegetation: "the richness of it, the riot of it, the variety of it . . . incredible and endless."[14] Heald herself cites the naturalist Berthold Seeman, a key figure in the discourses examined in this book: "In all the muddy places down to the verge of the ocean are impenetrable thickets of mangroves, chiefly rhizophoras and avicennias, which exhale putrid miasmata" (87). Against this tropical biopower, Heald sets the botanical and horticultural work of U.S. scientists and plant lovers, an early inkling of the ecotourism industry that now thrives in the region. At the Institute for Research Work in Tropical America at Gatun Lake, scientists "wrest from nature her inscrutable secrets, to discover the hidden forces that animate the world of the primeval jungle" (34) and realize the economic potential of plants such as the *Stevia Rebaudiana,* first discovered in 1899, that today is marketed to dieters worldwide as a popular sugar substitute. At the Canal Zone's Powell Orchid Garden, an offshoot of the Missouri Botanical Garden in St. Louis, workers cultivate "hundreds of varieties of orchids, all that are native to Panama and many other lands," including the most famous Panamanian flower of all, the *Espiritu Santo,* or Holy Ghost, an orchid that looks as if a small white dove is perched inside the flower (46).[15] It was sent to England in 1826, where it flowered in 1831, and was given its genus and species, *peristeria elata,* after the Greek for dove, by William Jackson Hooker, Regius Professor of Botany at Glasgow and director of Royal Botanic Gardens.[16] Panamanian writers, such as the romantic poet Tomás Martín Feuillet, later celebrated it in patriotic lyrics. By 1857, Feuillet's poem, *La flor del Espíritu Santo,* had already noted the flower's attraction to the forerunner of the ecological tourist, the foreign traveler ("el viajero del Atlántico") who braves the jungle to espy the rare flower.[17] As the orchids suggest, the United States conquered the jungle not only to open the canal but also to tame nature on a smaller scale, housing it in botanical gardens and domesticating it for the tourist. In Heald's day, the tourist could enjoy Panama's natural wonders without ever leaving the protected and Americanized precincts of the Canal Zone.[18]

Yet just beneath the smooth surface of U.S. dominion, barely repressed, lies a darker set of truths—truths that Heald cannot banish even as she strives to present a narrative of untroubled development. That narrative rests, as we have seen, on a binary and temporal divide: before the Canal Commission and after, before the U.S. "invasion" (69) and after. To illustrate the wonders of American engineering, Heald provides several pictures of canal works, such as the famed Gatun Locks, photographed to accentuate their titanic scale (fig. E.4). But to accentuate her contrastive logic of economic

RUINS OF OLD PANAMA.

FIGURE E.3. "Ruins of Old Panama," from Jean Salder Heald, *Picturesque Panama.*

FIGURE E.4. "Gatun Locks," from Jean Salder Heald, *Picturesque Panama*.

development, she sets these images against representations such as "Primitive Thatched House of Native near Monte Lirio" (fig. E.5). Despite enfolding them in the language of the picturesque by describing them as "charming views" (32), these pictures exemplify the allochronic logic that U.S. and British writers applied to Panamanian culture. They reinforce the temporal divide between modernity and primitiveness, development and stagnation, enlisting the reader in the ideological project that consigned Panama's rural people to a fast-vanishing world. Implicit in these contrastive images is nothing less than the disappearance—one might say extinction—of an entire way of life, marked as such by the adjective "primitive."

Evidence of this barely repressed colonial unconscious lies throughout Heald's text and speaks directly to the human cost of Panama's transformation, noted in previous chapters. In Heald's railroad journey from Colón to Panama, meant to illustrate by way of scenic imagery a gradually unfolding story of prosperity and progress, as well as the mobile possibilities of easy travel, she pauses at the Mount Hope cemetery. Here, she notes the "hundreds of brave adventurous dead who paid the price of their lives in building the railroad and digging the canal" (29). Although she moves quickly to an account of the flowering shrubs and "beautifully kept grounds (29), suggesting they befit a "botanical garden rather than a cemetery" (29), this evocation of touristic discourse is forced and unconvincing. Panama's status as a grave for subaltern labor was a widely known element of its history, endlessly rehearsed in travel accounts, poems, and guides. Pennell, the artist previously quoted, is quite clear about the human toll exacted by the canal, both in his prose descriptions and drawings, in which hoards of faceless workmen appear like ants among the colossal works of the construction sites. In one celebrated image, a group of men dangle precariously from a chain, hoisted up by a massive crane, their humanity reduced to simple mass (fig. E.6). Here is Heald's description of these images:

> In them one feels the charm of the vivid pictures of laborers lacquered in sweat, the thrill of achievement and the beauty in the great driving force of muscular arm strains, pulling at chains and the tense force of iron and steel. Here we catch the spontaneity of this force which was put into motion by human ingenuity, and here we see in the making the herculean miracle of the age—the Panama Canal. (42)

Heald reads these depictions of alienated labor through the prism of the capitalist picturesque, seeking to soften the rough edges of a painful modernity by the insistence on "charm," a keyword of the touristic imaginary. The language here, however, uncannily echoes Panamanian writing from roughly the same era,

PHOTO COURTESY OF LEWIS.

PRIMITIVE THATCHED HOUSE OF NATIVE NEAR MONTE LIRIO.

FIGURE E.5. "Primitive Thatched House of Native near Monte Lirio," from Jean Salder Heald, *Picturesque Panama*.

FIGURE E.6. Joseph Pennell, "Gatun Lock, End of the Day." Library of Congress.

which voices deep ambivalence about the American project. Heald's description of the earthworks required to dig the canal notes that "the *gaping wound*
from whence the canal locks drew a part of their firm foundations has not yet
healed, nor has the *deep gash* made for a roadway that encircles [Ancon hill]"
(45; emphasis mine).

This recognition of an injury to the land serves as a rhetorical bridge to
the literary tradition examined in this book and recent concerns about the
ecological costs of a widened Panama Canal and, more problematically, a new,

Chinese-funded canal through Nicaragua. To explore this point briefly in conclusion, I turn here to one of the many poems written in the immediate aftermath of the canal: Benigno Palma's 1916 sonnet, "Al Canal de Panamá." Palma (1882–1918) was a journalist and poet active in Panamanian politics whose literary and political career flourished at the turn of the century and after. He captured his reaction to the opening of the canal in a lyric poem, its small scale a formal contrast to the vast ambitions of the canal itself:

¡Salve! portento del esfuerzo humano;
de Libertad y del Progreso emblema;
de la Ciencia magnífica diadema;
Maravilla del Mundo Americano.

Salve a ti, Canal Interoceano;
del siglo XX encarnación suprema:
alto pregonas el preciado lema
de Orden y Paz, de un Pueblo soberano.

¡Grandiosa realidad! La Patria mía
lleva en su seno la profunda herida
que abrió esa arteria de la mar sombría.
Sus entrañas desgarra; y conmovida
se ofrece generosa al sacrificio,
para exclamar: ¡Pro mundi beneficio![19]

Hail, prodigy of human effort, emblem of freedom and progress, splendid crown of science, marvel of the American world!

Hail to you, Interoceanic Canal, highest incarnation of the Twentieth Century! You proclaim aloud a sovereign people's proud motto of Order and Peace.

Magnificent reality! My country bears in her breast the deep wound that opened this artery of the dark sea. It rends her entrails; and, with emotion, she offers herself nobly to the sacrifice, to exclaim: "For the good of the world!"[20]

The poem associates a foreign-backed engineering project with the advancement of cherished Spanish-American liberal ideals: order, progress, liberty, and scientific rationalism. It praises the canal as the "emblem" and "supreme incarnation" of the twentieth century, at once a "marvel" of the American world and of a modernity tightly bound to it. In these ways, the poem is utterly conventional, even a bit banal. There is little here to separate the work from the discourses of American exceptionalism found in writers such as Heald, nor from patriotic verses composed at the same time in Panama.[21]

The figurative language of Palma's final lines, however, suggests a rupture in this smooth surface—or rather, a scar. In writing "La Patria mía / lleva en su seno la profunda herida / que abrió esa arteria de la mar sombría," (My country carries in her breast the wound that opened this artery of the dark sea), Palma broaches the violence and rending of modernity. "Herida" can mean wound, hurt, or injury. Although "arteria" refers most directly to channel or communication, a metaphor we have seen before, the bodily allusion also carries the hint of a bleeding wound, a gash or rupture—in the land, in the social fabric, and in history itself. In her classic of Latina writing, *Borderlands/La Frontera,* Gloria Anzaldúa uses the same metaphor to remind us that "the U.S.-Mexican border *es una herida abierta* [an open wound], where the Third World grates against the first and bleeds," a place both of contact and colonial violence.[22] Indeed, Palma writes that the wound created by the big ditch is not superficial but "rends the country's entrails" ("sus entrañas desgarra"). As Palma suggests, and a complex literary and cultural tradition affirms, the new world of mobile modernity is double edged, creating on one side unprecedented possibilities for communication and movement, and on the other unhealed wounds that erupt in the fragmented spaces of history, memory, and representation.

NOTES

~

NOTES TO THE INTRODUCTION

1. Nathan Vanderklippe, "China Reveals Plans to Ship Cargo across Canada's Northwest Passage," *Globe and Mail,* April 20, 2016.

2. See Krauss et al., "As Polar Ice Turns to Water," A1, A10–11, and more recently Myers, "U.S. is Playing Catch-up," 1.

3. The Canadian attempt to rename the passage is reported in "The Northwest Passage is Already Canadian," *Globe and Mail,* October 26, 2009.

4. Throughout this book I use Panama (and Panamanian) as convenient shorthand for what is now the Republic of Panama. When the Spanish Empire broke apart in the second decade of the nineteenth century, Panama became part of the Republic of Gran Colombia, which included, among others, present-day Colombia, Ecuador, and Venezuela. In 1831, the union dissolved, and Panama became part of the Republic of Nueva Granada. As is well known, Panama seceded in 1903 with the backing of the United States, which led to its establishment as a nation and the building of the canal.

5. Taylor, *El Dorado,* 25; Grant, *Personal Memoirs,* 2:197. In the pages that follow, I use the admittedly clumsy adjective "U.S." instead of American, as the Spanish "estadounidenses" has no ready English equivalent, and it's important to draw the distinction between the United States and the Americas. Many Panamanian writers from the period, however, use "Americanos" to mark persons from the U.S., as well as the frequently derogatory "Yankees." All translations from the Spanish, as well, are mine unless otherwise noted.

6. The building of the canal has been exhaustively studied. Excellent sources include Mack, *Land Divided*; McCullough, *Path Between the Seas*; Parker, *Panama Fever.* A more critical tradition, which looks beyond celebratory narratives of U.S. technological prowess, includes Castillero Calvo, "Transitismo y dependencia"; Suárez, *Análisis regional y canal de Panamá*; Conniff, *Black Labor on a White Canal*; Lindsay-Poland, *Emperors in the Jungle*; Castro Herrera, *El agua entre los mares*; McGuinness, *Path of Empire*; Greene, *Canal Builders*; and Carse, et al., "Panama Canal Forum." For a recent and innovative ecocritical approach, focusing on the social justice consequences of environmental transformation, see Carse, *Beyond the Big Ditch.*

7. For the Panama expansion, see Muirhead, "Projected Effects." For the Nicaragua venture, see Lee Anderson, "Comandante's Canal"; Meyer and Huete-Pérez, "Conservation: Nicaragua Canal"; and, with a focus on Chinese investment in large-scale infrastructure, Chen and Chen, "China and Latin America." Cardenal is among the many who are opposed to Ortega's plan, argu-

ing that it "gravely threatens" Lake Nicaragua (Salinas, "Poesía contra el Canal"). If completed, the Nicaraguan canal will constitute the largest movement of earth in the planet's history.

8. "Short Cuts across the Globe," 68.

9. Belly, *Percement de l'isthme*, 6.

10. Pim and Seemann, *Dottings on the Roadside*, 59.

11. Castillero Calvo, "Transitismo y dependencia," 182. As he goes on to show, the reluctance of Great Britain to take the lead in building a crossing opened the door for the "nueva potencia," the United States, to step in. As Nicaragua embraces Chinese capital to build its canal, we may now be on the cusp of another imperial transformation.

12. Salvatore, "Imperial Mechanics," *passim*.

13. On these terms, see Gilroy's classic, *Black Atlantic*.

14. "Panama as a Home," 248. There were, however, several Anglo-American schemes for colonization, from Lincoln's ill-fated idea to establish a colony for U.S. blacks in Central America to hazier plans such as that of Berthold Seemann, who imagined that "our millions will pour into this long-neglected region, and found thriving colonies and happy homes along the magnificent mountain-ranges and on the splendid table lands" (Pim and Seemann, *Dottings on the Roadside*, 59).

15. Johnson, *Dictionary, s.v.* "network."

16. See, among many others, Kittler, *Discourse Networks*; Gitelman, *Paper Knowledge*; Siegert, *Relays*; Vismann, *Files*; and Menke, *Telegraphic Realism*.

17. For an analysis of the development of the telegraph system in the Americas, see Britton, *Cables, Crises, and the Press*.

18. Levander and Levine, *Hemispheric American Studies*, 2. In addition to Levander and Levine's collection, see, among many others, Fishkin, "Crossroads of Cultures"; Kaplan, "Violent Belongings"; Levander, "Introduction"; Elliott, "Diversity in the United States and Abroad"; Parrish, "'Hemispheric Turn.'"

19. Although it is outside the scope of my study, the history of French isthmian ventures has been extensively studied. For a crisp overview, see Parker, *Panama Fever*, 49–195.

20. Interest among literary scholars in British representations of Latin America has notably increased, though the focus of this work has largely been on South America and Mexico, and has paid little attention to the isthmus. See, among others, Beardsell, *Europe and Latin America*; Marshall, *English-Speaking Communities*; Aguirre, *Informal Empire*; Ramirez, *British Representations of Latin America*; Matthew Brown, *Informal Empire in Latin America*; Heinowitz, *Spanish America and British Romanticism*; Almeida, *Reimagining the Transatlantic*; and Reeder, "Forms of Informal Empire."

21. For a representative sampling, see Sheller and Urry, "New Mobilities Paradigm"; Cresswell, "Towards a Politics of Mobility"; Richardson, "Borders and Mobilities"; and Greenblatt, *Cultural Mobility*.

22. Sheller, "Aluminum across the Americas," 1.

23. Cresswell, "Towards a Politics of Mobility," 29. See also his "Mobilities II: Still."

24. Kemble, *Panama Route*, 254; LaRosa and Mejia, *United States Discovers Panama*, 1.

25. Muscatine, *Old San Francisco*, 71.

26. Maurer and Yu, *Big Ditch*, 37.

27. Otis, *Panama Railroad*, 49.

28. Chandler and Potash, *Gold, Silk, Pioneers and Mail*, 15.

29. Otis, *Panama Railroad*, 49. As I show in chapter 2, we must add the humble letter to the list of modern communications examined by mobilities research: "the telegraph, fax, telephone, mobile phone, as well as many-to-many communications effected through networked and increasingly embedded computers." See Sheller and Urry, "New Mobilities Paradigm," 212.

30. Pim and Seemann, *Dottings on the Roadside*, 14.

31. Qtd. in Niemeier, *Panama Story*, 25.

32. Otis, *Panama Railroad*, 15.

33. Hobsbawm, *Industry and Empire*, 88. For further analysis of timetables and schedules see Kern, *Culture of Time and Space*, 12–13; Ferguson, *Victorian Time*; Zerubavel, "Timetables and Scheduling, 48–49; idem, *Hidden Rhythms*; and the classic study of railroad time, Schivelbusch, *Railway Journey*, 33–45.

34. On the "sedentarist metaphysics" of place-bound meaning, see Cresswell, "Mobilities III," 712–21.

35. For a discussion of "non-place" see Marc Augé, who argues, with respect to modernity, that "non-places are the real measure of our time," and could be quantified by "totaling all the air, rail and motorway routes, the mobile cabins called 'means of transport' (aircraft, trains and road vehicles), the airports and railway stations . . . and finally the complex skein of cable and wireless networks" (*Non-Places*, 79).

36. David Harvey, *Justice, Nature, and the Geography of Difference*, 296.

37. Castillero Calvo, "Transitismo y dependencia," 184. ("Se desconoce sin embargo, qué grado de participación tuvo la vieja élite comerciante panameña en estos negocios").

38. Fabian, *Time and the Other*; McClintock, *Imperial Leather*.

39. McClintock, *Imperial Leather*, 30.

40. John Leary discusses the concept of development in U.S./Latin American affairs in *Cultural History of Underdevelopment*.

41. "Our Phantom Ship," 517. Charles Dickens and Wilkie Collins employ similar language in "The Perils of Certain English Prisoners" (1857).

42. Conrad, *Heart of Darkness*, 32–37.

43. Fabian, *Time and the Other*, 144.

44. As David Brading makes clear, the larger context for this thinking lies in a Protestant version of history with large implications for how Anglo-Americans viewed Spanish America. In this historical prism, "political freedom and commercial expansion proceeded together, flowering first in Holland and England, only then to find a lasting home in the United States." Such histories dismiss the "absolute monarchies of Spain and France, and still more the Catholic Church, as obstacles to progress, mere dwindling remnants of feudalism and superstition which were doomed to defeat when confronted with the rational, hardy virtue of northern Protestants" (*First America*, 631).

45. Duffy, *Speed Handbook*, 1, 5, 10–11. Filip Vostal examines recent developments in speed theory, arguing that speed "has become significant, indeed central, as a social scientific category and focus of attention today ("Thematizing Speed," 95).

46. Schivelbusch, *Railway Journey*, chs. 7–9; Grossman, *Charles Dickens's Networks*, 11. Michael Freeman writes that "to travel at rates of thirty miles an hour was sensational. Travelling in a carriage that was open to the air intensified the shock and exhilaration, as did passing through deep cuttings or tunnels" (*Railways and the Victorian Imagination*, 13). For further discussion, see ibid., 57–91; Schivelbusch, *Railway Journey*; Bagwell, *Transport Revolution from 1770*, 88–134; Turnock, *Railways in the British Isles*; Simmons, *Victorian Railway*; and Byerly, *Are We There Yet?*, 143–67. On the specific history of railways in Panama, see Castillero Reyes, *El ferrocarril de Panamá*.

47. Oliphant, *Patriots and Filibusters*, 215.

48. Duffy, *Speed Handbook*, 1.

49. David Harvey, *Condition of Postmodernity*, 240.

50. See "Short Cuts across the Globe"; "Short Cut to California"; "Our Phantom Ship"; "Five Travellers"; and "Crossing the Isthmus of Panama."

51. "Short Cuts across the Globe," 67.

52. Fabens, *Story of Life on the Isthmus*, 13.

53. Pim, *Gate of the Pacific*, 122.

54. "Short Cuts across the Globe," 65; Otis, *Panama Railroad*, 26.

55. "Panama to Chagres," 250.

56. Marryat, *Mountains and Molehills*, 18.

57. Seacole, *Wonderful Adventures*, 41.
58. Otis, *Panama Railroad*, 26–27.
59. Fabens, *Life on the Isthmus*, 146.
60. Taylor, *El Dorado*, 12.
61. Gisborne, *Isthmus of Darien*, 103–4.
62. Seacole, *Wonderful Adventures*, 14.
63. Lasso, "From Citizens to 'Natives,'" 41. Castillero Calvo argues convincingly that subsequent social unrest on the isthmus was directly related to the collapse of the local economy, when the railroad threw out of work the Chagres boatmen ("boteros o chateros") who were engaged in the diverse "facetas del tránsito" ("Transitismo y dependencia," 185). See also McGuinness, *Path of Empire*, 54–64.
64. See Stocking, "What's in a Name?" and, more expansively, Brantlinger, *Dark Vanishings*.
65. Bollaert, "Observations," 85; 77–78. For a list of Bollaert's writings on ethnology, see "Biographical Sketch."
66. Pim and Seemann, *Dottings on the Roadside*, 59.
67. "Iron Horse," 1. Subsequent citations are from this column.
68. Stoler, "Colonial Archives," 93–94.
69. Most famously in Gayatri Spivak's 1983 essay, which is reprinted along with commentary from other scholars, in Morris, *Can the Sublatern Speak?*
70. Szok, "*La Última gaviota*," 19; Watson, *Politics of Race*, 1–11; Mignolo, *Idea of Latin America*, 77–81; McGuiness, "Searching." The idea of a Hanseatic state, with trade and international commerce at its center, was codified in the 1826 *Acta hanseática*. See Castillero Calvo, "El movimiento anseática."
71. Szok, *Wolf Tracks*, 29.
72. Arosemena, "Estado económico del Istmo," 12.
73. Arosemena, *Exámen*, 3–9.
74. Ibid., 7. See also the 1844 treatise by Dénain, *Ensayo sobre los intereses*.
75. Burns, *Poverty of Progress*, 5.
76. Arosemena, "¡¡¡Alerta Istmeños!!!," 78.
77. Idem, *Estado Federal*, 98–99.
78. Idem, "Contra la expansión colonialista," 158–59.
79. Ibid., 158.
80. Idem, "La cuestión Americana," 249.
81. Ibid., 250.
82. Ibid., 251. Compare similar anti-imperialist comments of the Chilean writer Francisco Bilbao (1823–65), who wrote in his *Iniciativa de la América* (1856): "We are already witnessing fragments of America falling into the Saxon jaws of the magnetizing boa constrictor that is unrolling its tortuous coils. Yesterday it was Texas, then the north of Mexico, and then the Pacific that offered their submission to a new master" (qtd. in Mignolo, *Idea of Latin America*, 69).
83. Steven C. Ropp has argued that this tension forged a peculiar alliance: "Separated from the Hispanicized blacks by race and class, and separated even further from the new wave of Antillean blacks, the Panamanian upper class looked to the canal-building powers as countervailing forces in the domestic arena. . . . Commercial relations, administrative ties through the transit companies, common racial and class characteristics—all supported the formation of a tacit internal-external 'alliance'" (*Panamanian Politics*, 10).
84. The definitive account is McGuinness, *Path of Empire*, but see also Daley, "Watermelon Riot"; Castillero Calvo, "Un antecedente de la 'Tajada de Sandía'"; and Soler, *Panamá en el Mundo Americano*.
85. In the period covered in this book, the United States sent military forces to Panama to quell unrest and impose order several times, in periods lasting from one day to several weeks: 1860, Panama City; 1873, Panama; 1885, Colón and Panama City; 1895, Bocas del Toro; 1901, Panama City; November 1903 during Panamanian independence.

86. For analyses of the historical and philosophical formation of the term "Latin America," with specific reference to its racial implications, see Mignolo, *Idea of Latin America*; McGuiness, "Searching"; and more recently, Gobat, "Invention of Latin America." As Mignolo puts it succinctly, "The concept of 'Latinidad' . . . would ultimately rank [Latin Americans] below Anglo-Americans and . . . erase and demote the identities of Indians and Afro-South Americans" (*Idea of Latin America*, xv).

87. Martinez-Alier, *Marriage, Class and Colour*, 30–33. As Bradford Burns writes, Latin American elites "felt embattled. They feared the barbaric masses might engulf them and drown their cherished civilization" (*Poverty of Progress*, 23). See also Andrews, *Afro-Latin America, 1800–2000*, ch. 1–3, and Gudmundson and Wolfe, *Blacks and Blackness in Central America*, passim.

88. Arosemena, "La cuestión Americana," 256–57.

89. "Not by chance, then, did Arosemena begin to use the term 'Latin America' precisely when nonwhites were challenging the power of his class under the banner of democracy. To tame popular wrath against white elites like himself, Arosemena maintained that democratic development had to be led by the Latin race—a belief succinctly expressed in his use of the term 'Latin-American democracy'" (Gobat, "Invention of Latin America," 1363).

90. Miró, *Tomás Martín Feuillet*, 9–40.

91. Gruesz, *Ambassadors of Culture*, 168; Miró, *Tomás Martín Feuillet*, 29.

92. On the development of anti-imperialist thought in the press, see Miró, *La imprenta*, 82–90.

93. Feuillet, "Al ciudadano," in Miró, *Tomás Martín Feuillet*, 79.

94. Feuillet, "A un amigo," in Miró, *Tomás Martín Feuillet*, 90–92. McGuinness, citing from a secondary source, mistakenly identifies the poem as "How Much?" ("¿Cuánto tiene?") (*Path of Empire*, 79).

95. Mignolo, *Idea of Latin America*, 74.

96. On the use of dialect as a mode of stereotyping in Colombian literature, see Portillo, "Heterogeneidad." Thanks to Professor Victor Figueroa for this reference.

NOTES TO CHAPTER 1

1. Dimock, *Government-Operated Enterprises*, 26; Maurer and Yu, *Big Ditch*, 46–47.

2. Ralph Lee Woodward Jr. for example, attributes Belize's long economic decline to the railway's 1855 completion, which made it more profitable for Guatemala to route its commerce through Pacific ports, rather than through Belize, as formerly, with the greatest change occurring between 1855 and 1860 (*Rafael Carrera*, 308, 357–60). For a brief summary of Panama's modernization in response to the railroad, see Pérez-Venero, *Before the Five Frontiers*, 35–42.

3. Maurer and Yu, *Big Ditch*, 41–44. In 1857, the Panamanian historian Joaquin Posada Gutiérrez reckoned that thousands came from near and far to work on the railroad: "millares de hombres de los Estados Unidos, de Europa, de Chile, del Perú, de Haití, de Jamaica, de Curazao, de todas estas provincias litorales, de todas partes" (qtd. in Castillero Reyes's landmark study, *El ferrocarril de Panamá*, 11). The evidence for Africa comes from a recently discovered manuscript, which points to immigrant labor from African diasporic Islam. See Bayoumi, "Moving Beliefs."

4. Langley, *Americas*, 53. The arrival of immigrant labor also had lasting cultural repercussions on national formation and the politics of race. The desire among Panamanian elites to cultivate a Panamanian identity based on *hispanidad* entailed both anti-imperialism and racial discrimination against Panama's black immigrants-become-citizens (Watson, "Poetic Negrism").

5. Castillero Calvo, "Transitismo y dependencia," 184. For additional analysis of the railroad's economic consequences, see also his "Ciclos y coyunturas."

6. Pérez-Venero, *Before the Five Frontiers*, 91.

7. Pim, *Gate of the Pacific*, 208.

8. Qtd. in Castillero Reyes, *El Ferrocarril de Panamá*, 11–12.

9. Seacole, *Wonderful Adventures*, 14.

10. Ibid, 72–73. Seacole's "resistance to inhospitable Americans is indebted," as Goudie points out, to "black masculine maroon figures found across Panama whose acts of defiance she strategically recounts in the context of her own narrative ("New Regionalisms," 319).

11. McGuinness, *Path of Empire*, 22.

12. Pim, *Gate of the Pacific*, 206. McGuinness puts it this way: "As the railroad made its conflicted way across the isthmus, it captured more and more of the international traffic that crossed Panama, with the result that increasing numbers of boatmen, muleteers, and porters were driven out of their trades" (*Path of Empire*, 78).

13. For the history of this force, which was led by Ran Runnels, see Schott, *Rails across Panama*, 85–94.

14. On the "prosthetic imagination" in U.S. culture, see Bill Brown, "Science Fiction," 129–63, and Landsberg, *Prosthetic Memory*.

15. Ricardo D. Salvatore has argued that the construction of Latin America "as a territory for the projection of U.S. capital, expertise, dreams, and power required the channeling of massive energies into the production of images and texts" ("Enterprise of Knowledge," 71).

16. Von Hagen, *Maya Explorer*, 197.

17. For the history of Creole research on the Maya, see Chinchilla Mazariegos, "Archaeology and Nationalism."

18. Moro, *Observations*, 1.

19. Having time on his hands, Napoleon III penned his treatise in prison: "The more closely the body is confined, so much the more is the mind disposed to wander in unbounded space, and to canvas the feasibility of projects which it would scarcely be at leisure to entertain in a more active existence" (Bonaparte, *Canal of Nicaragua*, i). For an overview of these projects, see DuVal, *Cadiz to Cathay*, and McCullough, *Path Between the Seas*, 1–44.

20. Bolívar, *El Libertador*, 26. Bolivar later commissioned J. A. Lloyd to survey the prospects for a communication, the results of which were published in 1831 by Britain's newly established Royal Geographical Society. See Lloyd, "Notes Respecting the Isthmus."

21. McCullough erroneously sweeps aside Stephens's achievement: "Stephens had no more business issuing pronouncements on the feasibility of a Nicaragua canal from the little he had seen than had the engineer Horatio Allen from the comforts of his Manhattan office" (*Path Between the Seas*, 32).

22. Major works on the panorama include Altick, *Shows of London*; Oettermann, *Panorama*; Hyde, *Panoramania!*; Comment, *Painted Panorama*; and Galassi, *Before Photography*. For Catherwood's panorama of Jerusalem specifically, see John Davis, *Landscape of Belief*, 56–65; and Von Hagen, *Frederick Catherwood*, 23–37.

23. For Stephens's charge from Aaron Vail, Acting Secretary of State, see Manning, *Diplomatic Correspondence of the United States*, 3:22–24.

24. Pratt, *Imperial Eyes*, 59. For this trope in Robert Schomburgk's South American ventures, see Burnett, *Masters of All They Surveyed*.

25. Stephens, *Incidents of Travel in Central America, Chiapas, and Yucatan*. Further references given parenthetically.

26. In the 1830s, for example, U.S. politicians repeatedly fretted about British naval and commercial dominance in the hemisphere, imagining a ring of hostile, British-influenced territory formed by Canada, Oregon, California, Texas, and Cuba. See Haynes, "Anglophobia," 129.

27. For a discussion of belatedness in imperial travel, focused on Orientalist representation, see Behdad, *Belated Travelers*. It is important to note here, as well, the Honduran laws that governed the appropriation of monuments, which cast further doubt on Stephens's claims. See Rubín de la Borbolla and Rivas, *Honduras: Monumentos históricos*, 16, 27; and Agurcia Fasquelle, "La depredación del patrimonio."

28. Among others, see Bruce Harvey, *American Geographics*; and Greenberg, *Manifest Manhood*.

29. For discussions of nineteenth-century plans for a canal across Nicaragua, see Folkman, *Nicaragua Route*; Burns, *Patriarch and Folk*; and Herrera C., *Bongos*. For the larger context of U.S. intervention in Nicaragua, the best discussion is Gobat, *Confronting the American Dream*.

30. See Stephens to Forsyth, April 6, 1840, in Manning, *Diplomatic Correspondence*, 3:158–59, in which he informs the secretary of state that he has visited San Juan del Sur on his own initiative. His letter of August 17, 1840, written on his return to New York, summarizes his diplomatic work on behalf of the United States (ibid., 3:159–61).

31. On the Chinese workers see, among others, Chen P., *Comó, cuando, y por qué*; Chong Ruiz, *Los chinos*; Chou, *Los chinos*; and Cohen, "Chinese of the Panama Railroad." On the larger context of foreign labor in Panama see: Lewis, *West Indian in Panama*; Newton, *Silver Men*; Conniff, *Black Labor on a White Canal*; Frederick, *"Colón Man a Come*; and Parker, *Panama Fever*, 1–36.

32. On the European legal traditions behind this view, see Berkhofer, *White Man's Indian*, 120–21, and Pratt, *Imperial Eyes*, 61.

33. Greenberg, *Manifest Manhood*, 76; Horsman, *Race and Manifest Destiny*, 210–15.

34. Baily, *Central America*.

35. Later, advocates for a U.S.-controlled canal represented the Clayton-Bulwer Treaty as a mistake. In December 1857, Palmerston expressed his hope that the treaty would oppose "a barrier" to U.S. southward advance, "stopping the Yankees out of Central America." Van Alstyne, "Anglo-American Relations," 500. For Palmerston's later concession to *realpolitik*, see Bourne, "Clayton-Bulwer Treaty," 287–91.

36. Read, *Hand of God in History*, 136, 148, 142.

37. Bedell and Winston, "Report," 411.

38. *Papers of Henry Clay*, 263.

39. Martineau et al., *History of the Peace*, 2:406.

40. See Bancroft's chapter on interoceanic communication, in *History of Central America*, 8:688–754. See also Mack, *Land Divided*, 171–87.

41. O'Sullivan, "Annexation."

42. Panama Railroad Company, *Memorial of the Panama Rail-Road*, 24. This document prints both of Stephens' memorials: December 11, 1848 and December 10, 1849, though in reverse order. Further references given parenthetically.

43. Noted in *Journal of the House of Representatives*, 77–78.

44. The classic account is Merk, *Oregon Question*.

45. For a valuable reading of this treaty, focusing on its internal contradictions, see Mattox, "Claiming Panama," 117–47.

46. See Daley, "Watermelon Riot," and McGuinness, *Path of Empire*, 123–51.

47. Pérez-Venero, *Before the Five Frontiers*, 56.

48. See Liot, *Panama, Nicaragua and Tehuantepec*, and Bushell, *Royal Mail*, 86.

49. Alba C., *Cronología de los gobernantes*, 169; Russel, *Improvement of Communication*, 56.

50. Kemble, *Panama Route*, 25.

51. Weeks, *New Cambridge History of American Foreign Relations*, 203.

52. For the classic history of the spread of gold rush news, see Bieber, "California Gold Mania." The primary materials that supported this research are preserved in the Ralph P. Bieber collection in the Huntington Library, San Marino. For a more recent overview see Rohrbough, *Days of Gold*, ch. 2.

53. Bieber, "California Gold Mania," 12–15.

54. Stillson, *Spreading the Word*, 5.

55. Hughes, *Letter in Answer to the Hon. John M. Clayton*, 4.

56. Qtd. in Missal, *Seaway to the Future*, 41.

57. In October 1849, Stephens would lament that "instead of rolling in California gold, I am stuck in Panama mud" (Stephens, Letter to Blair, Huntington Library).

58. King's report to the Committee on Naval Affairs, January 16, 1849, qtd. from Hunt, "Proposed Railroad," 272. The cartographer and naval officer Matthew Maury put it this way: "The Panama improvement would bring us the travel from countries inhabited by millions, and send it through the length and breadth of the land, dispensing national, sectional, and particular benefits all the way" ("Maury's Estimate," 158).

59. Pim, *Gate of the Pacific*, 4–5.

60. Richards, *Imperial Archive*, 1.

61. On the power of simultaneity in forging "imagined communities" of national belonging, see the classic account in Benedict Anderson, *Imagined Communities*, 22–36, and Grossman's *Charles's Dickens Networks*, 79–181, which updates the concept for the Victorian novel.

62. Ibid. Similar arguments were later made for the overland transcontinental railroad, completed in 1867 (Deverell, *Railroad Crossing*, ch. 1).

63. *Oxford English Dictionary*, s.v. "communication," accessed March 18, 2016. http://www.oed .com.proxy.lib.wayne.edu/view/Entry/37309?redirectedFrom=communication#eid.

64. See, among others, Aparicio and Chávez-Silverman, *Tropicalizations*; and Driver and Martins, *Tropical Visions in an Age of Empire*.

65. Baucom, *Out of Place*, 84.

NOTES TO CHAPTER 2

1. Asa Briggs estimates that during the mid-nineteenth century British writers composed over two hundred travel volumes about the United States ("Trollope the Traveler," 89–115; 90). For a nuanced account of Trollope's work on North America, see Claybaugh, "Trollope and America."

2. Trollope, *West Indies*, 11. Further citations are given parenthetically.

3. Qtd. in Daunton, *Royal Mail*, 146.

4. "Instructions issued to Anthony Trollope, Esq. for his Guidance in the Survey of the Post-Offices in the West Indies," November 16, 1858, Post Office Records, "Instructions to Packet Agents, Colonial Administrators, &c.," Post 44/12, 95–101, British Postal Museum and Archive, London.

5. Trollope, *Autobiography*, 127–28.

6. Lambert, et al., "Currents," 486. Foucault concluded his 1967 lecture, "Of Other Spaces," by arguing that "the boat has not only been for our civilization, from the sixteenth century until the present, the great instrument of economic development . . . but has been simultaneously the greatest reserve of the imagination. The ship is the heterotopia *par excellence*" (27).

7. It is doubtful Trollope's motive was secrecy, for his employment at the Post Office was widely known. Trollope also hinted about mail delivery in the text: "My own opinion is that Jamaica should be the head-quarters of these packets; but the question is one which will not probably be interesting to the reader of these pages" (*West Indies*, 225). E. S. Dallas's *Times* review of *West Indies and the Spanish Main* also refers openly to the postal mission. For historical overviews of Trollope's postal work, see Super, *Trollope*, 38–44, and N. John Hall, *Trollope*, 171–82. For the correspondence, see Trollope, *Letters*, 1:78–88.

8. Gikandi, *Maps*, 92–94, 96, 109.

9. Catherine Hall, *Civilising Subjects*, 212. Behind Gikandi and Hall lies a tradition of postcolonial Caribbean writing. See Derek Walcott: "So a hole in their parchment opens, and suddenly, in a vast / dereliction of sunlight, there's that island known / to the traveller Trollope, and the fellow traveler Froude, / for making nothing. Not even a people" (*Midsummer*, 11). See also the infamous passage from Froude that serves as the epigraph to Naipaul's *Middle Passage*. For

other relevant studies, see Bury, "Trollope"; Brandenstein, "Representations"; and Dickerson, *Dark Victorians*.

10. Torres-Saillant, *Intellectual*, 84–85.

11. Morse, *Reforming Trollope*, 114.

12. Said, *Culture and Imperialism*, 11; emphasis in original.

13. Mobilities research, though cognizant of paper-based communication, stresses electronic forms: "The concept embraces one-to-one communications such as *the telegraph, fax, telephone, mobile phone, as well as many-to-many communications effected through networked and increasingly embedded computers*" (Sheller and Urry, "New Mobilities Paradigm," 212; emphasis mine).

14. Joyce, *State of Freedom*, 20. A sophisticated analysis of the interplay between these imperatives and British literary culture is Grossman's *Charles Dickens's Networks*.

15. For a sense of how perilous but also important the fate of a letter could be at this time, see "History of a Letter," which follows a letter along its path of delivery from faraway sender, to steamship, to final delivery in a California post office.

16. Daunton, *Royal Mail*, 146.

17. Ibid., 151.

18. The uncertainty is captured nicely in Elizabeth Gaskell's 1853 novel, *Cranford,* where a letter to India is imagined to be "tossed about on the sea, and stained with sea-waves perhaps. . . . The little piece of paper, but an hour ago so familiar and commonplace, had set out on its race to the strange wild countries beyond the Ganges!" (153). I am grateful to Kevin Sigerman of Rutgers University for this reference.

19. Headrick, *Tools of Empire*, 130. In addition to Daunton, for studies of the British post and communication see Bushell, *Royal Mail*; Howard Robinson, *Britain's Post Office*; Campbell-Smith, *Masters of the Post*; Headrick, *When Information Came of Age*; Rotunno, *Postal Plots*; and Kate Thomas, *Postal Pleasures*.

20. Daunton, *Royal Mail*, 23.

21. Super, *Trollope*, 21.

22. Ibid.

23. Zieger, "Affect and Logistics," 227.

24. Super, *Trollope*, 36.

25. British Postal Museum and Archive, "Instructions issued to Anthony Trollope," 98–99.

26. For another example of his meticulous calculations of time and distance, see his eight-page report of September 6, 1859, written at the conclusion of his journey back in London, in which he sets forth an argument for making Jamaica, not St. Thomas, the central point for mail distribution. The report, with detailed accountings of the speed of ships, with and against the prevailing winds, reads like a legal brief (British Postal Archive, Post 29/93). See also the twenty-two-page report of July 16, 1859 (British Postal Archive, Post 29/93).

27. See Aguirre, *Informal Empire*.

28. Trollope to Rowland Hill, May 8, 1859, from Panama, Post 29/103, British Postal Archive. Trollope's letter of July 25, 1859, Post 29/103, British Postal Archive, refers to negotiations with Totten to secure an annual charge for mail to Australia.

29. Arosemena, "Cuestión Americana," 255. Celestino Araúz argues that U.S. and British consulates encouraged their countrymen not to pay passenger taxes, which led to Panama's further economic prostration. "Justo Arosemena" 47–52. See also Celestino Araúz and Gelós P. Pizzurno, *El Panamá Colombiano*, 169–73.

30. MacQueen, *General Plan*, 1. MacQueen's charts include one just of the West Indies and Central America and a larger one, drawn by John Arrowsmith, of the entire globe, setting forth "all the routes of both steamers and sailing-packets, to every quarter of the world that has been adverted to" (xi).

31. Bushell, *Royal Mail*, 86.

32. Liot, *Panama, Nicaragua and Tehuantepec.*

33. "Short Cuts across the Globe," *Household Words*, April 13, 1850, 66.

34. Bidwell, *Isthmus of Panamá*, 28.

35. *Correspondence and Other Papers*, "Copy of Despatch from Governor Douglas to the Right Hon. Sir E. B. Lytton, Nov. 5, 1858," 298. Indeed, as Bushell argues, Canada might have had a much longer western coastline had trade between the west coast and Europe not been hampered by the lack of a transisthmian route (*Royal Mail*, 87).

36. MacQueen, *General Plan*, 85. See also Bidwell, cited above, on the importance of the isthmian passage to Britain's connection with British Columbia: "Panamá has been particularly brought under the notice of England and English travellers of late by the establishment of the colony of British Columbia, and the reports of the recent gold discoveries therein. During the year 1862 particularly, hardly a steamer arrived at the Atlantic port of the Isthmus that did not bring a hundred or two of stout young Englishmen full of life and energy, bound for the new colony" (305).

37. Ibid., 100.

38. Jones, among others, points out that Trollope's summary of the blacks' intellectual capacities echoed Carlyle ("Trollope," 192). According to G. H. Lewes, "Carlyle had read and *agreed* with the West Indian book, and the two got along very well together" (N. John Hall, *Trollope*, 274). For more general treatments of Carlyle and Trollope, see apRoberts, "Carlyle and Trollope"; N. John Hall, "Trollope and Carlyle;" and Goveia, *Study*. For a broader discussion of Trollope and race, with particular reference to his travel writing, see Buzard, "Portable Boundaries."

39. Froude, *English in the West Indies*, 42–43.

40. Pim and Seemann, *Dottings on the Roadside*, 220–21.

41. On coolie labor, see Lai, *Indentured Labor*, and Jung, *Coolies and Cane*.

42. Goodlad, "Trollopian 'Foreign Policy,'" 445, treated at greater length in her *Victorian Geopolitical Aesthetic*.

43. For an influential critique of Trollope's ideas, see Eric Williams, *British Historians*, 89–97.

44. Foner gives an excellent overview of the U.S./Cuban relationship in *History of Cuba*. Volume 2 deals with the period discussed here. For a recent survey of British periodical coverage of Cuba in the period discussed here, see Pionke, "Excavating Victorian Cuba."

45. Qtd. in Foner, *History of Cuba*, 1:145.

46. The Ostend report of October 18, 1854, originally a dispatch from Buchanan to U.S. Secretary of State William Marcy, is reprinted in Buchanan, *Works*, 9:260–66.

47. *Correspondence Respecting American*, Earl of Malmesbury to Lord Lyons, May 6, 1859, 15:702.

48. Van Alstyne, "British Diplomacy"; idem, "Central American Policy"; and Naylor, "British Role in Central America."

49. Bidwell, *Isthmus of Panamá*, 307; emphasis in original.

50. Norton to Ephraim G. Squier, 2 November 1851, Ephraim George Squier Papers, Library of Congress.

51. Woodward, *Rafael Carrera*, 231.

52. Arosemena, *Panamá y Nuestra América*, 157.

53. MacQueen, *General Plan*, 3.

54. Pim, *Gate of the Pacific*, 6, 287; my emphasis.

55. For other flashpoints, see Rippy, *Latin America*, 24–103, and Leonard, "'Keeping the Europeans Out.'"

56. Hugh Thomas, "Cuba," 288; Pérez, *Cuba*, 79.

57. "Short Cuts Across the Globe," 66.

58. Otis, *Panama Railroad*, 22. A 1918 Canal Zone public relations bulletin described the typical Panamaian worker as "energetic and faithful to a marked degree," but claimed that "the ease with which he can obtain a living in a country so rich as Panama, makes it unnecessary for him to do work that he does not choose to do," qtd. in Frenkel, "Geographical Representations," 88.

59. Darwin, *Journal*, 390.

60. On the theme of imperial lament, see Schmitt, *Darwin*, 95.

61. McGuinness, *Path of Empire*, 86.

62. The phrase comes in a somewhat different form from Carlyle's *History of Friedrich II*, 1:23–24. Paul Giles argues that views such as Trollope's, discredited as they are today, were "abstract rationalizations that commanded fervent loyalties in their own time" (*Antipodean America*, 216).

63. All quotations from Seacole, *Wonderful Adventures*, 44–45.

64. See McGuinness, *Path of Empire*, 84–122; and Lasso, "From Citizens to 'Natives,'" 39–41.

65. Trollope, "Journey to Panama," 189. For other stories inspired by the journey, see "Miss Sarah Jack, of Spanish Town, Jamaica," and "Returning Home," collected in Trollope, *Complete Short Stories*.

66. For a discussion of railway junctions as "nonspaces," see Byerly, *Are We There Yet?*, 187–90.

NOTES TO CHAPTER 3

1. Clippings from *Panama Star*, March 16, 1875, and May 1, 1875, Muybridge Scrapbook, Muybridge Collection, Kingston Museum. Muybridge wrote in his prospectus that "the object of the Company in having these views executed, was to stimulate commercial intercourse, by exhibiting to the Merchant and the Capitalist in a convenient and popular manner the ports, and facilities of commerce of a country which presents such vast fields of profitable enterprize; and the principal industries of a people with whom until recently we have had comparatively little intercourse. And at the same time to gratify the tourist and lovers of the picturesque with a glimpse of the wonderfully beautiful scenes that have hitherto remained unexplored" (qtd. in Mozley, *Eadweard Muybridge*, 55).

2. Tracy Robinson, *Panama*, 51.

3. Haas, *Muybridge*, 81. For a detailed account of the murder and trial, see ibid., 63–78, and Braun, *Eadweard Muybridge*, 88–113. Muybridge's critics have largely accepted that the Panama journey belongs in a biographical or psychological context. The Corcoran Gallery catalogue, for example, maintains that "Muybridge hoped that by peering into [Central America's] deep past he would be able to transcend his own recent suffering" (Brookman, *Helios*, 71).

4. Since Haas's pioneering work, scholarship on Muybridge has grown apace and is too large to summarize here. His work for Leland Stanford is well covered in Mozley, *Eadweard Muybridge*. Brookman, *Helios*, is comprehensive, and contains a particularly good bibliography. Other general studies include Braun, *Eadweard Muybridge*; Solnit, *River of Shadows*; Clegg, *Man Who Stopped Time*; Hendricks, *Eadweard Muybridge*. Byron Wolfe's forthcoming *Phantom Skies* will examine Muybridge's photographs through the context of Wolfe's own photographic re-creations. The Guatemala portion of the journey is covered particularly well by Bradford Burns, who argues that the steamship company hoped to stimulate interest in that country's nascent coffee industry, whose shipment it also controlled (*Eadweard Muybridge in Guatemala*, 21). As Burns notes, the coffee business boomed in this period, with imports to the United States alone rising from 82,243 tons in 1851 to 166,463 tons in 1880 (92). The definitive study remains Cambranes, *Café y campesinos*. For a comparison of Muybridge's Guatemalan images to other pictorial works of the time, see Manthorne, "Plantation Pictures."

5. The Panama Railroad Company erected telegraph wires in 1855 to send messages from coast to coast, and in 1870 the West India and Panama Telegraph Company commenced laying a transoceanic cable.

6. *Brunel's Mammoth Ship*.

7. See Willumson, *Iron Muse*, ch. 1.

8. Haas, *Muybridge*, 14, 16.

9. The Alaskan pictures are listed in *Catalogue of Photographic Views,* 39–40.

10. For a study of the larger encounter, and Muybridge's role in it, see Gmelch, *Tlingit Encounter,* esp. 22–24 and 149–50.

11. Prospectus, May 1872, in Muybridge Scrapbook, Muybridge Collection, Kingston Museum.

12. Qtd. in Hendricks, *Eadweard Muybridge,* 25.

13. This process involved "using a tripod-mounted camera, composing the scene through the lens while hidden underneath a black cloth, then emerging to prepare the glass plate with chemicals, then disappearing again under the cloth to expose the image" (Gmelch, *Tlingit Encounter,* 149). Several images, as Gmelch points out, show evidence of the Tlingit "fully cooperating with the camera" (150).

14. As Jonathan Crary notes, "the stereoscope discloses a fundamentally disunited and aggregate field of disjunct elements" (*Techniques,* 125).

15. I have discovered the Helios signature in several though not all of the Alaskan landscapes. It is always quite cleverly hidden—written on rocks, among shrubbery, on the sloping roofs of buildings. Muybridge appears to have experimented widely with this practice in the early period of his career, when he was establishing his artistic identity. Although Muybridge took steps to protect his work by filing for copyright, Haas maintains that some of the photographs were sold without mention of Muybridge's name (*Muybridge,* 14).

16. Qtd. in Solnit, *River of Shadows,* 87.

17. Wolfe's archival research has resulted in the identification of eleven of Muybridge's volumes. Wolfe maintains an excellent website at www.byronwolfe.com/muybridge.

18. Muybridge also issued the Guatemala photographs in an affordable stereograph format.

19. Crary, *Techniques,* 124–29. Crary argues that "the most pervasive means of producing 'realistic' effects in mass visual culture, such as the stereoscope, were in fact based on a radical abstraction and reconstruction of optical experience, thus demanding a reconsideration of what 'realism' means in the nineteenth century" (9).

20. Poole, *Vision,* 7.

21. Rosenblum, *World History of Photography,* 35.

22. Selfridge, *Reports of Explorations and Surveys.*

23. Study of O'Sullivan's survey work is enjoying a renaissance. See *Framing the West*; and Keith Davis and Jane Aspinwall, *Timothy H. O'Sullivan.* In 1871, John Moran traced O'Sullivan's footprints, producing a number of stereograph views of the isthmus, a selection of which is preserved at the George Eastman House Museum in Rochester, NY.

24. Some of the difficulties Darien explorers faced can be grasped in the following description: "No matter whether at work in the hills or in the swamps or on the open river, there are hardships all around. To follow a trail avoiding rivers is to suffer thirst; to follow one crossing streams is to pass, while overheated, into the cool waters of the river; if in the swamps, freedom is circumscribed for days by the limits of a small flat-boat; and if on the open river pursuing a canoe journey, sitting tailor-fashion on the bottom of the canoe in an inch or more water, for hours, may at least be regarded as monotonous. . . . It will be readily conceded that Darien placed a heavy tax upon those who struggled to learn her secrets" (Sullivan, *Report of Historical and Technical Information,* 81). For more on the Darien expedition, see Horan, *Timothy O'Sullivan,* 215–22.

25. *Views on the Isthmus.*

26. The dedication of the church is mentioned in "Panama Railroad," 366.

27. The Spanish photographer Rafael Castro y Ordoñez produced approximately two dozen photographs of Panama while serving on the *Comisión Científica del Pacífico,* 1862–66. See Miller, *For Science and National Glory*; López-Ocón, "La comisión científica del Pacífico"; and the brief entry on Castro y Ordoñez in Palmquist and Kailbourn, *Pioneer Photographers of the Far West,* 161–62. The images themselves are in the photographic archives of the Museo Nacional de Ciencias Naturales in Madrid.

28. Muybridge, "Aspinwall," Lantern Slide #7720, Box 10C, Lantern Slide Collection, Muybridge Collection, Kingston.

29. I provide Muybridge's image numbers from *Isthmus of Panama and Central America*, which were printed in an ascending list on the verso of each stereograph.

30. Solnit argues that even within Muybridge's experiments in various panoramic forms, his perspective is often fragmented (Brookman, *Helios*, 184).

31. Qtd. in Mozley, *Eadweard Muybridge*, 11.

32. The publication of Charnay's Mexican photographs in Paris coincides with Muybridge's so-called lost years in Europe (1861–65), which included at least one visit to the French capital. During this period, Muybridge may have seen, for example, Roger Fenton's photographs of ruined medieval cathedrals, which were exhibited at the 1862 International Exhibition in Kensington. In San Francisco, he may have seen the daguerreotypes of Robert Vance, who had traveled in South and Central America. In his 1851 catalogue, Vance listed a "Panoramic View of Panama, taken from the Cathedral, showing the surrounding country, Island of Bogata, and others in the Pacific, ruins of various churches and monasteries" (*Catalogue*).

33. Qtd. in Campbell, *Hermit in the Garden*, 36.

34. Keith F. Davis, *Désiré Charnay*, 130.

35. See Garrigan, *Collecting Mexico*, 74–76, and Tenorio-Trillo, *Mexico at the World's Fairs*, 74–78.

36. See Gordon, "Out of Sequence."

37. Benjamin, "Work of Art," 237.

38. Roth, *Irresistible Decay*, 28.

39. Charnay, *Ancient Cities of the New World*, 46.

40. Maudslay and Maudslay, *Glimpse at Guatemala*, 12.

41. A surviving lantern slide of the same scene shows two standing figures, not one, but otherwise the composition is the same and gives the same lonely effect. Muybridge, "Suburbs of Panama," Lantern Slide Collection, #7639, Box 10A, Muybridge Collection, Kingston.

42. Solnit, *River of Shadows*, 225; Haas, *Muybridge*, 9.

43. On the Modoc, see Palmquist, "Photographing the Modoc Indian War."

44. Marixa Lasso points out the enduring generic quality of the term itself, noting that in a later period correspondence from the Isthmian Canal Commission reveals "that terms like 'native house' and 'native hut' were used regardless of the characteristics of the house or its inhabitants" (Lasso, "From Citizens to 'Natives,'" 41).

45. Stephanie Hawkins, in her discussion of the "anthro-pornography" of the *National Geographic*, notes that visual synecdoche of this kind is a "method of decontextualization. While photographs of individual types in *National Geographic* use one person to secure the whole group in a static image of cultural timelessness, synecdoche also makes the circulation of images and their global diffusion possible" (*American Iconographic*, 70).

46. In one of his large-plate versions of "Native Hut," Muybridge also used the sheet, suspending it behind the family pictured in the image. See "Suburban Residence, Panama" at the Center for Creative Photography, University of Arizona, Accession no. 76.253.34.

47. Stepan, *Picturing Tropical*, 95.

48. Hodgkin and Cull, "Manual of Ethnological Inquiry," 195. Photography as an instrument of data collection assumed increased importance in subsequent versions of these traveler's guides, such as *Notes and Queries on Anthropology*. On these guides more generally, see Stocking, "Reading the Palimpsest of Inquiry." For the broader context, see Frank Spencer, "Some Notes"; Maxwell, *Picture Imperfect*, 29–47; and Hochmann, *Savage Preservation*.

49. Kuhn discusses the increased emphasis on measurement in social science after 1840 in "Function of Measurement."

50. Stepan, *Picturing Tropical*, 102.

51. For Muybridge's racially inflected photographs in *Animal Locomotion*, see Elspeth H. Brown, "Racialising the Virile Body."

52. See, for example, Linda Williams, "Film Body"; Braun, "Muybridge's Scientific Fictions"; and Gordon, "Sanctioning the Nude."

53. Braun, *Eadweard Muybridge*," 215.

54. Ibid., 207.

55. Muybridge, *Animal Locomotion*, plates 401, 402, 433, 434, 435, 436, 32, and 34, respectively.

56. For a discussion of Arthur Munby and Hannah Cullwick's fetishization of domestic labor, and its links to Victorian racial thought, see McClintock, *Imperial Leather*, 132–80.

57. The French naturalist Armand Reclus, who traveled in the region in 1876, described the stifling conditions under which the Panamanian washerwomen worked, noting the oppressive heat and the difficult manual labor that laundering in these conditions involved (*Panama*, 80).

NOTES TO CHAPTER 4

1. Spanish newspapers included: *La crónica official* (1849), *El Panameño* (1849), *La voz del istmo* (1852), *El correo del istmo* (1851), *El arriero* (1852), *El vigilante* (1852), *La estrella de Panamá* (1853), *La gaceta del Estado* (1855), *El pensamiento* (1856), *Boletin oficial del Estado Soberano de Panamá* (1862), and many others. On the development of the Spanish language press, see Arias, *Orígenes de la prensa*; Recuero, *Breve historia del periodismo*; and Miró, *La imprenta*. For a brief English-language overview of Panamanian literature, see Salgado, "Panama." More extensive treatments include García S., *Historia de la literatura panameña*; Miró, *Literatura*; and with a special focus on the canal, Sepúlveda, *El tema*.

2. For the early history of the *Star*, see Niemeier, *Panama Story*, 1–32.

3. Gilbert's importance as a figure in the Panamanian literary tradition is indicated by his inclusion in a recent anthology of the country's verse: Vega et al., *Antología de la poesía colonense*.

4. Bristow, "Whither 'Victorian' Poetry," 96.

5. *Gilbertianae* contained eleven poems, including some of his most famous work: "John Aspinwall," "Beyond the Chagres," "A Frejoles Washer-Girl" [*sic*], "The Isthmian Way," and "Sunset." *Panama Patchwork*, which was reprinted thirteen times from 1906–35, contained 103 poems. Hereafter all quotations are from the second edition of 1905, published by the Star and Herald Press, and cited by line number only.

6. At the end of his life Gilbert was considered an important isthmian writer (Tracy Robinson, *Fifty Years in Panama, 1861–1911*, 257–58). However, his popularity plummeted, and despite the advent of hemispheric approaches to American studies, there has been no critical attention to his oeuvre.

7. Idem, "Forward to the Third Edition," xvii–xviii.

8. Unfortunately, by the time the review was written, Gilbert had died, and the article became an obituary. Montgomery Schuyler, "The Poet of the Isthmus," *New York Times*, September 8, 1906. For a reading of Stedman on the Caribbean, with brief attention to Panama, see Mary Loeffelholz, "Edmund Clarence," 198–204.

9. See McCullough, *Path*, 45–101.

10. For the Canal Zone's manifestation of this rhetoric, see Frenkel "Geographical Representations."

11. Tracy Robinson, *Song of the Palm*, 100, italics in original. Individual poems hereafter cited by line numbers.

12. Compare Eric Walrond's discussion of dredges from a later period: "It dug deep down, too, far into the recesses of its sprawling cosmos. Back to a pre-geological age it delved, and brought up things. . . . Dross surged up; guava stumps, pine stumps, earth-burned sprats, river stakes" (*Tropic Death*, 87).

13. Fabens, *Story of Life on the Isthmus*, 134.

14. Grant, *Papers of Ulysses S. Grant*, 252.

15. Jameson, *Political Unconscious*, 102.

16. Froude, *English in the West Indies*, 156.

17. Howe, *Chiefs, Scribes, and Ethnographers*, 2.

18. On the palm as tropical sign of prodigality and fertility, see Manthorne, *Tropical Renaissance*, 13.

19. Joseph Davis, "On Some of the Bearings of Ethnology," 317. See also Stocking, "What's in a Name"; Rainger, "Race, Politics, and Science"; Brantlinger, "Victorians and Africans"; Lorimer, "Theoretical Racism"; and Hume, "Quantifying Characters."

20. Bollaert, "Observations," 85.

21. Squier, *Notes on Central America*, 55.

22. Seemann, *Narrative*, 2:302.

23. Herbert Spencer, *Herbert Spencer on Social Evolution*, 163.

24. Young, *Colonial Desire*, 2.

25. Herrick, *Poetical Works*, 28.

26. "Panama Poet Breathes his Last at the Age of Sixty-One Years," *Washington Post*, September 9, 1906, E3.

27. Reclus, *Panama*, 80.

28. Abbot, *Panama and the Canal in Picture and Prose*, 38.

29. Gilbert, *Panama Patchwork*, 2, 13.

30. Gilbert, "At the Grave of John Aspinwall," in *Fall of Panama*, 101. The inscrutable native is a repeated figure in European colonial discourse, and we should be careful that we do not simply "replicate what in the context of imperialist discourse was the familiar category of the exotic" (Suleri, *Rhetoric of English India*, 12).

31. Mignolo, *Idea of Latin America*, 4.

NOTES TO THE EPILOGUE

1. Sarah J. Moore examines the fair in *Empire on Display*.

2. The accounts written by canal administrators are particularly fascinating. See, for example, Goethals, *Government of the Canal Zone*, and Gorgas, *Sanitation in Panama*. Goethals was famously immortalized in Percy MacKaye's poem, which is quoted in *Picturesque Panama*: "A man went down to Panama / Where many a man had died, / To slit the sliding mountains / And lift the eternal Tides."

3. The classic Marxist study is MacCannell, *Tourist*. More recently, see Löfgren, *On Holiday*; and Zuelow, *History of Modern Tourism*. For the Caribbean and Panama specifically, see Klytchnikova and Dorosh, "Tourism Sector in Panama"; Merrill, *Negotiating Paradise*; Sheller, *Consuming the Caribbean*; and Scott, "From Disease to Desire."

4. Caren Kaplan, *Questions of Travel*, 3.

5. Aspinall, *Pocket Guide*; Haskins, *Canal Zone Pilot*.

6. Jean Sadler Heald, *Picturesque Panama*, 9. Further references provided in the text. The literature on the picturesque is extensive. For a brisk précis, see Kim Ian Michasiw, "Nine Revisionist Theses on the Picturesque."

7. See Pratt, *Imperial Eyes*, 54.

8. Already by 1890, the Census Bureau had declared the closing of the U.S. frontier (McCullough, *Path Between the Seas*, 252).

9. Kincaid, *Small Place*, 18–19.

10. Heald also lists the "Gilbert House," where the poet lived, as one of the area's main tourist attractions.

11. Duffy, *Speed Handbook*, 1–11.

12. For efforts to deal with the *Aedes aegypti* mosquito, see McNeill, *Mosquito Empires,* 308–14, and Sutter, "'The First Mountain to be Removed.'"

13. Quoted in Scott, "Disease to Desire," 70.

14. Pennell, *Joseph Pennell's Pictures of the Panama Canal,* 10.

15. John Dwyer, describing the botanical gardens, uses touristic language for natural history, referring to Panama as a "naturalist's paradise" and a "mecca" ("Panama, Plant Collection, and the Missouri Botanical Garden," 109–10).

16. See Lindley, *Genera and Species,* 160–61.

17. Feuillet, "La flor del Espíritu Santo," in Miró, *Tomás Martín Feuillet,* 77–78.

18. For an excellent discussion of early twentieth-century scientific surveys of the Canal Zone, especially the Smithsonian Biological Survey (1910–12), see Henson, "Baseline Environmental Survey." On the relationship between botany and empire more broadly, see Brockway, *Science and Colonial Expansion*; Schiebinger, *Plants and Empire*; Schiebinger and Swan, *Colonial Botany*; and Drayton, *Nature's Government.*

19. Palma, *Horas áticas,* 21.

20. Translation by Alice Stone Blackwell, *Some Spanish-American Poets,* 526.

21. Cf. Enrique Geenzier's much more patriotic poem, "La epopeya del hierro" ("The Iron Epic"), which associates the canal with liberal ideals of progress, liberty, and freedom, and declares it, without ambivalence or hesitation, "the glory of all humankind and a gift for the entire world." On this period in Panama's literary history, see Garcia S., *Historia de la literatura Panameña,* ch. 2 and 3, and Barragán de Turner, *Letras de Panamá,* 17–44. For a discussion of the bitter Colombian poetic reaction to the canal and Panamanian independence, including denunciations of both a rapacious United States and a treasonous Panama, see Arbena, "Loss of Panama."

22. Anzaldúa, *Borderlands/La Frontera,* 3.

BIBLIOGRAPHY

Abbot, Willis J. *Panama and the Canal in Picture and Prose*. London: Syndicate Publishing, 1913.

Aguirre, Robert D. *Informal Empire: Mexico and Central America in Victorian Culture*. Minneapolis: University of Minnesota Press, 2004.

Agurcia Fasquelle, Ricardo. "La depredación del patrimonio cultural en Honduras: El caso de la arqueología." *Yaxkin* 8, no. 2 (1984): 83–91.

Alba C., Manuel M. *Cronología de los gobernantes de Panamá, 1510–1967*. Panamá: n.p., 1967.

Almeida, Joselyn M. *Reimagining the Transatlantic, 1780–1890*. Aldershot: Ashgate, 2011.

Altick, Richard D. *The Shows of London*. Cambridge: Belknap Press, 1978.

Anderson, Benedict. *Imagined Communities: Reflections on the Origins and Spread of Nationalism*, rev. ed. London: Verso, 1991.

Anderson, Lee. "The Comandante's Canal." *New Yorker*. March 10, 2014, 50–61.

Andrews, George Reid. *Afro-Latin America, 1800–2000*. Oxford: Oxford University Press, 2004.

Anzaldúa, Gloria. *Borderlands/La Frontera: The New Mestiza*. San Francisco, CA: Spinsters/Aunt Lute Books, 1987.

Aparicio, Frances R., and Susana Chávez-Silverman, eds. *Tropicalizations: Transcultural Representations of Latinidad*. Hanover, NH: University Press of New England, 1997.

Araúz, Celestino A. "Justo Arosemena ante el expansionismo de los Estados Unidos." *Revista Tareas* (Panamá), 94 (1996): 36–68.

Araúz, Celestino A., and Gelós P. Pizzurno. *El Panamá Colombiano (1821–1903)*. Panamá: Primer Banco de Ahorros y Diario La Prensa de Panamá. 1993.

Arbena, Joseph L. "The Loss of Panama and Colombian Poetry of the Early Twentieth Century." *Annals of the Southeastern Conference on Latin American Studies* 6 (1975): 94–103.

apRoberts, Ruth. "Carlyle and Trollope." In *Carlyle and his Contemporaries: Essays in Honor of Charles Richard Sanders*, edited by John Clubbe, 204–26. Durham, NC: Duke University Press, 1976.

Arías, Euologia R. de. *Orígenes de la prensa y aspecto evolutivo en Hispanoamérica y Panamá*. Panamá, n.p., 1987.

Arosemena, Justo. ¡¡¡Alerta Istmeños!!! To Be or Not to Be, That Is the Question. Shakespeare." In Arosemena, *Escritos,* 74–78.

———. "Contra la expansión colonialista de Estados Unidos." In Arosemena, *Panamá y nuestra América,* 157–61.

———. *Escritos de Justo Arosemena. Estudio introductorio y antología.* Ed. Argella Telo Burgos. Panamá: Universidad de Panamá, 1985.

———. "Estado económico del Istmo." In Arosemena, *Escritos,* 3–13.

———. *Estado Federal.* In Arosemena, *Panamá y nuestra América,* 6–114.

———. *Examen sobre la franca comunicación entre los dos océanos por el Istmo de Panamá.* Bogotá: Imp. de José a Cualla, 1846.

———. "La cuestión Americana." In Arosemena, *Escritos,* 247–63.

———. *Panamá y nuestra América.* Ed. Ricuarte Soler. México: Universidad Nacional Autónoma de México, 1981.

Aspinall, Algernon E. *The Pocket Guide to the West Indies.* London: Edward Stanford, 1907.

Augé, Marc. *Non-Places: Introduction to an Anthropology of Supermodernity.* Trans. John Howe. London: Verso, 1995.

Bagwell, Philip S. *The Transport Revolution from 1770.* London: B. T. Batsford, 1974.

Baily, John. *Central America: Describing Each of the States of Guatemala, Honduras, Salvador, Nicaragua, and Costa Rica; Their Natural Features, Products, Population, and Remarkable Capacity for Colonization, with Three Views.* London: Trelawney Saunders, 1850.

Bancroft, Hubert Howe. *History of Central America.* Vols. 6–8, *The Works of Hubert Howe Bancroft.* San Francisco, CA: A. L. Bancroft, 1883.

Barragán de Turner, Isabel. *Letras de Panamá: Historia compendiada de la literatura panameña.* Panamá: Universidad de Panamá, 2008.

Baucom, Ian. *Out of Place: Englishness, Empire, and the Locations of Identity.* Princeton, NJ: Princeton University Press, 1999.

Bayoumi, Moustafa. "Moving Beliefs: The Panama Manuscript of Sheik Sana See and African Diasporic Islam. *Interventions* 5, no. 1 (2003): 58–81.

Beardsell, Peter. *Europe and Latin America: Returning the Gaze.* Manchester: Manchester University Press, 2000.

Bedell, G. T., and Fred S. Winston. "Report of a Special Committee of the Foreign Committee in Relation to a Proposed Mission to Central America." *Spirit of the Missions* 17 (1852): 410–13.

Behdad, Ali. *Belated Travelers: Orientalism in the Age of Colonial Dissolution.* Durham, NC: Duke University Press, 1994.

Belly, Félix. *Percement de l'isthme de Panama par le canal de Nicaragua: Exposé de la question.* Paris: Aux Bureaux de la Direction du Canal, 1858.

Benjamin, Walter. "The Work of Art in the Age of Mechanical Reproduction." In *Illuminations: Essays and Reflections,* edited by Hannah Arendt, translated by Harry Zohn, 217–51. New York: Schocken Books, 1969.

Berkhofer, Robert F., Jr. *The White Man's Indian: Images of the American Indian from Columbus to the Present.* New York: Knopf, 1978.

Bidwell, Charles Toll. *The Isthmus of Panamá.* London: Chapman and Hall, 1865.

Bieber, Ralph P. "California Gold Mania." *Mississippi Valley Historical Review* 35, no. 1 (1948): 3–48.

"Biographical Sketch of Mr. W. Bollaert." *Journal of the Anthropological Institute of Great Britain and Ireland* 6 (1877): 510–13.

Blackwell, Alice Stone. *Some Spanish-American Poets.* Trans. Alice Stone Blackwell. Philadelphia: University of Pennsylvania Press, 1937.

Bolívar, Simón. *El Libertador: Writings of Simón Bolívar.* Ed. David Bushnell. Trans. Fred Fornoff. New York: Oxford University Press, 2003.

Bollaert, William. "Observations on the Past and Present Populations of the New World." *Memoirs Read before the Anthropological Society of London* 1 (1863–64): 72–119.

Bonaparte, Napoleon Luis. *Canal of Nicaragua: Or, a Project to Connect the Atlantic and Pacific Oceans by Means of a Canal.* London: Mills & Son, 1846.

Bourne, Kenneth. "The Clayton-Bulwer Treaty and the Decline of British Opposition to the Territorial Expansion of the United States, 1857–60," *Journal of Modern History* 33, no. 3 (1961): 287–91.

Brading, David A. *The First America: Spanish Monarchy, Creole Patriots, and the Liberal State, 1492–1867.* Cambridge: Cambridge University Press, 1991.

Brandenstein, Claudia. "Representations of Landscape and Nature in Anthony Trollope's *The West Indies and the Spanish Main* and James Anthony Froude's *The English in the West Indies.*" In *Five Emus to the King of Siam: Environment and Empire,* edited by Helen Tiffin, 15–29. Amsterdam: Rodopi, 2007.

Brantlinger, Patrick. *Dark Vanishings: Discourse on the Extinction of Primitive Races, 1800–1930.* Ithaca, NY: Cornell University Press, 2003.

———. "Victorians and Africans: The Genealogy of the Myth of the Dark Continent." *Critical Inquiry* 12, no. 1 (1985): 166–203.

Braun, Marta. *Eadweard Muybridge.* London: Reaktion Books, 2010.

———. "Muybridge's Scientific Fictions." *Studies in Visual Communication* 10, no. 3 (1984): 2–22.

Briggs, Asa. "Trollope the Traveler." In *The Collected Essays of Asa Briggs.* 3 vols. Urbana: University of Illinois Press, 1985, 2:89–115.

Bristow, Joseph. "Whither 'Victorian' Poetry: A Genre and its Period." *Victorian Poetry* 42, no.1 (2004): 81–109.

British Association for the Advancement of Science. *Notes and Queries on Anthropology, for the Use of Travellers and Residents in Uncivilized Lands.* London: E. Stanford, 1874.

British Postal Museum and Archive, London.

Britton, John A. *Cables, Crises, and the Press: The Geopolitics of the New International Information System in the Americas, 1866–1903.* Albuquerque: University of New Mexico Press, 2013.

Brockway, Lucille. *Science and Colonial Expansion: The Role of the British Royal Botanic Garden.* New Haven, CT: Yale University Press, 2002.

Brookman, Philip, ed. *Helios: Eadweard Muybridge in a Time of Change.* Gottingen: Steidl, 2010.

Brown, Bill. "Science Fiction, the Word's Fair, and the Prosthetics of Empire, 1910–1915." In *Cultures of United States Imperialism,* edited by Amy Kaplan and Donald E. Pease, 129–63. Durham, NC: Duke University Press, 1993.

Brown, Elspeth H. "Racialising the Virile Body: Eadweard Muybridge's Locomotion Studies 1883–1887." *Gender and History* 17, no. 5 (2005): 627–56.

Brown, Matthew. *Informal Empire in Latin America: Culture, Commerce, and Capital.* Oxford: Blackwell, 2008.

Brunel's Mammoth Ship: View, Section, Plan, and Description of the Great Eastern Steam Ship: Building at Millwall for the Eastern Steam Navigation Company, and Designed to Carry Ten Thousand Persons. San Francisco, CA: E. J. Muygridge, 1857.

Buchanan, James. *The Works of James Buchanan, Comprising His Speeches, State Papers, and Private Correspondence,* edited by John Bassett Moore. 10 vols. New York: New York Antiquarian Press, 1960.

Burnett, D. Graham. *Masters of All They Surveyed: Exploration, Geography, and a British El Dorado.* Chicago: University of Chicago Press, 2000.

Burns, E. Bradford. *Eadweard Muybridge in Guatemala, 1875: The Photographer as Social Recorder.* Berkeley: University of California Press, 1986.

———. *Patriarch and Folk: The Emergence of Nicaragua, 1798–1858.* Cambridge, MA: Harvard University Press, 1991.

———. *The Poverty of Progress: Latin America in the Nineteenth Century.* Berkeley: University of California Press, 1980.

Bury, Laurent. "Trollope et l'empire." *Cahiers Victoriens et Edouardiens* 39 (1994): 177–86.

Bushell, T. A. *Royal Mail: A Centenary History of the Royal Mail Line, 1839–1939.* London: Trade and Travel Publications, 1939.

Buzard, James. "Portable Boundaries: Trollope, Race, and Travel." *Nineteenth-Century Contexts* 32, no. 1 (2010): 5–18.

Byerly, Alison. *Are We There Yet? Virtual Travel and Victorian Realism.* Ann Arbor: University of Michigan Press, 2013.

Cambranes, J. C. *Café y campesinos: los orígenes de la economía de plantación moderna en Guatemala, 1853–1897.* Madrid: Catriel, 1996.

Campbell, Gordon. *The Hermit in the Garden: From Imperial Rome to Ornamental Gnome.* Oxford: Oxford University Press, 2013.

Campbell-Smith, Duncan. *Masters of the Post: The Authorized History of the Royal Mail.* London: Allen Lane, 2011.

Carlyle, Thomas. *History of Friedrich II of Prussia, called Frederick the Great.* 4 vols. London: Chapman and Hall, 1858–65.

Carse, Ashley. *Beyond the Big Ditch: Politics, Ecology, and Infrastructure at the Panama Canal.* Cambridge: MIT Press, 2015.

Carse, Ashley, Christine Keiner, Pamela M. Henson, Marixa Lasso, Paul S. Sutter, and Megan Raby. "Panama Canal Forum: From the Conquest of Nature to the Construction of New Ecologies." *Environmental History* 21, no. 2 (2016): 206–87.

Castillero Calvo, Alfredo. "Ciclos y coyunturas en la economía panameña: 1645–1869. Interpretación sumaria (segunda parte)." *Revista Tareas: Historia ambiental Latinoamericana* 120 (May–Aug. 2005): 113–30.

———. "El movimiento anseático de 1826. Primera tentativa autonomista de los istmeños después de la anexión a Colombia." *Tarejas* 4 (1960): 3–25.

———. "Transitismo y dependencia: El caso del istmo de Panamá." *Anuario de Estudios Centroamericanos* 1 (1974): 165–86.

———. "Un antecedente de la 'Tajada de Sandía.'" *Lotería* 6, no. 69 (1961): 20–23.

Castillero Reyes, Ernesto. *El ferrocarril de Panamá y su historia.* Panamá: Imprenta Nacional, 1932.

Castro Herrera, Guillermo. *El agua entre los mares.* Panama City: Ciudad de Saber, 2007.

Catalogue of Photographic Views illustrating the Yosemite, Mammoth Trees, Geyser Springs, and other Remarkable and Interesting Scenery of the Far West, by Muybridge. San Francisco, CA: Bradley & Rulofson, 1873.

Chandler Robert J. and Stephen J. Potash. *Gold, Silk, Pioneers and Mail: The Story of the Pacific Mail Steamship Company.* Pacific Maritime History Series, no. 6. San Francisco: Friends of the San Francisco Maritime Museum Library, 2007.

Charnay, Désiré. *The Ancient Cities of the New World, Being Voyages and Explorations in Mexico and Central America from 1857–1882.* Translated by J. Gonino and Helen S. Conant. New York: Harper and Brothers, 1887.

Chen, Kayla, and Xiangming Chen. "China and Latin America: Connected and Competing." *European Financial Review.* March 10, 2013: 56–58.

Chen P., Berta Alicia. *Cómo, cuando y por qué llegaron los chinos a Panamá.* Panamá: MDC, 2010.

Chinchilla Mazariegos, Oswaldo. "Archaeology and Nationalism in Guatemala at the Time of Independence." *Antiquity* 72 (1998): 376–86.

Chong Ruiz, Eustorgio. *Los chinos en la sociedad panameña.* Panamá: Instituto Nacional de Cultura, 1992.

Chou, Diego L. *Los chinos en Hispanoamérica.* San José de Costa Rica: Facultad Latinoamericana de Ciencias Sociales, 2002.

Clay, Henry. *The Papers of Henry Clay, Volume 4, Secretary of State, 1825.* Ed. James F. Hopkins. Louisville: University Press of Kentucky, 1972.

Claybaugh, Amanda. "Trollope and America." In *The Cambridge Companion to Anthony Trollope,* edited by Carolyn Dever and Lisa Niles, 211–23. Cambridge: Cambridge University Press, 2011.

Clegg, Brian. *The Man Who Stopped Time: The Illuminating Story of Eadweard Muybridge, Pioneer Photographer, Father of the Motion Picture, Murderer.* Washington, DC: Joseph Henry Press, 2007.

Cohen, Lucy M. "The Chinese of the Panama Railroad: Preliminary Notes on the Migrants of 1854 Who 'Failed.'" *Ethnohistory* 18, no. 4 (1971): 309–20.

Comment, Bernard. *The Painted Panorama.* Trans. by Anne-Marie Glasheen. New York: H. N. Abrams, 2000.

Conniff, Michael L. *Black Labor on a White Canal: Panama, 1904–1981.* Pittsburgh, PA: University of Pittsburgh Press, 1985.

Conrad, Joseph. *Heart of Darkness.* Ed. Robert Kimbrough, 3rd ed. New York: W. W. Norton, 1988.

Correspondence and Other Papers Relating to Hudson's Bay Company, The Exploration of the Territories [Captain Palisser's Expedition], and Other Affairs in Canada, 1859. Vol. 22 of *Irish University Press Series of British Parliamentary Papers: Colonies, Canada, 1802–99.* Shannon: Irish University Press, 1969.

Correspondence Respecting American and British Affairs in Central and South America, 1850–96. Vol. 15 of *Irish University Press Series of British Parliamentary Papers: British Parliamentary Papers, Area Studies; United States of America.* Shannon: Irish University Press, 1971.

Crary, Jonathan. *Techniques of the Observer: On Vision and Modernity.* Cambridge, MA: MIT Press, 1992.

Cresswell, Tim. "Mobilities II: Still." *Progress in Human Geography* 36, no. 5 (2012): 645–53.

———. "Mobilities III: Moving On." *Progress in Human Geography* 38, no. 5 (2014): 712–21.

———. "Towards a Politics of Mobility." *Environment and Planning D: Society and Space* 28 (2010): 17–31.

"Crossing the Isthmus of Panama." *Household Words.* February 12, 1853, 521–24.

Daley, Mercedes Chen. "The Watermelon Riot: Cultural Encounters in Panama City, April 15, 1856." *Hispanic American Historical Review* 70, no. 1 (1990): 85–108.

Dallas, E. S. Review of *West Indies and the Spanish Main,* by Anthony Trollope. *Times* (London), January 9, 1860, and January 18, 1860.

Darwin, Charles. *Journal of Researches into the Natural History and Geology of the Countries Visited during the Voyage Round the H.M.S. Beagle.* 11th ed. London: John Murray, 1913.

Daunton, Martin J. *Royal Mail: The Post Office since 1840.* London: Athlone Press, 1985.

Davis, John. *The Landscape of Belief: Encountering the Holy Land in Nineteenth-Century American Art and Culture.* Princeton, NJ: Princeton University Press, 1996.

Davis, Joseph Barnard. "On Some of the Bearings of Ethnology upon Archaeological Science." *Archaeological Journal* 13 (1856): 315–27.

Davis, Keith F. *Désiré Charnay, Expeditionary Photographer.* Albuquerque: University of New Mexico Press, 1981.

Davis, Keith F., and Jane L. Aspinwall. *Timothy H. O'Sullivan: The King Survey Photographs.* New Haven, CT: Yale University Press, 2011.

Dénain, A. *Ensayo sobre los intereses políticos y comerciales del Istmo de Panamá.* Panamá: José Maria Bermudez, 1844.

Deverell, William. *Railroad Crossing: Californians and the Railroad, 1850–1910.* Berkeley: University of California Press, 1994.

Dickens, Charles and Wilkie Collins. *The Perils of Certain English Prisoners, and Their Treasure in Women, Children, Silver, and Jewels. Household Words* (Extra Christmas Number). December 7, 1857, 1–36.

Dickerson, Vanessa D. *Dark Victorians.* Urbana: University of Illinois Press, 2008.

Dimock, Marshall E. *Government-Operated Enterprises in the Panama Canal Zone.* Chicago: University of Chicago Press, 1934.

Drayton, Richard. *Nature's Government: Science, Imperial Britain, and the "Improvement" of the World.* New Haven, CT: Yale University Press, 2000.

Driver, Felix, and Luciana Martins, eds. *Tropical Visions in an Age of Empire.* Chicago: University of Chicago Press, 2005.

Duffy, Enda. *The Speed Handbook: Velocity, Pleasure, Modernism.* Durham, NC: Duke University Press, 2009.

DuVal, Miles P. *Cadiz to Cathay: The Story of the Long Struggle for a Waterway across the American Isthmus.* Stanford, CA: Stanford University Press, 1940.

Dwyer, John D. "Panama, Plant Collection, and the Missouri Botanical Garden." *Annals of the Missouri Botanical Garden* 51, no. 1 (1964): 109–17.

Elliot, Emery. "Diversity in the United States and Abroad: What Does It Mean When American Studies Is Transnational?" *American Quarterly* 59, no. 1 (2007): 1–22.

Fabens, Joseph W. *A Story of Life on the Isthmus.* New York: George P. Putnam, 1853.

Fabian, Johannes. *Time and the Other: How Anthropology Makes Its Object.* New York: Columbia University Press, 1983.

Fergson, Trish, ed. *Victorian Time: Technologies, Standardizations, Catastrophes.* Houndmills, Basingstoke: Palgrave Macmillan, 2013.

Fishkin, Shelley Fisher. "Crossroads of Cultures: The Transnational Turn in American Studies—Presidential Address to the American Studies Association, November 12, 2004." *American Quarterly* 57, no. 1 (2005): 17–57.

"Five Travellers." *Household Words.* December 27, 1851, 318–21.

Folkman, David I., Jr. *The Nicaragua Route.* Salt Lake City: University of Utah Press, 1972.

Foner, Philip S. *A History of Cuba and Its Relations with the United States.* 2 vols. New York: International Publishers, 1963.

Foucault, Michel. "Of Other Spaces." Trans. by Jay Miskowiec. *Diacritics* 16 (1986): 22–27.

Framing the West: The Survey Photographs of Timothy H. O'Sullivan. Ed. Toby Jurovics, Carol M. Johnson, Glenn Willumson, William F. Stapp, and Page Stegner. New Haven, CT: Yale University Press, 2010.

Frederick, Rhonda. *"Colón Man a Come": Mythographies of Panama Canal Migration.* Lanham, MD: Lexington Books, 2005.

Freeman, Michael. *Railways and the Victorian Imagination.* New Haven, CT: Yale University Press, 1999.

Frenkel, Stephen. "Geographical Representations of the 'Other': The Landscape of the Panama Canal Zone." *Journal of Historical Geography* 28, no. 1 (2002): 85–99.

Froude, James A. *The English in the West Indies, or the Bow of Ulysses.* London: Longmans, Green, 1888.

Galassi, Peter. *Before Photography: Painting and the Invention of Photography.* New York: Museum of Modern Art, 1981.

García S., Ismael. *Historia de la literatura Panameña.* México: Universidad Nacional Autónoma de México, 1972.

Garrigan, Shelley E. *Collecting Mexico: Museums, Monuments, and the Creation of National Identity.* Minneapolis: University of Minnesota Press, 2012.

Gaskell, Elizabeth. *Cranford.* New York: Barnes and Noble, 2005.

Geenzier, Enrique. "La epopeya de hierro." In Octavio Méndez Pereira, *Parnaso panameño,* 337–42. Panamá: Tipografía el istmo, 1916.

Gikandi, Simon. *Maps of Englishness: Writing Identity in the Culture of Colonialism.* New York: Columbia University Press, 1996.

Gilbert, James Stanley. *The Fall of Panamá and other Isthmian Rhymes and Sketches.* New York: n.p., 1894.

———. *Gilbertianae: Isthmian Rhymes.* Great Barrington, MA: Douglas Brothers, 1891.

———. *Panama Patchwork: Poems by James Stanley Gilbert.* 2nd ed. Panama: Star and Herald, 1905.

Giles, Paul. *Antipodean America: Australasia and the Constitution of U.S. Literature.* Oxford: Oxford University Press, 2013.

Gilroy, Paul. *The Black Atlantic: Modernity and Double Consciousness.* Cambridge, MA: Harvard University Press, 1993.

Gisborne, Lionel. *The Isthmus of Darien in 1852: Journal of the Expedition of Inquiry for the Junction of the Atlantic and Pacific Oceans.* London: Saunders and Stanford, 1853.

Gitelman, Lisa. *Paper Knowledge: Toward a Media History of Documents.* Durham, NC: Duke University Press, 2014.

Gmelch, Bohn. *The Tlingit Encounter with Photography.* Philadelphia: University of Pennsylvania Museum of Archaeology and Anthropology, 2008.

Gobat, Michael. *Confronting the American Dream: Nicaragua under U.S. Imperial Rule.* Durham, NC: Duke University Press, 2005.

———. "The Invention of Latin America: A Transnational History of Anti-imperialism, Democracy, and Race." *American Historical Review* 118, no. 5 (2013): 1345–75.

Goethals, George. *Government of the Canal Zone.* Princeton, NJ: Princeton University Press, 1915.

Goodlad, Lauren M. E. "Trollopian 'Foreign Policy': Rootedness and Cosmopolitanism in the Mid-Victorian Imaginary." *PMLA* 142, no. 2 (2009): 437–54.

———. *The Victorian Geopolitical Aesthetic: Realism, Sovereignty, and Transnational Experience.* Oxford: Oxford University Press, 2015.

Gordon, Sarah. "Out of Sequence: Suspended and Spectacular Bodies in Eadweard Muybridge's *Animal Locomotion* Series." *Spectator* 28, no. 2 (2008): 10–22.

———. "Sanctioning the Nude: Production and Reception of Eadweard Muybridge's *Animal Locomotion*, 1887." PhD diss., Northwestern University, 2006.

Gorgas, William. *Sanitation in Panama.* New York: D. Appleton and Company, 1915.

Goudie, Sean X. "New Regionalisms: US-Caribbean Literary Relations." In Levander and Levine, *Hemispheric American Studies*, 310–24.

Goveia, Elsa V. *A Study on the Historiography of the British West Indies to the End of the Nineteenth Century.* Washington, DC: Howard University Press, 1980. Reprint of edition published in Mexico by Pan American Institute of Geography and History, 1956.

Grant, Ulysses S. *The Papers of Ulysses S. Grant, Volume 1, 1837–1861.* Ed. John Y. Simon. Carbondale: Southern Illinois University Press, 1967.

———. *Personal Memoirs of U.S. Grant.* 2 vols. New York: Charles L. Webster, 1885.

Greenberg, Amy S. *Manifest Manhood and the Antebellum American Empire.* Cambridge: Cambridge University Press, 2005.

Greenblatt, Stephen, ed. *Cultural Mobility: A Manifesto.* Cambridge: Cambridge University Press, 2010.

Greene, Julie. *The Canal Builders.* New York: Penguin, 2009.

Grossman, Jonathan. *Charles Dickens's Networks: Public Transport and the Novel.* Oxford: Oxford University Press, 2012.

Gruesz, Kirsten Silva. *Ambassadors of Culture: The Transamerican Origins of Latino Writing.* Princeton, NJ: Princeton University Press, 2002.

Gudmundson, Lowell, and Justin Wolfe, eds. *Blacks and Blackness in Central America: Between Race and Place.* Durham, NC: Duke University Press, 2010.

Haas, Robert Hartlett. *Muybridge: Man in Motion.* Berkeley: University of California Press, 1976.

Hall, Catherine. *Civilising Subjects: Metropole and Colony in the English Imagination, 1830–1867.* Chicago: University of Chicago Press, 2002.

Hall, N. John. *Trollope: A Biography.* Oxford: Clarendon Press, 1991.

———. "Trollope and Carlyle." *Nineteenth-Century Fiction* 27, no. 2 (1972): 197–205.

Harvey, Bruce A. *American Geographics: U.S. National Narratives and the Representation of the Non-European World, 1830–1865.* Stanford, CA: Stanford University Press, 2002.

Harvey, David. *The Condition of Postmodernity: An Enquiry into the Origins of Cultural Change.* London: Blackwell, 1990.

———. *Justice, Nature, and the Geography of Difference.* London: Blackwell, 1996.

Haskins, William C. *Canal Zone Pilot: Guide to the Republic of Panama, and Classified Business Directory.* Panama: Star and Herald, 1908.

Hawkins, Stephanie L. *American Iconographic: National Geographic, Global Culture, and the Visual Imagination.* Charlottesville: University of Virginia Press, 2010.

Haynes, Sam W. "Anglophobia and the Annexation of Texas: The Quest for National Security." In *Manifest Destiny and Empire: American Antebellum Expansionism,* edited by Sam W. Haynes and Christopher Morris, 115–45. College Station: Texas A&M University Press, 1997.

Headrick, Daniel R. *The Tools of Empire: Technology and European Imperialism in the Nineteenth Century.* New York: Oxford University Press, 1981.

———. *When Information Came of Age: Technologies of Knowledge in the Age of Reason and Revolution, 1700—1850.* Oxford: Oxford University Press, 2000.

Heald, Jean Sadler. *Picturesque Panama.* Chicago: C. Teich, 1928.

Heinowitz, Rebecca C. *Spanish America and British Romanticism, 1777–1826: Rewriting Conquest.* Edinburgh: Edinburgh University Press, 2010.

Hendricks, Gordon. *Eadweard Muybridge: The Father of the Motion Picture.* London: Secker and Warburg, 1975.

Henson, Paula M. "A Baseline Environmental Survey: The 1910–12 Smithsonian Biological Survey of the Panama Canal Zone." *Environmental History* 21, no. 2 (2016): 18–26.

Herrera C., Miguel Angel. *Bongos, bogas, vapores y marinos: Historia de los 'marineros' del río San Juan, 1849–55.* Managua: Centro Nicaragüense de Escritores, 1999.

Herrick, Robert. *The Poetical Works of Robert Herrick.* Ed. F. W. Moorman. London: Oxford University Press, 1921.

"The History of a Letter." *Hutchings California Magazine* 2, no. 19 (January 1858): 289–300.

Hobsbawm, Eric J. *Industry and Empire from 1750 to the Present Day.* New York: New Press, 1999.

Hochmann, Brian. *Savage Preservation: The Ethnographic Origins of Modern Media Technology.* Minneapolis: University of Minnesota Press, 2014.

Hodgkin, Thomas, and Richard Cull. "A Manual of Ethnological Inquiry." *Journal of the Ethnological Society of London* 3 (1854): 193–208.

Horan, James D. *Timothy O'Sullivan: America's Forgotten Photographer.* New York: Bonanza Books, 1966.

Horsman, Reginald. *Race and Manifest Destiny: The Origins of American Racial Anglo-Saxonism.* Cambridge, MA: Harvard University Press, 1981.

Howe, James. *Chiefs, Scribes, and Ethnographers: Kuna Culture from Inside and Out.* Austin: University of Texas Press, 2009.

Hughes, George W. *Letter in Answer to the Hon. John M. Clayton, Secretary of State, on Intermarine Communications.* Washington, DC: J. T. Towers, 1850.

Hume, Brad D. "Quantifying Characters: Polygenist Anthropologists and the Hardening of Heredity." *Journal of the History of Biology* 41, no. 1 (2008): 119–58.

Hunt, Freeman. "Proposed Railroad across the Isthmus of Panama." *Merchants' Magazine and Commercial Review* 20, no. 3 (March 1849): 269–78.

Hyde, Ralph. *Panoramania! The Art and Entertainment of the 'All-Embracing' View.* London: Barbican Art Gallery, 1988.

"Iron Horse." *Panama Star.* August 4, 1849: 1.

Jameson, Frederick. *The Political Unconscious: Narrative as a Socially Symbolic Act.* Ithaca, NY: Cornell University Press, 1981.

Johnson, Samuel. *Johnson's Dictionary.* 1755.

Jones, Iva G. "Trollope, Carlyle, and Mill on the Negro: An Episode in the History of Ideas." *Journal of Negro History* 5, no. 3 (1967): 185–99.

Joyce, Patrick. *The State of Freedom: A Social History of the British State since 1800.* Cambridge: Cambridge University Press, 2013.

Jung, Moon-Ho Jung. *Coolies and Cane: Race, Labor, and Sugar in the Age of Emancipation.* Baltimore: Johns Hopkins University Press, 2006.

Kaplan, Amy. "Violent Belongings and the Question of Empire Today—Presidential Address to the American Studies Association." *American Quarterly* 56, no. 1 (2004): 1–18.

Kaplan, Caren. *Questions of Travel: Postmodern Discourses of Displacement.* Durham, NC: Duke University Press, 1996.

Kemble, John Haskell. *The Panama Route, 1848–1869.* Berkeley: University of California Press, 1943.

Kern, Stephen. *The Culture of Time and Space, 1880–1918.* Cambridge, MA: Harvard University Press, 1983.

Kincaid, Jamaica. *A Small Place.* New York: Farrar, Strauss, and Giroux, 1988.

Kittler, Friedrich. *Discourse Networks 1800/1900.* Trans. Michael Metteer, with Chris Cullens. Stanford, CA: Stanford University Press, 1992.

Klytchnikova, Irina, and Paul Dorosh. "Tourism Sector in Panama: Regional Economic Impacts and the Potential to Benefit the Poor." *Investigación y pensamiento crítico* 2, no. 4 (2014): 59–83.

Krauss, Clifford, Steven Lee Myers, Andrew C. Revkin, and Simon Romero. "As Polar Ice Turns to Water, Dreams of Treasure Abound." *New York Times (1923-Current file):* A1, A10–11. October 10, 2005. *ProQuest.* Web. March 11, 2016.

Kuhn, Thomas S. "The Function of Measurement in Modern Physical Science." *Isis* 52, no. 2 (1961): 161–93.

Lai, Walton Look. *Indentured Labor, Caribbean Sugar: Chinese and Indian Migrants to the British West Indies, 1838–1918.* Baltimore: Johns Hopkins University Press, 1993.

Lambert, David, Luciana Martins, and Miles Ogbern. "Currents, Visions and Voyages: Historical Geographies of the Sea." *Journal of Historical Geography* 32, no. 3 (2006): 479–93.

Landsberg, Alison. *Prosthetic Memory: The Transformation of American Remembrance in the Age of Mass Culture.* New York: Columbia University Press, 2004.

Langley, Lester D. *The Americas in the Modern Age.* New Haven, CT: Yale University Press, 2003.

LaRosa, Michael J., and Germán R. Mejia, eds. *The United States Discovers Panama: The Writings of Soldiers, Scholars, Scientists, and Scoundrels, 1850–1905.* Lanham, MD: Rowman and Littlefield, 2003.

Lasso, Marixa. "From Citizens to 'Natives': Tropical Politics of Depopulation at the Panama Canal Zone." *Environmental History* 21, no. 2 (2016): 37–46.

Leary, John P. *A Cultural History of Underdevelopment: Latin America in the U.S. Imagination*. Charlottesville: University of Virginia, 2016.

Leonard, Thomas M. "'Keeping the Europeans Out': The United States and Central America since 1823." In *Central America: Historical Perspectives on the Contemporary Crises*, edited by Ralph Lee Woodward Jr., 5–19. New York: Greenwood Press, 1988.

Levander, Caroline. "Introduction: Hemispheric American Literary History." *American Literary History* 18, no. 3 (2006): 397–405.

Levander, Caroline, and Robert S. Levine, eds. *Hemispheric American Studies*. New Brunswick, NJ: Rutgers University Press, 2008.

Lewis, Lancelot S. *The West Indian in Panama: Black Labor in Panama, 1850–1914*. Washington, DC: University Press of America, 1980.

Lindley, John. *The Genera and Species of Orchideous Plants*. London: Treuttel, 1830.

Lindsay-Poland, John. *Emperors in the Jungle: The Hidden History of the U.S. in Panama*. Durham, NC: Duke University Press, 2003.

Liot, W. B. *Panama, Nicaragua and Tehuantepec; or, Considerations upon the Questions of Communication between the Atlantic and Pacific Oceans*. London: Simpkin and Marshall, 1849.

Lloyd, J. A. "Notes Respecting the Isthmus of Panama." *Journal of the Royal Geographical Society of London* 1 (1831): 69–191.

Loeffelholz, Mary. "Edmund Clarence Stedman's Black Atlantic." *Victorian Poetry* 43, no. 2 (2005): 198–204.

Löfgren, Ovar. *On Holiday: A History of Vacationing*. Critical Studies in Critical Human Geography. Berkeley: University of California Press, 2002.

López-Ocón, Leoncio. "La comisión científica del Pacífico: de la ciencia imperial a la ciencia federativa." *Bulletin de l'Institut Francais d'Etudes Andines* 32, no. 3 (2003): 479–515.

Lorimer, Douglas. "Theoretical Racism in Late-Victorian Anthropology, 1870–1900." *Victorian Studies* 31, no. 3 (1988): 405–30.

MacCannell, Dean. *The Tourist: A New Theory of the Leisure Class, with a New Introduction*. Berkeley: University of California Press, 2013.

Mack, Gerstle. *The Land Divided: A History of the Panama Canal and Other Isthmian Canal Projects*. New York: Knopf, 1944.

MacQueen, James. *A General Plan for a Mail Communication by Steam, between Great Britain and the Eastern and Western Parts of the World*. London: B. Fellowes, 1838.

Manning, William R., ed. *Diplomatic Correspondence of the United States, Inter-American Affairs, 1831–1860*. 12 vols. Washington, DC: Carnegie Endowment for International Peace, 1932–39.

Manthorne, Katherine. "Plantation Pictures in the Americas, circa 1880: Land, Power, and Resistance." *Nepantla: Views from the South* 2, no. 2 (2001): 317–53.

———. *Tropical Renaissance: North American Artists Exploring Latin America, 1839–1879*. Washington, DC: Smithsonian Institution Press, 1989.

Marryat, Frank. *Mountains and Molehills; or, Recollections of a Burnt Journal*. New York: Harper and Brothers, 1855.

Marshall, Oliver. *English-Speaking Communities in Latin America Since Independence*. London: Palgrave Macmillan, 2000.

Martineau, Harriet, George Lillie Craik, and Charles Knight. *History of the Peace: Being a History of England from 1816 to 1854. With an Introduction 1800 to 1815.* 4 vols. Boston: Walker, Wise, 1865.

Martinez-Alier, Verena. *Marriage, Class and Colour in Nineteenth-Century Cuba: A Study of Racial Attitudes and Sexual Values in a Slave Society.* Cambridge: Cambridge University Press, 1974.

Mattox, Jake. "Claiming Panama: Genre and Gender in Antebellum U.S. Isthmiana." *American Studies* 53, no. 1 (2014): 117–47.

Maudslay, Anne Cary Morris, and Alfred Percival Maudslay. *A Glimpse at Guatemala, and Some Notes on the Ancient Monuments of Central America.* London: John Murray, 1899.

Maurer, Noel, and Carlos Yu. *The Big Ditch: How American Took, Built, Ran, and Ultimately Gave Away the Panama Canal.* Princeton, NJ: Princeton University Press, 2011.

Maury, M. F. "Maury's Estimate of the Resources of the Gulf of Mexico and of the Caribbean Sea, and of the Importance of Interoceanic Communication." In Sullivan, *Historical and Technical,* 149–58.

Maxwell, Anne. *Picture Imperfect: Photography and Eugenics, 1870–1940.* Eastbourne: Sussex University Press, 2008.

McClintock, Anne D. *Imperial Leather: Race, Gender, and Sexuality in the Colonial Conquest.* New York: Routledge, 1995.

McCullough, David. *The Path Between the Seas: The Creation of the Panama Canal, 1870–1914.* New York: Simon and Schuster, 1977.

McGuinness, Aims. *Path of Empire: Panama and the California Gold Rush.* Ithaca, NY: Cornell University Press, 2008.

———. "Searching for 'Latin America': Race and Sovereignty in the Americas in the 1850s." In *Race and Nation in Modern Latin America,* edited by Nancy P. Applebaum, Anne S. Macpherson, Karin Alejandra Rosemblatt, 87–107. Chapel Hill: University of North Carolina, Press, 2003.

McNeill, John Robert. *Mosquito Empires: Ecology and War in the Greater Caribbean, 1620–1914.* Cambridge: Cambridge University Press, 2010.

Menke, Richard. *Telegraphic Realism: Victorian Fiction and Other Information Systems.* Stanford: Stanford University Press, 2007.

Merk, Frederick. *The Oregon Question: Essays in Anglo-American Diplomacy and Politics.* Cambridge, MA: Harvard University Press, 1967.

Merrill, Dennis. *Negotiating Paradise: U.S. Tourism and Empire in Twentieth-Century Latin America.* Chapel Hill: University North Carolina Press, 2009.

Meyer, Axel and Jorge A. Huete-Pérez. "Conservation: Nicaragua Canal Could Wreak Environmental Ruin." *Nature* 506, no. 7488 (2014), 287–89.

Michasiw, Kim Ian. "Nine Revisionist Theses on the Picturesque." *Representations* 38 (Spring 1992): 76–100.

Mignolo, Walter D. *The Idea of Latin America.* London: Blackwell Publishing, 2005.

Miller, Robert Ryall. *For Science and National Glory: The Spanish Scientific Expedition to America, 1862–1866.* Norman: University of Oklahoma Press, 1968.

Miró, Rodrigo. *La imprenta y el periodismo en Panamá durante la primera mitad del siglo XIX.* Panamá: Instituto de Investigaciones Históricas Ricardo J. Alfaro: 1976.

———. *La literatura panameña (origen y proceso).* San José, CR: Imprenta Trejos Hermanos, 1972.

———. *Tomás Martín Feuillet, prototipo romántico: estudio y selección.* Panamá: Impr. Nacional, 1962.

Missal, Alexander. *Seaway to the Future: American Social Visions and the Construction of the Panama Canal.* Madison: University of Wisconsin Press, 2008.

Moore, Sarah J. *Empire on Display: San Francisco's Panama-Pacific Exhibition of 1915.* Norman: University of Oklahoma Press, 2013.

Moro, Gaetano. *Observations in Relation to a Communication between the Atlantic and Pacific Oceans, through the Isthmus of Tehuantepec.* New York: R. Craighead, 1849.

Morris, Rosalind C., ed. *Can the Subaltern Speak?: Reflections on the History of an Idea.* New York: Columbia University Press, 2010.

Morse, Deborah Denenholz. *Reforming Trollope: Race, Gender, and Englishness in the Novels of Anthony Trollope.* Burlington, VT: Ashgate, 2013.

Mozley, Anita Ventura. *Eadweard Muybridge: The Stanford Years, 1872–1882.* Stanford, CA: Stanford University Museum of Art, 1972.

Muirhead, Jim R., Mark S. Minton, Whitman A. Miller, and Gregory M. Ruiz. "Projected Effects of the Panama Canal Expansion on Shipping Traffic and Biological Invasions." *Diversity and Distributions: A Journal of Conservation Biogeography* 21 (2014): 75–87.

Muscatine, Doris. *Old San Francisco: The Biography of a City from Early Days to the Earthquake.* New York: G. P. Putnam's Sons, 1975.

Muybridge Collection. Kingston Museum and History Centre. Kingston Upon Thames, UK.

Muybridge, Eadweard. *Animal Locomotion: An Electro-Photographic Investigation of Consecutive Phases of Animal Movements.* 11 vols. Philadelphia: J. B. Lippincott, 1887.

Myers, Steven Lee. "U.S. Is Playing Catch-Up in Scramble for the Arctic." *New York Times,* August 30, 2015.

Naipaul, V. S. *The Middle Passage: Impressions of Five Societies—British, French, and Dutch—in the West Indies and South America.* New York: Vintage Books, 1981.

Naylor, Robert A. "The British Role in Central America Prior to the Clayton-Bulwer Treaty of 1850." *Hispanic American Historical Review* 40, no. 3 (1960): 361–82.

Newton, Velma. *The Silver Men: West Indian Labour Migration to Panama, 1850–1914.* Kingston, Jamaica: Institute of Social and Economic Research, 1984.

Niemeier, Jean G. *The Panama Story.* Portland, OR: Metropolitan Press, 1968.

Norton, Charles Eliot. Charles Eliot Norton to Ephraim G. Squier, November 2, 1851. Ephraim George Squier Papers, Library of Congress.

Oettermann, Stephan. *The Panorama: History of a Mass Medium.* Trans. by Deborah Lucas Schneider. New York: Zone Books, 1997.

Oliphant, Laurence. *Patriots and Filibusters, or Incidents of Political and Exploratory Travel.* Edinburgh: W. Blackwood, 1860.

O'Sullivan, John. "Annexation." *United States Magazine and Democratic Review* 17, no. 1 (July–August 1845): 5–10.

Otis, Fessenden N. *History of the Panama Railroad; and of the Pacific Mail Steamship Company: Together with a Traveller's Guide and Business Man's Hand-Book for the Panama Railroad.* New York: Harper and Brothers, 1867.

"Our Phantom Ship, Central America." *Household Words,* February 22, 1851, 516–24.

Palma, Benigno. *Horas áticas.* Colón: n.p., 1916.

Palmquist, Peter E. "Photographing the Modoc Indian War: Louis Heller versus Eadweard Muybridge." *History of Photography* 2, no. 3 (1978): 187–205.

Palmquist, Peter E., and Thomas R. Kailbourn, eds. *Pioneer Photographers of the Far West: A Biographical Dictionary, 1840–1865* Stanford, CA: Stanford University Press, 2000, s.v. "Castro y Ordoñez."

"Panama as a Home." *All the Year Round.* May 9, 1863, 246–48.

"Panama Poet Breathes His Last at the Age of Sixty-One Years." *Washington Post,* September 9, 1906.

"The Panama Railroad." *New Monthly Magazine* 135 (1865): 366.

Panama Railroad Company. *Memorial of the Panama Rail-Road Company to the Congress of the United States, 10th December, 1849.* New York: Van Norden and Amerman, Printers, 1850.

"Panama to Chagres." *Chambers's Edinburgh Journal* 381 (April 1851): 248–51.

Parker, Matthew. *Panama Fever: The Epic Story of the Building of the Panama Canal.* New York: Anchor, 2009.

Parrish, Susan S. "The 'Hemispheric Turn' in Colonial American Studies." *Early American Literature* 40, no. 3 (2004): 545–53.

Pennell, Joseph. *Joseph Pennell's Pictures of the Panama Canal: Reproductions of a Series of Lithographs Made by Him on the Isthmus of Panama, January–March 1912, Together with Impressions and Notes by the Artist.* Philadelphia: J. B. Lippincott Co, 1913.

Pérez, Louis A. *Cuba: Between Reform and Revolution,* 3rd ed. New York: Oxford University Press, 2006.

Pérez-Venero, Alex. *Before the Five Frontiers: Panama from 1821–1900.* New York: AMS Press, 1978.

Pim, Bedford. *The Gate of the Pacific.* London: L. Reeve, 1863.

Pim, Bedford, and Berthold Seemann. *Dottings on the Roadside in Panama, Nicaragua and Mosquito.* London: Chapman and Hall, 1869.

Pionke, Albert. "Excavating Victorian Cuba in the British Periodicals Database." *Victorian Periodicals Review* 47, no. 3 (Fall 2014): 369–97.

Poole, Deborah. *Vision, Race and Modernity.* Princeton, NJ: Princeton University Press, 1997.

Portilla, Mario. "Heterogeneidad lingüística en *La Varágine.*" *Filología y Lingüística* 39, no. 2 (2013): 61–74.

Pratt, Mary Louise. *Imperial Eyes: Travel Writing and Transculturation.* New York: Routledge, 1992.

Rainger, Ronald. "Race, Politics, and Science: The Anthropological Society of London in the 1860s." *Victorian Studies* 22, no. 1 (1978): 51–70.

Ramirez, Luz E. *British Representations of Latin America.* Gainesville: University Press of Florida, 2007.

Read, Morris. *The Hand of God in History.* London: James Blackwood, 1850.

Reclus, Armand. *Panama et Darien, voyages d'exploration."* Paris: Hachette, 1881.

Recuero, Maria T. *Breve historia del periodismo en Panamá.* Panamá, 1935.

Reeder, Jessie. "The Forms of Informal Empire: Narrating British and Latin American Relations, 1810–1900." PhD diss., University of Wisconsin-Madison, 2014.

Richards, Thomas. *The Imperial Archive: Knowledge and the Fantasy of Empire.* London: Verso, 1993.

Richardson, Tim. "Borders and Mobilities: Introduction to the Special Issue." *Mobilities* 8 (2013), 1–6.

Rippy, J. Fred. *Latin America in World Politics*. New York: F. S. Crofts, 1931.

Roberts, Ruth. "Carlyle and Trollope." In *Carlyle and His Contemporaries: Essays in Honor of Charles Richard Sanders*, edited by John Clubbe, 204–26. Durham, NC: Duke University Press, 1976.

Robinson, Howard. *Britain's Post Office: A History of Development from the Beginnings to the Present Day*. Oxford: Oxford University Press, 1953.

Robinson, Tracy. *Fifty Years in Panama, 1861–1911*. 2nd ed. New York: Trow Press, 1907.

———. "Forward to the Third Edition." In *Panama Patchwork* by James Stanley Gilbert. 3rd ed., xvii–xviii. New York: Star and Herald, 1908.

———. *Panama: A Personal Record of Forty-Six Years, 1861–1907*. New York: Star and Herald Company, 1907.

———. *Song of the Palm*. New York: Brentanos, 1889.

Rohrbough, Malcolm. *Days of Gold: The California Gold Rush and the American Nation*. Berkeley: University of California Press, 1997.

Ropp, Steven C. *Panamanian Politics: From Guarded Nation to National Guard*. Stanford, CA: Hoover Institution Press, 1982.

Rosenblum, Naomi. *A World History of Photography*. 3rd ed. New York: Abbeville, 1997.

Roth, Michael S., ed. *Irresistible Decay: Ruins Reclaimed*. Los Angeles: Getty Research Institute, 1997.

Rotunno, Laura. *Postal Plots in British Fiction, 1840–1898: Readdressing Correspondence in Victorian Culture*. Houndsmills: Palgrave Macmillan, 2013.

Rubín de la Borbolla, Daniel F., and Pedro Rivas. *Honduras: Monumentos históricos y arqueológicos*. México: Consejo Internacional de la Filosofía y de las Ciencas Humanas, 1953.

Russel, Robert Royal. *Improvement of Communication with the Pacific Coast as an Issue in American Politics, 1783–1864*. Cedar Rapids, MI: Torch Press, 1948.

Said, Edward. *Culture and Imperialism*. New York: Knopf, 1993.

Salgado, María A. "Panama." In *Handbook of Latin American Literature*, edited by David William Foster, 453–68. New York: Garland, 1987.

Salinas, Carlos. "Poesía contra el Canal en Nicaragua." *El País* (Managua), February 19, 2015, accessed March 15, 2016, http://cultura.elpais.com/cultura/2015/02/18/actualidad/1424277917_785420.html.

Salvatore, Ricardo D. "The Enterprise of Knowledge: Representational Machines of Informal Empire." In *Close Encounters of Empire: Writing the Cultural History of U.S.-Latin American Relations*, edited by Gilbert M. Joseph, Catherine C. LeGrand, and Ricardo D. Salvatore, 69–106. Durham, NC: Duke University Press, 1998.

———. "Imperial Mechanics: South America's Integration in the Machine Age." *American Quarterly* 58, no. 3 (2006): 662–91.

Schiebinger, Londa. *Plants and Empire: Colonial Bioprospecting in the Atlantic World*. Cambridge: Harvard University Press, 2007.

Schiebinger, Londa, and Claudia Swan, eds. *Colonial Botany: Science, Commerce, and Politics in the Early Modern World*. Philadelphia: University of Pennsylvania Press, 2005.

Schivelbusch, Wolfgang. *The Railway Journey*. Berkeley: University of California Press, 1986.

Schmitt, Cannon. *Darwin and the Memory of the Human: Evolution, Savages, and South America.* Cambridge: Cambridge University Press, 2009.

Schott, Joseph L. *Rails across Panama: The Story of the Building of the Panama Railroad, 1849–1855.* Indianapolis, IN: Bobbs-Merrill, 1967.

Scott, Blake. "From Disease to Desire: The Rise of Tourism at the Panama Canal." *Environmental History* 21, no. 2 (2016): 67–74.

Seacole, Mary. *Wonderful Adventures of Mrs. Seacole in Many Lands.* The Schomburg Library of Nineteenth-Century Black Women Writers. New York: Oxford University Press, 1988.

Seemann, Berthold. *Narrative of the Voyage of H.M.S. Herald during the Years 1845–51, under the Command of Captain Henry Kellett, R. N., C. B.* 2 vols. London: Reeve, 1853.

Selfridge, Thomas Oliver. *Reports of Explorations and Surveys to Ascertain the Practicability of a Ship-Canal Between the Atlantic and Pacific Oceans by the way of the Isthmus of Darien.* Washington, DC: Government Printing Office, 1874.

Sepúlveda, Mélida Ruth. *El tema del Canal en la novelística panameña.* Caracas: Universidad Católica "Andres Bello," 1975.

Sheller, Mimi. "Aluminum across the Americas: Caribbean Mobilities and Transnational American Studies." *Journal of Transnational American Studies* 5 (2013), http://escholarship.org/uc/item/7bb5c9j6.

———. *Consuming the Caribbean: From Arawaks to Zombies.* International Library of Sociology. New York: Routledge, 2003.

Sheller, Mimi, and John Urry. "The New Mobilities Paradigm." *Environment and Planning A* 38 (2006), 207–26.

"Short Cut to California." *Household Words.* March 15, 1851, 597–98.

"Short Cuts across the Globe: Panama." *Household Words.* April 13, 1850, 65–69.

Siegert, Bernhard. *Relays: Literature as an Epoch of the Postal System.* Stanford, CA: Stanford University Press, 1999.

Simmons, Jack. *The Victorian Railway.* New York: Thames and Hudson, 1991.

Soler, Ricarte. *Panamá en el Mundo Americano.* Panama City: Ediciones de la Revista Tareas, 1985.

Solnit, Rebecca. *River of Shadows: Eadweard Muybridge and the Technological Wild West.* New York: Viking, 2003.

Spencer, Frank. "Some Notes on the Attempt to Apply Photography to Anthropometry during the Second Half of the Nineteenth Century." In *Anthropology and Photography, 1860–1920,* edited by Elizabeth Edwards, 99–107. New Haven, CT: Yale University Press, 1992.

Spencer, Herbert. *Herbert Spencer on Social Evolution.* Ed. J.D.Y. Peel. Chicago: University of Chicago Press, 1972.

Squier, Ephraim George. *Notes on Central America; Particularly the States of Honduras and San Salvador.* New York: Harper and Brothers, 1855.

Steadman, Edmund Clarence. *NY Times,* September 8, 1906, BR553.

Stepan, Nancy Leys. *Picturing Tropical Nature.* Ithaca, NY: Cornell University Press, 2001.

Stephens, John Lloyd. *Incidents of Travel in Central America, Chiapas, and Yucatan.* 2 vols. New York: Harper and Brothers, 1841.

———. *Incidents of Travel in Yucatan.* New York: Harper and Brothers, 1843.

——. Letter to James Lawrence Blair, October 16, 1849. Janin Family Collection, Correspondence. Huntington Library, San Marino.

Stillson, Richard T. *Spreading the Word: A History of Information in the California Gold Rush.* Lincoln: University of Nebraska Press, 2006.

Stocking, George W. "Reading the Palimpsest of Inquiry: *Notes and Queries* and the History of British Social Anthropology." In *Delimiting Anthropology: Occasional Essays and Reflections,* 164–206. Madison: University of Wisconsin Press, 2001.

——. "What's in a Name? The Origins of the Royal Anthropological Institute (1837–71)." *Man* 6 (1971): 369–90.

Stoler, Ann Laura. "Colonial Archives and the Arts of Governance." *Archival Science* 2, nos. 1–2 (2002): 87–109.

Suárez, Omar J. *Análisis regional y canal de Panamá: Ensayos geográficos.* Panama City: Editorial Universitaria, 1981.

Suleri, Sara. *The Rhetoric of English India.* Chicago: University of Chicago Press, 1992.

Sullivan, John T. *Report of Historical and Technical Information relating to the Problem of Interoceanic Communication by way of the American Isthmus.* Washington, DC: Government Printing Office, 1883.

Super, R. H. *Trollope in the Post Office.* Ann Arbor: University of Michigan Press, 1981.

Sutter, Paul S. "'The First Mountain to be Removed': Yellow Fever Control and the Construction of the Panama Canal." *Environmental History* 21, no. 2 (2016): 47–56.

Szok, Peter A. *"La última gaviota": Liberalism and Nostalgia in Early Twentieth-Century Panamá.* New York: Praeger, 2001.

——. *Wolf Tracks: Popular Art and Re-Africanization in Twentieth-Century Panama.* Caribbean Studies. Jackson: University Press of Mississippi, 2012.

Taylor, Bayard. *El Dorado; or, Adventures in the Path of Empire, Comprising a Voyage to California, via Panama; Life in San Francisco and Monterey; Pictures of the Gold Region, and Experiences of Mexican Travel.* 18th ed. New York: G. P. Putnam, 1864.

Tenorio-Trillo, Mauricio. *Mexico at the World's Fairs: Crafting a Modern Nation.* Berkeley: University of California Press, 1996.

Teran, Oscar. *Panamá, del tratado Herrán-Hay al tratado Hay-Bunau Varilla: Historia crítica del atraco yanqui mal llamado en Colombia la perdida de Panamá, y en Panamá, nuestra independencia de Colombia.* Bogotá: C. Valencia Editores, 1976.

Thomas, Hugh. "Cuba from the Middle of the Eighteenth Century to c. 1870." In *The Cambridge History of Latin America, Volume III, From Independence to c. 1870,* edited by Leslie Bethell, 277–96. Cambridge: Cambridge University Press, 1985.

Thomas, Kate. *Postal Pleasures: Sex, Scandal, and Victorian Letters.* Oxford: Oxford University Press, 2012.

Torres-Saillant, Silvio. *An Intellectual History of the Caribbean.* Basingstoke: Palgrave Macmillan, 2006.

Trollope, Anthony. *An Autobiography.* Ed. by Michael Sadleir and Frederick Page. Oxford: Oxford University Press, 1980.

——. *The Complete Short Stories,* Vol. 3, *Tourists and Colonials,* edited by Betty Jane Slemp Breyer. Fort Worth: Texas Christian University Press, 1981.

———. "The Journey to Panama." In *The Victoria Regia: A Volume of Original Contributions in Poetry and Prose,* edited by Adelaide A. Procter, 187–214. London: Emily Faithfull, 1861.

———. *The Letters of Anthony Trollope.* Ed. N. John Hall. 2 vols. Stanford: Stanford University Press, 1983.

———. *The West Indies and the Spanish Main.* New York: Carroll and Graf, 1999.

Turnock, David. *Railways in the British Isles: Landscape, Land Use and Society.* London: Black, 1982.

Van Alstyne, Richard W. "Anglo-American Relations, 1853–57." *American Historical Review* 42, no. 3 (1937): 491–500.

———. "British Diplomacy and the Clayton-Bulwer Treaty, 1850–60." *The Journal of Modern History* 11, no. 2 (1939): 149–83.

———. "The Central American Policy of Lord Palmerston, 1846–48," *Hispanic American Historical Review* 16, no. 3 (1936): 339–59.

Vance, Robert H. *Catalogue of Daguerreotype Panoramic Views in California.* New York: Godwin, 1851.

Vega, Luis Wong, Orlando Segura J., Winston Churchill James, and Jorge Luis Macías Fonseca, eds. *Antología de la poesía colonense, 1900–2012.* Panamá: Editorial La Antigua USMA, 2012.

Views on the Isthmus, Special Collections, Getty Research Institute, Los Angeles.

Vismann, Cornelia. *Files: Law and Media Technology.* Trans. Geoffrey Winthrop-Young. Stanford, CA: Stanford University Press, 2008.

Von Hagen, Victor Wolfgang. *Frederick Catherwood, Archt.* New York: Oxford University Press, 1950.

———. *Maya Explorer: John Lloyd Stephens and the Lost Cities of Central America and Yucatán.* Norman: University of Oklahoma Press, 1947.

Vostal, Filip. "Thematizing Speed: Between Critical Theory and Cultural Analysis." *European Journal of Social Theory* 17, no. 1 (2014): 95–114.

Walcott, Derek. *Midsummer.* New York: Farrar, Straus, Giroux, 1983.

Walrond, Eric. *Tropic Death.* New York: Collier, 1926.

Watson, Sonja Stephenson. "Poetic Negrism and the National Sentiment of Anti-West Indianism and Anti-Imperialism in Panamanian Literature." *Callaloo* 35, no. 2 (2012): 459–74.

———. *The Politics of Race in Panama: Afro Hispanic and West Indian Literary Discourses of Contention.* Gainesville: University Press of Florida, 2014.

Weeks, William Earl. *The New Cambridge History of American Foreign Relations: Dimensions of the Early American Empire, 1754–1865.* Cambridge: Cambridge University Press, 2013.

Williams, Eric. *British Historians and the West Indies.* 1966. New York: Africana Books, 1972.

Williams, Linda. "Film Body: An Implantation of Perversions." *Cine-tracts* 3, no. 4 (1981): 19–36.

Willumson, Glenn. *Iron Muse: Photographing the Transcontinental Railroad.* Berkeley: University of California Press, 2013.

Woodward, Ralph L., Jr. *Rafael Carrera and the Emergence of the Republic of Guatemala, 1821–1871.* Athens: University of Georgia Press, 1993.

Young, Robert J. C. *Colonial Desire: Hybridity in Theory, Culture, and Race.* New York: Routledge, 1995.

Zerubavel, Eviatar. *Hidden Rhythms: Schedules and Calendars in Social Life.* Berkeley: University of California Press, 1981.

———. "Timetables and Scheduling: On the Social Organization of Time." *Sociological Inquiry* 46 (1976): 87–94.

———. "Timetables and Scheduling: On the Social Organization of Time." *Sociological Inquiry* 46 (1976): 87–94.

Zieger, Susan. "Affect and Logistics: Trollope's Postal Work." *Victorians Journal of Culture and Literature* 128 (Fall 2015): 226–44.

Zuelow, Eric G. E. *A History of Modern Tourism.* New York: Palgrave Macmillan, 2015.

INDEX

~

Russell, Andrew, 80; "Meeting of the Rails," 80

Said, Edward, 57
San Blas Indians. *See* Kuna people
Schivelbush, Wolfgang, 12; *Railway Journey,* 12
Seacole, Mary, 14, 16, 31, 71, 73–74; *Wonderful Adventures,* 31, 73
Seeman, Berthold, 4, 8, 17, 134, 157, 166n14
Selfridge, Thomas Oliver, 88
sexualization, 107–16, 135–41, 177n45
shortcuts, 14
sickness. *See* illness
slavery, 22, 64–66, 70, 73, 151
Song of the Palm (Robinson), 121, 124–25
"Song of the Prickly Heat" (Gilbert), 128
Spanish-American War, 7, 123, 148
speed, 12–14, 18, 80, 167n46
Spencer, Herbert, 134
Squier, Ephraim George, 36, 67, 134
Stanford, Leland, 26
Steadman, Edmund Clarence, 121
steamers. *See* steamships
steam packets. *See* steamships
steamships, 4, 20, 44–45, 47–49, 62–64, 80–81
Stephens, John Lloyd, 25, 32–50, 57, 94, 149; *Incidents of Travel in Central America, Chiapas, and Yucatan,* 32, 38, 40, 42, 45
stereographs, 26, 79–119, 136–39
stereotypes, 16–17, 107, 179n30. *See also* racism
Stillson, Richard T., 46
subaltern people, 19, 22, 24, 39, 50. *See also* Kuna people; Maya people; Tlingit people
sublime, 34–35, 37–38
Suez Canal, 13
systems. *See* communication; infrastructure; mail; networks

Taylor, Bayard, 2, 16
technology, 5, 16, 18, 76, 91. *See also* mobility; network; railroad; steamships

Thomas, Hugh, 69
time, 9, 10–12, 34, 38, 96–102, 104–5, 116–17, 135–36, 143–45, 152; allochronic, 11, 16, 18, 160
Tlingit people, 84–86, 103
Torres-Saillant, Silvio, 56
"To the Crab" (Gilbert), 126
Totten, George, 60–62, 145–46
tourism, 26
tourists, 27, 149–56
transportation, 4, 6, 17, 25–26, 31–32, 39–45, 74, 85
travelers, 2–27, 30–32, 48, 64, 72, 79, 99, 110, 130–31, 150, 170n27
Treaty of Guadalupe Hidalgo, 45
Trollope, Anthony, 25–26, 54–75, 149; *West Indies and the Spanish Main, The,* 54–75

United States, 165n5
United States Navy, 22, 45, 47

Views on the Isthmus (anon.), 88–89

Walker, William, 21, 67, 69
warships, 5
washerwomen. *See* laundry
Watermelon Riot. *See* "El incidente de la tajada de sandia"
West Indies and the Spanish Main, The (Trollope), 54–75
Wolfe, Byron, 86
women, representations of, 105–18, 131, 135–43, 150–51
Wonderful Adventures (Seacole), 31, 73
working class, 31
world fairs, 96–97, 148

Yankee Strip, 20–21, 25, 30, 57, 120, 123,149–56
"Yellow Eyes" (Gilbert), 129
Yosemite, 85, 93, 103, 107
Young, Robert, 134
Yu, Carlos, 8

Zieger, Susan, 59